Charles the Bold presides over a Chapter of the Golden Fleece

CAXTON
AND
HIS WORLD

N. F. Blake

ANDRE DEUTSCH

FIRST PUBLISHED 1969 BY
ANDRE DEUTSCH LIMITED
105 GREAT RUSSELL STREET
LONDON WCI

COPYRIGHT © 1969 BY N. F. BLAKE

PRINTED IN GREAT BRITAIN BY
TONBRIDGE PRINTERS LTD
TONBRIDGE KENT
SBN 233 96093 7

FOR VALERIE

ACKNOWLEDGEMENTS

Two friends, Yvonne Offord and Jean Imray, have advised me throughout the preparation of this volume and I am most grateful to them for their help. Donald Matthew read through my first draft and made many recommendations. Similarly I have received help from many colleagues in Liverpool, as well as from librarians and archivists in libraries and archives both in England and in the Low Countries. I gratefully acknowledge their assistance. I am indebted to the University of Liverpool for several research grants to enable me to visit various archives. I should like to thank the General Editor of the Language Library for including my book in his series and also for making many helpful suggestions. Mr Michael Alexander of André Deutsch has also offered me much valuable advice. Finally, I should like to thank my wife and Mrs Thompson and Miss Burton for their help in the preparation of the typescript.

During the preparation of this volume I have often enjoyed the hospitality of my uncle and aunt, Mr and Mrs A. F. Blake, on my frequent visits to London, and I owe them a special word of thanks.

I wish to thank the following for their permission to reproduce illustrations in their care: the Bodleian Library (plate 3); Boston Public Library, Mass. (plate 7); the Trustees of the British Museum (plates 4 & 5); the Worshipful Company of Mercers (plate 2); the Syndics of the Fitzwilliam Museum (frontispiece); Lambeth Palace Library (plate 6); and the Governors of the John Rylands Library (plates 1 & 8). Details of the provenance of these illustrations will be found in Notes on the Plates.

Some of the views expressed in this book have already appeared in articles. I should like to thank the editors of the following journals for their permission to reproduce material which was published in them: *Anglia; The Book Collector; Bulletin of the John Rylands Library; Essays and Studies; Leeds Studies in English; Notes and Queries* (and Oxford University Press, the publishers); and *Proceedings of the Suffolk Institute of Archaeology*. Details of these articles may be found in the Select Bibliography. I should also like to thank the editors of *Traditio* for permission to outline the general conclusions of my article 'The Biblical Additions in Caxton's *Golden Legend*', which they are to publish.

I acknowledge permission from Mr D. A. Pearsall and Thomas Nelson and Sons Ltd to reprint a passage from *The Floure and the Leafe* (Nelson's Medieval and Renaissance Library, 1962); and from the Council of the Early English Text Society to reprint a passage from A. T. P. Byles, *The Book of the Ordre of Chyualry* (1926).

Liverpool, 1968

CONTENTS

LIST OF PLATES

I

PROBLEMS
OF THE
EARLIEST YEARS

Most Englishmen know of William Caxton. Indeed, apart from those of the monarchs, his is the name from the fifteenth century most familiar today. Those who are unacquainted with writers like Malory or Lydgate, with humanists like Humphrey Duke of Gloucester or John Tiptoft, Earl of Worcester, or with politicians like Henry Duke of Bedford will nevertheless at least have heard of Caxton. Why is this so? He did not invent printing; he merely introduced it into England. He made no original contributions of note to English literature; the bulk of his literary output was translation. In outlook he was more medieval than modern. And although he took part in negotiations with foreign powers, he was not responsible for any English diplomatic triumph. His fame may be ascribed to the importance which we today attach to printing, the invention of which is regarded as a turning point in European history. The art was perfected by Johann Gutenberg at Mainz about 1450. Nevertheless, its introduction into England in 1476 is relatively late by European standards. This feat, it might be suggested, is hardly sufficient to support Caxton's present reputation. It will be one of the purposes of this book to see how far that reputation is justified and how it developed. Though the early history of the printing press in England is of greater importance than the man who brought it here, the two cannot easily be separated. England differs from most countries in that a merchant started the first press here. This fact poses several questions. Why should a merchant engaged in the cloth trade have taken up printing and brought a press to England? Did the fact that he was a merchant influence the books he chose to print and the way in which he printed them? These questions in their turn suggest a third which is far more difficult to answer: what sort of man was Caxton, the first English printer? Hence this book, which is an attempt to provide answers to these and similar questions, is divided

13

into two parts. The first is a biography of Caxton, the second an evaluation of his work, for the achievements of the first English press can be understood only against the background of his life. This book is not, however, concerned with the bibliography or typography of Caxton's output.

The first chapters of this book are thus devoted to an account of Caxton's life as an aid to understanding the history of the first English press, though his life is also of interest for its own sake and for what it reveals of fifteenth-century culture. However, despite his subsequent fame, to his contemporaries and immediate successors Caxton was not such an important person that they felt it necessary to record details of his life and work. It is not till he began to play a part in national life that we can with any confidence reconstruct his biography from the surviving documentary sources. His origins remain obscure; it is a case of choosing between possible hypotheses. Consequently this chapter is designed to illustrate the difficulties a biographer has to face. It will show how I have approached the sources and what sort of information I think they can yield. This approach is implicit in the later chapters as well, but the detailed investigation which lies behind my picture of his life as merchant and printer will not be given there. This chapter stands as a model for the rest of the book.

One important difficulty facing a biographer of William Caxton is the frequent occurrence of that name in fifteenth-century documents.[1] It is tempting to link all documents in which it occurs with the printer; but often the necessary proof is lacking. This frustrating state of affairs can be illustrated from a series of seventeen charters concerning the manor of Little Wratting in Suffolk.[2] The charters show that Little Wratting passed into the hands of a Philip Caxton about 1420. Philip had two sons, another Philip born in 1412 and William born about 1415. It has been suggested that this William is the same person as the printer; and at the Festival of Britain in 1951 the charters were exhibited at Tenterden as 'The Caxton Charters'. It may seem surprising that a series of charters which concern a William Caxton from Suffolk

[1] Thus from a quick survey of London documents I have found a William de Caxtone in Letter-Book K for 1444; a William Causton, tailor, in Plea and Memoranda Roll A 74 for 1448; and probably the same William Causton, tailor and citizen of London, in Hustings Roll 192 for 1462.

[2] These charters, all now in the British Museum, were found among the muniments of Lord Winterton of Shillinglee Park in 1922. For a discussion and abstracts of them see Blake, *The Proceedings of the Suffolk Institute of Archaeology*, xxix, 2 (1962), 139–53, and *ibid.*, xxx, 1 (1964), 112–15.

should have been associated with the printer, who was born in Kent and lived in London, but had no known connexion with East Anglia. There are, however, certain coincidences between the life of the printer and details in the charters. Thus charter 3, which records an indenture of sale by the younger Philip Caxton, was ratified by the seals of the London aldermen, Thomas Cateworthe and Robert Large, because Philip's seal was not well enough known. Robert Large was the mercer to whom William Caxton, the future printer, was apprenticed, and there may have been ties between the Larges and the Caxtons. One of the feoffees of Little Wratting in charter 12 is a Master Benedict Burgh. This is the man who was Archdeacon of Colchester and later High Canon of St Stephen's, Westminster, whose poetic translation *Cato* was printed by Caxton about 1477. He may also have been a friend of the family. There are other minor correspondences; but, on the other hand, there are difficulties in identifying Caxton of Little Wratting as the printer. In one of the later charters, for example, he is called a saddler. There is no known reason why the printer should be so designated since in all other documents he is referred to as a mercer.[1] There are other objections, though none is insuperable. The printer could have been born as early as 1415, though a later date for his birth has hitherto been preferred. Although he may have owned land in Kent where his son was born, Caxton's father could also have bought a manor in Suffolk as an investment or as a form of insurance for his wife in the event of his own death or even as a step towards rising in the social scale. Unless the family had been permanently resident at the manor in Suffolk, there would be no reason for the printer to refer to it in his own writings later in his life. However, despite the striking coincidences, conclusive proof to identify William Caxton of Little Wratting with the printer is wanting. Therefore, it ought not to be assumed that the two are identical, though the possibility cannot be ruled out. The problem of identification is one that recurs constantly in the documents relating to Caxton.

A biographer of the printer is in the happy position that he need not rely upon historical documents, for Caxton left a series of prologues and epilogues to the books he printed which contain a mass of informa-

---

[1] Miss Jean Imray has pointed out to me that there is no need to assume that the William Caxton, saddler, of this later charter is the same man as the William Caxton, son of Philip Caxton of Little Wratting, who is mentioned in many of the other charters. This is so; and it underlines my point that it is extremely difficult to identify people mentioned in such documents with any confidence.

tion about himself. With these there is no problem of identification, and they contain details about almost all periods of his life. Because of the reliance which recent biographers have placed in historical documents, the prologues and epilogues have not been fully exploited. I hope to show in this book that they should be used as our principal source for Caxton's life and work, and that the documentary evidence is best used in support of them. Hence for information about his birthplace the best source is his prologue to the *History of Troy*.[1] As the passage can show what type of information Caxton included in his prologues, I shall quote it in full.

> And afterward whan I remembryd my self of my symplenes and unperfightnes that I had in bothe langages, that is to wete in Frenshe & in Englissh, for in France was I never, and was born & lerned myn Englissh in Kente in the Weeld, where I doubte not is spoken as brode and rude Englissh as is in ony place of Englond; & have contynued by the space of xxx yere for the most parte in the contres of Braband, Flandres, Holand and Zeland. [4][2]

Caxton's words have been taken at their face value. However, although the prologues and epilogues are the major sources for our knowledge of the printer, the information they contain must be properly interpreted. He did not write them to inform posterity of details of his life; he used them to convince would-be purchasers of his books that they were worth buying. To do this he employed the fashionable formulas and modes of expression. So each passage must be examined to see whether it is based round such a formula and in the light of the particular purpose for which the complete prologue or epilogue was written. This applies particularly to the *History of Troy*; although it was the first book Caxton translated and printed, it was completed under the patronage of Margaret of Burgundy and was directed towards a noble clientele. Stories of Troy were popular with the polite classes, and Caxton has tried to capitalize on this interest by translating a recently made version in French for the Burgundian court. Yet in his prologue he goes out of his way to impress upon his

---

[1] I have abbreviated Caxton's titles. For the full titles and details of the books see the appendix, Caxton's Publications.

[2] In all quotations from Caxton's works the punctuation is my own and I have modernized the usage of *u* and *v*. References in brackets after quotations from the prologues and epilogues are to the pagination in Crotch 1928, which has the original punctuation.

readers that his qualifications for such a translation were limited. His knowledge of French was sketchy because he had never been to France, and his English was likewise not of the best because he had been born in Kent, where a regional dialect was spoken, and because he had lived abroad for thirty years among people who, it is implied, spoke no English at all. These details do not add up to an autobiography. Caxton simply selected those facts which threw his knowledge of French and English into the worst possible light. But we know from other sources that he had lived in London, where he could have heard the London English which was becoming accepted as the standard literary language; that his writings contain no traces of the Kentish dialect; and that while abroad he had some connexion with Margaret of Burgundy, Edward IV's sister, he was Governor of the English Nation, and he often returned to London. If he had wished to emphasize his command of English rather than otherwise, he could have written that he had spent his youth in London, that he had later moved in merchant and aristocratic circles, and that he had conversed even with members of the nobility. The details he supplied of his life may be true, but they are certainly not the whole truth.

Why then did he wish to throw his attainments into such a poor light? It is difficult for us today to imagine that anyone could have thought that a relative incompetence in command of French and English would have recommended a translation from one language into the other to any buyer. The fifteenth-century reader, however, would have immediately realized that the disclaimer was a traditional formula. It was common in the Middle Ages for writers, translators or adaptors to disparage their own ability in order that the reader's indulgence could be won over. This practice is called the 'humility formula' by modern scholars.[1] Based ultimately on Latin authors, the convention was popularized in the early Middle Ages by writers of saints' lives and became especially common among writers in the fifteenth century. To illustrate its popularity, let me quote what a modern editor of a fifteenth-century English poem has written on this theme.

In the fifteenth century the most elaborate submission formulas were reserved for 'commanded' works, prepared at the request of some powerful patron . . .; the examples in Lydgate are prolonged and

[1] E. R. Curtius (trans. W. R. Trask), *European Literature and the Latin Middle Ages* (New York, 1953), Excursus II.

effusive. The full modesty epilogue has an initial command, 'Go, little boke' . . .; an apology for the author's inadequacy, for his 'rude langage' and 'rurall termes'; a request for the reader to make corrections and improvements where he thinks fit; an assertion that all lies 'under support of' the patience and tolerance of the reader, and that the author would never have presumed to trespass so far had it not been for his patron's insistence; and a final commendation of the poem, with all its faults, to the mercy of the reader. . . . Chaucer draws on the tradition once only, in the noble and moving epilogue to *Troilus*; but the fifteenth century, with the increasing importance of patrons, is profuse in examples . . . Caxton follows the convention closely in his Prologues and Epilogues.[1]

Caxton's use of the humility or submission formula shows that, though he was a mercer dealing in cloth, he nevertheless knew what the fashionable literary formulas were and felt obliged to use them. This is a matter to which I shall return. In so far as the formula affects what he tells us of his birthplace and career, its use must lead to an emphasis on those parts of his life which reflect unfavourably upon his command of English and to an exaggeration of them in order to cast them in as unfavourable a light as possible.

This exaggeration is convincingly illustrated by his statement in the passage above about his thirty years' residence abroad. Previous biographers have accepted this figure as reliable and have dated his departure from England thirty years before their chosen date for the composition of the prologue to the *History of Troy*. Thirty is a round figure, and in the Middle Ages such figures as thirty and sixty were used to suggest a large, rather than to give a specific, number. Readers of Anglo-Saxon poetry will remember that in *Beowulf* Grendel took thirty thanes from the hall at Heorot (ll. 122–3) and that Beowulf himself swam from Frisia to his home with thirty suits of armour (ll. 2361–2). The English author of the Middle English romance *Beves of Hamtoun* altered the height of the giant in his French source from nine to thirty feet (l. 1860). A particularly interesting example of the use of thirty concerns John Pickering, who succeeded Caxton as Governor of the English Nation at Bruges.[2] As we shall see, the exact date that Caxton relinquished this post is unknown, though he still occupied it in 1470. As Pickering died in 1498, he cannot have been

---

[1] D. A. Pearsall, *The Floure and the Leafe* (London and Edinburgh, 1962), p. 152.
[2] Bone, *The Library*, 4th Series xii (1931–2), 284–306.

Governor for more than twenty-eight years, though his tenure of the office was probably shorter. Yet in accordance with Weever's *Ancient Funerall Monuments* (1631), his tomb had the following inscription:

> The honorable Merchant *ION PICKERING*,
> And *ELISABYTH*, lie vndyr this ston:
> Of the English merchant Venturers vndyr the kyng,
> In the Martis beyond See, gouernor was this ION,
> Thirty yeere and mor that roome he did manteyn, ... (p. 399)

Thirty is here a round figure, as the *and more* bears out. Similarly Caxton's *thirty years* means no more than 'a great many years'; it is used emotively. This does not mean that Caxton was trying to deceive his readers and us. His prologues and epilogues are literary, not autobiographical, writings, to which the standards of accuracy we expect from historical documents cannot be applied.

This example of how Caxton manipulated details of his career to make a particular point more telling warns us to approach his information about his birthplace with caution. He was born, he said, in the Weald of Kent. He included this reference to the Weald because he wanted to suggest that he came from an uncivilized part of the country, for in the fifteenth century and later the Weald was associated with wildness. This association may have been helped by the alliteration and assonance of 'wild' and 'Weald'; but other, more important factors are involved. The Weald was a large tract of wooded country in close proximity to London. To a Londoner, and Caxton was no doubt looking at things here with the eye of a Londoner, Kent was a wild, barbarous region and the direction from which trouble was most likely to come. The men of Kent had marched on London in 1381, 1450 and 1471. An example of what Londoners might expect from Kent is provided by a letter by the Duke of Norfolk concerning the troubles following the death of Edward IV: 'It is soo that the Kentysshmen be up in the weld, and sey that they wol come and robbe the cite, which I shall lett yf I may'.[1] A similar attitude to Kent can be found in contemporary literature. Thus in *The Pastime of Pleasure* (c. 1505) by Stephen Hawes, Kent is the home of the foolish dwarf, Godfrey Gobylyve:

[1] J. Gairdner, *The Paston Letters: 1422–1509 A.D.* (Edinburgh, 1910), iii, 308.

Sotheych quod he whan I cham in kent
At home I cham though I be hyther sent
I cham a gentylman of moche noble kynne
Though Iche be cladde in a knaues skynne.[1]

His language confirms that he came from an area of little refinement.
Kent created a very different image in the mind of a fifteenth-century
Londoner from the one it creates in ours today. Caxton added the
words 'in the Weeld' to his statement about being born in Kent to
create in the minds of his noble audience a feeling of barbarousness and
lack of refinement. It is used symbolically, and not to give accurate
geographical information. So it is conceivable, for example, that he
was born in Canterbury, even though it lies outside the area which we
today think of as the Weald and even though it is also very different
in character from it. After all Lyly, who is thought to have been born
in Canterbury, could also write in his *Euphues and his England*: 'I was
borne in the wylde of *Kent*'. Consequently Caxton's words do not
necessarily mean that he was born in the country rather than a town,
or that his birthplace is to be located in that area now delineated as the
Weald in a purely geographical sense.

Previous attempts to localize Caxton's place of birth have taken two
forms. One has been to connect the personal name Caxton with the
place name Caxton in any of its variant spellings. The other has been
to associate him with one of the known Caxton families in Kent at the
beginning of the fifteenth century. Neither approach is satisfactory,
for there is no proof to associate Caxton with any of the places or
families which have been suggested. Recently a different method has
been put forward to arrive at a solution.[2] This method relies upon
Caxton's translations. Caxton added small points of information to the
books he translated, and this is especially true of the *Golden Legend*.[3] In
that work, a collection of saints' lives, there is a reference to Strood in
Kent which could have been inserted by Caxton. The legend of St
Augustine of Canterbury records how when Augustine was preaching
in Dorset, he was pelted with fishtails by the local inhabitants. As a

---

[1] W. E. Mead, *The Pastime of Pleasure* (London, 1928), p. 134. Even as late as
Spenser's time the more rugged aspects of Kent predominated. The annotator
E.K. in his gloss to the June eclogue of *The Shepherdes Calendar* described Kent as
'very hillye and woodye'.

[2] Blake, *Notes and Queries*, ccxi (1966), 52–54.

[3] Jeremy, *Modern Language Notes*, lxiv (1949), 259–61.

result their 'chyldren that were borne after in that place had tayles, as it is sayde, tyl they had repented them'. The version in Caxton's text does not finish there, as one might expect, but it contains one final remark: 'It is sayd comynly that thys fyl at Strode in Kente, but blessyd be God at this day is no suche deformyte'.[1] Although it cannot be proved that Caxton added this sentence, such evidence as there is suggests he did. He took the lives of the English saints from an earlier English translation of the *Golden Legend*. The only manuscript of that work which contains the story of the men of Dorset, Lambeth MS 72, does not include the sentence about Strood. As the Lambeth manuscript is closely related to the one Caxton used, the implication is that he added this sentence. Furthermore, the connexion of Strood with tailed men is found only in his version. Originally they were associated with Dorset. But in Laʒamon's *Brut* (l. 29585) although the Caligula manuscript has Dorchester, the Otho manuscript has Rochester as the scene of this episode. Possibly this transference to Rochester was a scribal error, for it is the first time that tailed men are associated with Kent. From then onwards the account is often linked with Rochester, as in Robert of Brunne's *Chronicle of England* (ll. 15188–212). As Strood is near Rochester, the imputation could easily have been extended there. Often the accusation was levelled against Englishmen in general without reference to a particular locality. That Caxton was sensitive to this charge is suggested by his omission of the reference to the tails of Englishmen in his translation of the *Mirror of the World*.[2] Since Caxton was touchy about the subject of tailed Englishmen, and since his version of the *Golden Legend* is the only one to link the story of tails to Strood, probably he added the reference to Strood. This being so, one could assume that he identified himself with this part of Kent and possibly even that he was born near here. The evidence is certainly far from conclusive and the suggestion should be considered as tentative. Strood is not in the Weald, but, as we have seen, this need not be regarded as an insuperable objection.

The historical documents in which Caxton is mentioned must be submitted to the same scrutiny as the prologues and epilogues. As an

[1] Ellis 1892 p. 504. (Details of abbreviated titles of modern editions of Caxton's works will be found in Caxton's Publications.)

[2] Prior 1913 p. xviii. At Bergen-op-Zoom in 1457 a citizen said to an English merchant that he lied *comme Englois coué*. The English community was so insulted that the Governor, William Obray, ordered them to leave Bergen and cease trading there; see Thielemans 1966 pp. 277–8.

example of how such a critical scrutiny may affect our understanding
of details of his life, I shall consider his date of birth, for which the
prologues and epilogues provide no evidence. Since the work of
Blades in the last century, most writers have accepted a date between
1421 and 1424. This dating is based on an entry in the Wardens'
Account Book of the Mercers' Company.[1] William Caxton became a
member of the Mercers' Company and he served his apprenticeship
under Robert Large. When a master enrolled a new apprentice he had
to pay a fee of two shillings to the company. In the Account Book it is
recorded that two shillings each for William Caxton and John Large,
apprentices of Robert Large, were paid in 1438. Assuming this to mean
that Caxton embarked upon his apprenticeship in 1438, Blades went on
to argue that, since the period of apprenticeship was so arranged to
terminate when the apprentice was twenty-four years old, and since
the normal period of apprenticeship was from seven to ten years,
Caxton was between fourteen and seventeen in 1438. This reasoning is
based on three doubtful assumptions: that Caxton started his apprenticeship in 1438, that he would have served from seven to ten years,
and that he would have issued from his apprenticeship at the age of
twenty-four.

That Robert Large paid the two-shilling fee for his apprentice
William Caxton in 1438 is no guarantee that Caxton actually started
his apprenticeship in that year. The Account Book is, as its name
implies, a record of payments to and by the company; it is not a record
of when apprentices were enrolled or issued. A master was supposed to
pay the fee as soon as his apprentice was enrolled, but payment was not
made promptly. Large was no exception. The two-shilling fee for one
of his apprentices, Christopher Heton, was paid in 1443, two years
after Large's death. Yet in his will of 1441 Large left to a 'Christopher,
my apprentice' the sum of twenty pounds; this Christopher must be
Christopher Heton. Furthermore, that the date of Heton's entry into
apprenticeship was not 1443 is confirmed by the record for his issue
from apprenticeship which is also given as 1443 in the Account Book.
Large also bequeathed twenty marks to his apprentice Robert Dedes;
but there is no record in the Account Book of any payment of his
apprenticeship fee. As this bequest was for the same amount as Caxton's,
it seems probable that Dedes had already been an apprentice for some
time before 1441. For two of his apprentices Large failed to pay the

[1] Blades 1861 i. 3-4.

entry fee promptly, and the Account Book shows that he was dilatory in the payment of his other dues. Consequently although Caxton had started his apprenticeship by 1438, it is not necessary to assume that he became an apprentice in that year.

Blades's second assumption was that an apprentice served his master for from seven to ten years. This was the length of service which Blades arrived at from a consideration of the dates for entry into and issue from apprenticeship in the Account Book. We have just seen that its dates are not reliable. Furthermore, in the Account Book the length of service actually differs from no years at all, as in the case of Heton mentioned in the preceding paragraph, to twenty-one years, for John Harow, another of Large's apprentices, entered in 1423 and issued in 1454. In neither case can the Account Book reflect the real length of service; Harow is known to have issued by 1450. A study of those who entered upon their apprenticeships with the Mercers' Company in the first thirty years of Henry VI's reign has revealed that only a little more than half served from seven to ten years.[1] So not only is the Account Book unreliable, but also Blades's interpretation of its evidence is inaccurate. A more accurate assessment of the length of an apprentice's service can be made from the Plea and Memoranda Rolls of the City of London.[2] In these records the length of service extends from seven to fifteen years, and there is no indication that the longer periods were in any way unusual. From some of the entries, however, it appears that it was not legal to take on an apprentice who was under the age of fourteen.

The third assumption made by Blades, that the length of an apprenticeship was so arranged that the apprentice would issue at the age of twenty-four, cannot be substantiated. Blades himself argued that this was so on the basis of a law passed in 1693, though this enactment need have no significance for the fifteenth century. In fact the Common Council of the City of London passed a similar requirement in the 1550s,[3] though the wording is such that it implies an apprentice should not be less than twenty-four years old when he issued. I have found no similar decree for the fifteenth century. There is, however, evidence that many apprentices issued who were either younger or older than twenty-four. Thrupp in a comparison of the registers of freemen of the mercers and grocers with wills and inquisitions showed that

---

[1] Blake, *The Book Collector*, xv (1966), 283–95.
[2] Thomas 1943, and Jones 1954.
[3] Court of the Common Council of the City of London, Journal 17, fol. 6ᵛ.

apprentices took the freedom of their company at ages ranging from twenty-one to twenty-six.[1]

What can we conclude about the date of Caxton's birth? He was an apprentice by 1438, and it is a reasonable assumption that he was fourteen by then, though he could have been considerably older. Unfortunately the Wardens' Account Book has no record of the payment for his issue from apprenticeship. As he is referred to as an apprentice in Robert Large's will, he cannot have issued before 1441. If we accept twenty-six as the highest age at which an apprentice would issue, Caxton was born between 1415 and 1424. A more accurate dating is not possible, for there is no other evidence which can be objectively assessed. If we could accept the identification of William Caxton of Wratting with the printer, his date of birth would be about 1415. This suggestion, like those made by former scholars for a more accurate dating, is too speculative to be acceptable. However, it could be suggested that Caxton's career followed the same pattern as that of his good friend William Pratt. Both their apprenticeship fees were paid in 1438; Pratt issued in 1450; both paid their first livery dues in 1453; Pratt died in 1486 and Caxton in 1491. That Caxton was about the same age as Pratt is likely, but far from certain. They were not apprenticed to the same master and may have become friends at a later date. And unfortunately, we do not know the date of Pratt's birth. For the present we must be content to accept the limits 1415–1424 for Caxton's birth.

There is little to add to this scant picture of Caxton's first years. In his prologue to *Charles the Great* Caxton himself informs us that he went to school.[2] That information implies that his parents were members of the middle classes who were hoping that their son would make use of his education to rise in the administrative or merchant class, a view which is supported by his apprenticeship to Robert Large. Large was an important member of the Mercers' Company who became Lord Mayor of the City of London in 1439. It was probably not easy to get one's son accepted as an apprentice with Large. So we shall not be far wrong if we think of Caxton's father as a merchant or member of the professional or administrative class. If so, it would be natural to suppose that he lived in or near one of the more important centres in Kent, such as Canterbury or Rochester, unless he had acquired sufficient wealth to buy a manor for himself in an attempt to become a member

[1] Thrupp 1948 p. 193.
[2] Crotch 1928 p. 96.

of the landed gentry. Where Caxton's school was we cannot tell. It is not necessary to assume that it was in Kent, since children were sent away to school then, as now. At school he would have acquired an ability to read and write, and no doubt he mastered the rudiments of Latin grammar. He certainly knew Latin, for he translated Latin texts. It is possible that he also learned French at school. His claim in *Charles the Great* that he earned his living from his schooling is too general to be regarded as significant. Yet the letters of merchants do employ French epistolary forms,[1] and it is conceivable that future merchants were given some training in French. Caxton certainly knew French at a later date, as his translations from that language show. Possibly he learned it at school; though he might have picked it up in his business life later on.

The conclusions of this chapter are twofold. Firstly, we have the meagre results of this somewhat involved investigation into Caxton's early years. He was born between 1415 and 1424 in Kent, though not necessarily in the geographical area of the Weald. Indeed, there is a slender possibility that he may have been born in or near Strood. His parents were probably members of the professional or merchant class. When he was old enough he was sent to school, where he would have learned how to read and write, and some Latin. He remained at school till he was fourteen or a little older, when he was apprenticed as a mercer to Robert Large. Secondly, we have learned how complicated it can be to use the evidence found in the sources for Caxton's biography. The results gained from the investigation may hardly seem commensurate with the detailed labour involved. It is, however, necessary to examine the sources in depth because Caxton's life is a subject which has attracted numerous writers, many of whom have not been of a scholarly inclination. In assessing the available evidence we can often appreciate why the theories hitherto accepted are untenable, even if it is not always possible to replace them. Even if it leads to no certainty about individual details in Caxton's life, an examination of the evidence for his biography reveals much about the fifteenth century, and this in turn provides a useful basis from which to understand him and the contribution he made to fifteenth-century culture.

[1] Thrupp 1948 p. 166. See also K. Lambley, *The Teaching and Cultivation of the French Language in England during Tudor and Stuart Times* (Manchester, 1920), and C. P. McMahon, *Education in Fifteenth-Century England* (Baltimore, 1947).

2

MERCER AND MERCHANT ADVENTURER

Whatever the date of Caxton's enrolment as an apprentice with Robert Large may have been, the event itself may be considered the most important one in his life for it meant that he could in due course become a member of the powerful Mercers' Company. The development of his later career was largely determined by his membership of this company. By becoming an apprentice to Large, he also became a member of a rich merchant's household, for the duties of a master included feeding and clothing the apprentices as well as instructing them in the trade. Large was an important and influential merchant. His family was not from London,[1] and Large may himself have come as a young apprentice to London to make his fortune. In this he succeeded, for he died a rich man. Within the company and in the city his talents were recognized: in 1427 he was elected a warden of the company, in 1430 a sheriff of the city, and finally in 1439 Lord Mayor.

Caxton had thus become apprentice to one of the more important men in the city. On becoming an apprentice he would have taken up his lodgings in Large's house situated at the north end of the Old Jewry. This house was extensive, for it housed the family and all the apprentices. In all we know of eleven of his apprentices by name, though they were not all resident in the house at the same time. Some of these apprentices, such as John Harow, became influential men in their time and played a part in the Wars of the Roses. Others, such as Thomas Nyche, appear to have continued working for Large after completing their apprenticeship, possibly as factors. There is no reason to think that Caxton was any different from the other apprentices.[2]

[1] This can be seen from his will, for the original Latin and a translation of which see Blades 1861 i. 95–104. Most of the documents used in this chapter are printed in this book or in Crotch 1928.

[2] It is fortuitous that Caxton's name is linked with that of Large's son, John, in the entry in the Wardens' Account Book recording payment for their enrolment as apprentices.

It is possible that the majority came from good homes and that they received financial support from their fathers when embarking on their mercantile careers. Caxton would have fitted comfortably into this environment for, as suggested in the last chapter, his father may well have been a prosperous member of the middle classes. That Large was his master would have been of great value to him. He became part of what was certainly a flourishing business, which would have provided him with useful contacts and future trading partners.

The Mercers' Company, which Caxton had joined, was particularly associated with the trade between England and north-west Europe. Large himself would have visited the Low Countries in the course of his business, though the only extant evidence for such visits is a brief entry in the Wardens' Account Book for 1432. It is difficult to be certain what goods were included in the trade of 'mercery' which grew up between England and the continent. Mercers dealt in haberdashery, cloth and silks. In the 1330s or 1340s the custody of the Small Beam, the balance belonging to London which was used for weighing small, fine goods, including silk, was entrusted to the care of the Mercers' Company, who appointed a keeper. It was presumably goods of this type which mercers sold retail in London, though London documents also refer to the sale of other forms of merchandise. However, any limitations about what a particular company might sell applied to the retail, not the wholesale, trade. As far as the latter was concerned it appears that, apart from wool, there were few restrictions as to the type of goods which could be exported or imported by members of any company. It was also in this import-export business that the largest fortunes were made; and mercers played a prominent part in it.[1] Large presumably made his fortune from participating in this wholesale trade. He would have imported a wide range of textiles and luxury items and exported cloth and other products in exchange.

The London livery companies originated as trade guilds, which were associations of men engaged in a particular craft to protect the interests of that craft. The Mercers' Company was one of the oldest-established. It had already been organized into a fraternity with its own livery and priest by the beginning of the fourteenth century. By Caxton's time, however, the original purpose of the company was becoming blurred, as were many of the differences between the various companies. The

---

[1] I am indebted to Miss Jean Imray, Archivist of the Mercers' Company, for much of my information about the mercers and the merchant adventurers.

mercers were governed by four wardens, elected annually. A boy entered the company by becoming an apprentice to a freeman. After his apprenticeship, which lasted anything from seven to fifteen years, the apprentice issued to take up the freedom of the company. Among the benefits a freeman possessed were to do business as a member of the company and to enrol apprentices. He was also entitled to take the company livery. There appears to have been no fixed waiting period between taking the freedom and making one's livery payments. A liveryman was eligible for the offices within the company, after which he could look forward to promotion within the city hierarchy. As we saw, the evidence of the Wardens' Account Book is limited because it is far from complete. Thus, although it contains evidence only for Caxton's enrolment as an apprentice and a disputed entry for his first livery payment, there seems no reason to doubt that he progressed normally through the lower ranks of the company. The dates for this progress remain uncertain.

He was an apprentice by 1438, the year in which Large paid his entrance fee to the company, though he may have started his apprenticeship earlier, and he was still an apprentice in 1441, the year in which Large made his will and died. In it Large bequeathed twenty marks to Caxton, his 'apprentice'. Other apprentices were similarly remembered by Large, though some, perhaps the more senior ones, received fifty marks. The date at which Caxton issued from his apprenticeship is not clear. The *terminus ad quem* is 1453, the date of his first livery payment. But as a document in Bruges shows that he was an independent merchant by 1450, he had presumably issued by that date. It has been suggested that on Large's death Caxton would have been transferred as an apprentice to another merchant and even that it was for this assumed new master that he went to the Low Countries.[1] Although the Wardens' Account Book does reveal that some apprentices were transferred to a different master on the death of their first one, this was not a regular practice and there is no need to assume that it happened in Caxton's case. From the Plea and Memoranda Rolls of the City of London it is clear that a widow was expected to carry on her husband's trade and teach his apprentices.[2] Indeed, it would be silly to wind up a flourishing business merely because its manager died. So we may assume that Johanna, Large's second wife, would have taken over the general supervision of the business and the training of the apprentices.

[1] Crotch 1928 pp. xxxvii–xxxviii.
[2] Thomas 1943 pp. 230–1, and Jones 1954 pp. 31, 46, etc.

The business would then have passed to Large's son Richard in 1444. In that year Richard attained the age of twenty-four, and was thus enabled to take over the inheritance which his father had put in trust for him; whereupon Johanna married John Gedney, a draper. So Caxton probably continued as an apprentice in the business after Large's death until he issued from his apprenticeship to become a freeman of the company. It is natural to think that this happened early rather than late in the 1440s, but there is little evidence either way, though the date of his issue may be related to the date of his departure for Bruges.

Under the year 1444 there is an entry in one of the City of London Letter-Books recording payment for certain tenements. This list includes the name William de Caxtone, who paid one penny for his tenement. The editor of the Letter-Books surmised that this William was 'not improbably the famous printer'.[1] If the entry refers to the printer, though there is no proof that it does, it would suggest that he had finished his apprenticeship by 1444, since he was now living in his own tenement, and that he had not left London to go abroad permanently as yet. Both statements seem quite reasonable from what we know of Caxton's life. The only other piece of evidence concerning the date of his departure for the Low Countries is his statement in the prologue to the *History of Troy* that he had been for 'the space of xxx yere for the most parte in the contres of Braband, Flandres, Holand and Zeland' [4]. Previous scholars have taken this to mean that Caxton left England in 1441 shortly after Large's death.[2] There are two points to bear in mind here: the date of the prologue and the interpretation of the thirty years. Caxton informs us that he finished translating the *History of Troy* in September 1471. As we shall see, the book was not printed till late 1473 or early 1474. Thus although the translation was finished in 1471, it is quite probable that the prologue itself was not written till shortly before the book was printed, that is in 1473. Even if we take the thirty years of his prologue literally, it need not mean that he left England before 1443. However, as we saw in the last chapter, we cannot rely upon the accuracy of the figure thirty. It is impossible, therefore, to date his departure to the Low Countries accurately. He was certainly there by 1450. It is doubtful whether he would have left immediately after Large's death in 1441; and even taking the thirty years literally, we have no reason to put his departure before 1443.

[1] *Calendar of Letter-Books: Letter Book K*, edited by R. R. Sharpe (London, 1911), p. 305.
[2] Crotch 1928 p. xxxviii.

Presumably he left England for the first time between 1444 and 1449; there is nothing which favours an early rather than a late date in this period.

It is necessary to pause here to understand why Caxton should have gone to spend so much of his life in Bruges. Today it is a quiet town in Belgium overshadowed by Ostend, Ghent and Brussels. In the fourteenth century it was a thriving merchant town, as many of the houses yet testify. It was possible for ships to sail into the city and unload their merchandise at what is now the Jan van Eyck Plaats. In the fifteenth and sixteenth centuries, the gradual silting up of the River Zwyn made it increasingly difficult for ships to come into the town, which thus lost its position to Ghent and Antwerp. Bruges and Ghent owed their importance to the weaving trade which had developed there. Their artisans produced a fine cloth which was much in demand. Because merchants came to buy this cloth, their presence led to the establishment of a market for a much wider range of goods. The English visited these markets, not only to buy the Flemish cloth and other goods, but also to sell their own cloth and wool. Wool, the export of which was in the hands of English merchants known as the Staplers and which was carefully regulated by the English kings, was used in the production of Flemish cloth. Not unnaturally, therefore, there was a close relationship between England and Flanders. This is not to say that the relationship was always cordial, for both sides tried to take advantage of their position. The Flemings frequently objected to the competition of the English cloth and raised tariff barriers against it. The English retaliated by withholding their wool. When they did so the repercussions were felt all over England, so that the wool export and the trade with Flanders were always of primary political importance.

The county of Flanders was ruled by an independent count in the thirteenth and fourteenth centuries. At the end of the fourteenth century the county passed into the hands of the Dukes of Burgundy through the marriage of Philip the Bold to Margaret of Maele, daughter of Louis II of Flanders. Although their duchy was centred on Burgundy and Dijon, the Dukes had managed later to extend their territory by marriage and diplomacy to include a large part of the north and west of France as well as much of the Low Countries. The emergence of this dukedom as a power in Europe had a profound effect on European political life as well as producing tensions in the Low Countries. For although the great Flemish towns resembled their Italian counterparts, they had never been able to free themselves from the domination of their counts. And if it had been difficult for them to influence the decisions of their counts at an early period, it was even more so when the county was absorbed into the Duchy of Burgundy, for the Dukes made international alliances for wider political considerations than the mercantile self-interest of the Flemish towns.

Nevertheless, despite piracy and the periodic outbreak of war and the squabbling over commercial privileges, the merchant towns in Flanders prospered in the fifteenth century. As we can tell from the account of the fifteenth-century traveller, Pero Tafur, the people of Bruges were prosperous, the houses were solid, and the town was crammed with merchandise of all sorts. He saw there oranges and lemons from Castile, wine and fruits from Greece, spices from Alexandria, furs from the Black Sea, brocades, silks and armour from Italy, and, of course, wool and manufactured textiles.[1] Because of its predominance as a market, merchants from all over Europe gathered at Bruges and established themselves in national communities. Each nation had its own privileges granted both by its rulers and the local authorities, and each was ruled by a governor. This official acted as the spokesman of his own community, tried to extend its privileges, and disciplined its members. The English, like other nations, had established their own settlement in Bruges—and these merchants were known as the Merchant Adventurers. A merchant adventurer is essentially any English merchant, other than a stapler, who engaged in the overseas trade. Originally there were English merchant adventurers in several countries, but the company in the Low Countries was the most important as well as the longest lived. The merchant adventurers came from many towns in England, though London provided the largest contingent. Apart from being organized in the Merchant Adventurers' Company overseas, they were also enrolled in local Merchant Adventurer guilds in their home towns, as the Merchant Adventurers' Hall in York bears witness. In London the position was different, because there was an intimate connexion between the Mercers' Company and that of the Merchant Adventurers. In London, Mercers' Hall acted as the headquarters for the merchant adventurers and housed their records.[2] In the fifteenth century there was no independent Merchant Adventurers' Company as such in London. So,

---

[1] M. Letts, *Pero Tafur* (London, 1926), pp. 198–200.
[2] See Imray, *Journal of the Society of Archivists*, ii (1960–4), 457–67, and works quoted there.

many mercers became merchant adventurers, as Caxton did. Since the mercers dominated the London group of merchant adventurers and since the London merchants formed the most powerful section of the English community abroad, many mercers reached important positions in the Merchant Adventurers' Company. Almost all its Governors in the Low Countries in the fifteenth and sixteenth centuries were mercers. It was thus common for a mercer to seek advancement in the Merchant Adventurers' Company abroad instead of within the Mercers' Company at home.

The preceding paragraphs underline the importance of that first major event in Caxton's life, becoming an apprentice to a mercer. By that step he joined a powerful company which played a dominant role in the trade with the Low Countries. Most mercers were engaged in this trade, and the young Caxton would have become involved in it almost as a matter of course. Once he started to trade in cloth and other wares, he would naturally have visited Bruges, which was at that time the headquarters of the merchant adventurers in the Low Countries. However, the common view that once Caxton left England in the 1440s he never returned to England before 1476 is absurd. It has sprung from a misconception of the life of the merchant adventurers and a misunderstanding of the passage in his prologue to the *History of Troy*, which has been read to mean that he spent thirty years without a break away from England. His 'the space of xxx yere for the most parte in the contres of Braband', in which *for the most parte* has been overlooked, must mean that he also spent some of this time in England. The merchant adventurers, whose company Caxton would have joined on going abroad, may well have spent several months each year visiting foreign markets and commercial centres, but their homes were in England. Some of course may have stayed abroad longer; but even then, since the journey from Bruges to London was relatively easy, they surely returned home periodically.

Thus when Caxton left England in the 1440s, he went to build up a trade, either alone or in partnership, between England and the Low Countries. It is unlikely that he intended to settle permanently in Bruges or any other foreign town, though later when he rose in the hierarchy of the Merchant Adventurers' Company, its business would have protracted his periods of residence there. At first he might have returned frequently to London; and this fact makes the precise date of his first journey to Bruges relatively unimportant. His departure was not a dramatic termination of his life in England in order to begin a new one abroad; it was merely the first of many voyages to the Low Countries he was to make. It is likely, for example, that he was in England in 1453 and 1455. Under 1453 the Account Book contains details of his first livery payment and of the fine he paid for not attending the mayor on his visit to Westminster. Under 1455 his testimony in a lawsuit heard by the Court of the Common Council is recorded in the Journal Books.[1] There is no reason to believe that these two years were exceptional: it is the paucity of the records which prevents us from tracing all his visits to London. That he was often in London may be inferred from the entry in the Wardens' Account Book recording his failure to pay the livery dues (see plate 2). When a mercer was eligible to take up the company livery he paid twenty shillings to the company in three annual instalments of 6s. 8d. each. The Account Book records these payments and whether they were for the first, second or third year. In 1453 seventeen mercers are entered in the accounts for payment of livery dues: sixteen are recorded for paying the 6s. 8d. for their first year, and the seventeenth paid for all three years in a lump sum of twenty shillings. Of the sixteen, fourteen are recorded in the accounts as paying their next instalments in 1454 and 1455. However, the other two, William Caxton and Richard Burgh, do not appear in any later livery payment and their names in the account for 1453 are crossed out and a note is added in the margin to the effect that they were in debt to the company for their fees. At the end of the account these two are duly entered in the list of the company's debtors. Presumably when the clerk was copying out the accounts and came to the list of debtors, he remembered that Caxton and Burgh had already been listed for payment of their dues and so turned back a page to cross out their names. However the error came to be made and whatever the reason may be for Caxton's failure to pay his livery dues in time, presumably he intended to pay them in three annual instalments (there is no indication of his paying a composition fee for the three years), and he expected to be in London for three consecutive years to do so. Indeed, it is probable that he was in London again in 1455, since his testimony in a lawsuit is recorded in the Journal Books of the Court of the Common Council for that year. For the first ten to fifteen years of his life as a merchant adventurer, he may well have spent as much time in London as Bruges. His home and his wife (whose existence is assumed from a reference to his daughter) may

---

[1] Blake, *Notes and Queries*, ccxii (1967), 86-87.

B

have been in London; while abroad, he would have rented lodgings or perhaps stayed at the *domus Anglorum*.[1]

Caxton went abroad to trade. Although later he also became an administrator, negotiator, arbitrator, translator and printer, he remained basically a buyer and seller of goods for the rest of his life. Doubtless textiles were his principal commodity, as was true of all merchant adventurers, but we also have evidence of his dealing in pewter.[2] Otherwise there is little extant documentary evidence as to the goods he traded in. The major English exports to the Low Countries were wool and cloth; and when the Duke of Burgundy prevented the import of these two items into Flanders in 1464, the English community moved in a body to Utrecht. This move, led by Caxton as Governor, emphasizes the importance of these two commodities. Wool was normally in the hands of the staplers, and the merchant adventurers exported the cloth. So we may assume that Caxton, like any other Adventurer, played his part in this trade. On the homeward journey the merchant adventurers shipped luxury items. These presumably included the articles Pero Tafur saw for sale in Bruges as well as such things as pins, hats, tennis balls and feather-beds, which appear in the Customs Accounts of the Port of London. In the fifteenth century Bruges was also the centre of a flourishing trade in manuscripts and paintings. The two businesses went hand in hand, since it was the elaborate and luxurious miniatures in the Bruges manuscripts which made them so sought after by the nobility and merchants of Europe. Many of these manuscripts found their way to England in the fifteenth century, and some excellent examples can still be seen in the Royal Library, now in the British Museum. They were imported by merchant adventurers. An interesting record of the importance of books in their trade is provided by an entry in the Acts of Court of the Mercers' Company for 1479. In that year it was agreed to standardize the arrangement of a bill of custom, and a specimen of how such bills were to be set out in future was drawn up. The wares included in the specimen were no doubt those handled most frequently by the Adventurers—hence their inclusion. They include manufactured cloth from various centres in the Low Countries, taffeta, satin, damask and fustian, cotton kerchiefs—and paper books.[3]

[1] The manuscript 'Register of Privileges: English Merchants' [Mercers' Hall] records that the English merchants usually owned a house in important towns and that they all tended to rent lodgings in the same street.

[2] Blake, *Notes and Queries*, ccxii (1967), 86–87.

[3] Lyell and Watney 1936 p. 118; cf. also p. 509.

This evidence supports the assumption that Caxton sold manuscripts during his career as a merchant adventurer. On the other hand, the view that there was a sharp break in his life when he began printing lacks conviction. Those who think along these lines usually imply that for the first half of his life he was solely a merchant, possibly with some scholarly interests, and that later he ceased to be a merchant to become a scholar-printer. But in the latter part of his life he remained a merchant selling wares, even if those wares were his books. If as a merchant adventurer he sold manuscripts as well as cloth and other goods, there is no need to assume a drastic change in his way of life. From a seller of manuscripts he could easily become a printer and seller of books. Indeed, it could have been from his activities as a seller of manuscripts that he realized what opportunities were afforded by the new art of printing and decided to explore them. Later when he had settled at Westminster, he imported books and manuscripts from the continent,[1] which suggests that he may also have done so earlier. Furthermore, as he acquired books from the continent so quickly, it is likely that he was familiar with the pattern of book-distribution in Europe and that he had acquired this knowledge while abroad. Then in his prologues and epilogues Caxton refers to the sale of manuscripts to English customers and to his own reading of manuscripts while on the continent. For example, he wrote in the prologue to *Blanchardin and Eglantine* that he had sold the manuscript of the French text to Margaret, Duchess of Somerset, 'longe to fore' [105]; and in his prologue to *King Arthur* that 'many noble volumes be made of hym [i.e. Arthur] & of his noble knyghtes in Frensshe, which I have seen & redde beyonde the see' [94]. There are several similar references, and although it is not possible to prove that any of them refer to the period before he learned printing in 1471, it is quite possible that some of them do. In one instance there is good evidence that it does. Caxton made his English translation of the *Mirror of the World* (1481) from a French text written in Bruges in 1464. He also used the French prologue in this manuscript as a model for his own, as we shall see in Chapter Eight where the two prologues are printed in full. But one important detail has been added in Caxton's translation: where the French manuscript (now British Museum, Royal 19 A IX) states that it was made in Bruges in 1464, Caxton's prologue puts the date more specifically as June 1464. Since there is nothing in the manuscript which could have given him this information, it is likely that he knew it because he had purchased the

[1] Kerling, *The Book Collector*, iv (1955), 190-9.

manuscript from the Bruges bookseller in June 1464. One cannot be certain that he bought the manuscript, since he made the translation for Hugh Bryce, and possibly Bryce lent the manuscript to Caxton for the purposes of the translation. But usually when a manuscript was loaned to him Caxton informs us of it, which he does not in this case. If the manuscript had belonged to someone else it is perhaps rather unlikely that the information that it was finished in June 1464, information which is unique in his prologues, would have been added. It is not improbable that Bryce came to Caxton wishing to have a translation made, but left the choice of text to the printer. So Caxton may have bought the French manuscript in 1464 and it may have been in his possession till the translation was made.[1] If so, it would be a good example of his interest in the book trade before he turned to printing.

Although none of these points is conclusive in itself, together they build up a strong case. There is also the evidence of the style of his prologues, in which he used many formulas. Significantly, they appear even in his earliest texts. Usually they are based more on French than on English models. The occurrence of these formulas proves that he had some acquaintance with contemporary French literature before he started translating. Without such knowledge he could not have aped the words and clichés of his contemporaries so closely. He probably acquired this knowledge of literary formulas from French manuscripts produced in Bruges in the fifteenth century. If an English merchant was familiar with the contents of French manuscripts, his familiarity presumably sprang from a trade in manuscripts, for there is little evidence that Caxton was a scholar. Furthermore, when Caxton returned from Cologne after learning how to print, he entered into a partnership with Colard Mansion, a prominent Bruges bookseller who became dean of the booksellers' guild in 1471. This partnership could easily have arisen from an earlier business association by which Caxton bought manuscripts from Mansion's workshop. It would have been from a bookseller like Mansion that he acquired the manuscript of the French *History of Troy* which he used for his own translation of that work.

There is one piece of possible evidence that ought also to be considered. A manuscript in Boston, Massachusetts, contains a collection of poems and proseworks in French and English (see plate 7). The manuscript was copied in Calais and bound in north-western France or Flanders in the fifteenth century. The importance of this manuscript

[1] Blake, *Notes and Queries*, ccxii (1967), 205–7.

is that according to a contemporary note it belonged to a William Caston, who gave it to William Sonnyng in 1471. Nothing is known of Moris, the scribe, or of Sonnyng, but it is conceivable that the William Caston should be identified with William Caxton, the printer.[1] If the identification could be accepted, it would show that Caxton had owned at least one manuscript before he started printing. However, since the identification of Caston with Caxton is not definite, this evidence remains of uncertain value.

Although we may thus assume that Caxton was engaged in the book trade for some time before he started printing, his main business was doubtless the buying and selling of cloth. This business is mentioned in the same documents which refer to his dealings in pewter. We have otherwise little evidence about his life as a trader, for the surviving documents deal mainly with lawsuits. He also refers occasionally in his books to various episodes in his life on the continent. One might think from these references that he had never been a merchant. For whereas in the documents we see him settling differences between merchants at Antwerp,[2] or being engaged in litigation on his own behalf, in his writings he referred only to such events as attending divine service in the Church of Our Lady, Antwerp, talking with the Benedictines of Ghent, or discussing David's psalms with Sir John Capons. The discrepancy is explained by the different nature of the two sources. The documents are records of legal business, whereas Caxton's writings were moral and edifying treatises intended for a courtly audience. Chivalry and religion have no part in the former, just as the marketplace is out of keeping with the latter. In order to understand his life fully it is necessary to keep both sides of it in mind. He did not cease to be a worldly man in order to develop an interest in moral questions when he became a printer. He was a religious man and a merchant all his life.

The earliest document from Bruges in which Caxton is mentioned is dated 2 January 1450.[3] It records a lawsuit, in which he was involved because he and another Englishman, John Selle, had stood surety to John Granton, a stapler from Calais, for a sum of £110. Since Granton had not paid this debt to William Craes, another English merchant, when it was due, he had been imprisoned in Bruges, but had subsequently fled. As a result Caxton and Selle were forced to pay the

---

[1] Thus McCusker, More Books, 6th Series xv (1940), 275–84.
[2] Antwerp: Stadtsarchief, Schepenbrieven No. 69 [1465].
[3] Misdated by Blades 1861 i. 105 to 1449.

debt, though they assured the court that Granton could easily meet the obligation. The case raises two interesting points. Firstly, though the lawsuit took place in Bruges, all the merchants involved were English. Consequently we may wonder whether this document proves that Caxton was by then settled in Bruges. The transaction could have been made in London or elsewhere. As suggested earlier, he may still at this time have been resident as often in London as in Bruges. Secondly, as he was standing surety to a stapler from Calais, he may have visited Calais and perhaps had some connexion with the wool trade carried out by the staplers. In his prologue to the *History of Troy* he wrote that he had never been to France. But by France he probably meant the kingdom of France, of which Calais did not form a part in the fifteenth century. As there were often close dealings between the staplers and merchant adventurers who often infringed on what was properly the Staple trade, Caxton may have been involved at some time in the wool trade.

This suggestion receives support from two charters referred to by Thielemans concerning a William Caxton of the Staple at Calais, dated 1453 and 1458 respectively.[1] The first concerns the arrest of some goods belonging to Caxton and other English merchants at the customs in Nieuport; they included cloth, furs, silk, ermine and saffron. It was disputed how much duty should be paid for the wares, particularly as the saffron had been concealed in a cask—though Caxton pleaded ignorance of its existence. When the amount of duty was settled, the goods were returned to Caxton. The second document records the grant of a safeconduct to Caxton and Anthoine de la Tour to take part in the Anglo-Burgundian negotiations at Bruges. Unfortunately, it is not certain whether these documents, particularly the first one, refer to the future printer, for he is never referred to as a stapler elsewhere. The first one might refer to another Caxton, perhaps the William Caston who owned the manuscript made in Calais and now in Boston (cf. p. 36). If it does refer to the printer, it confirms that he was trading in luxury items at an early stage in his career, for the wares mentioned are exceptional in their quantity and richness; other documents do not record that English merchants were exporting so many luxury items from the continent to England. The second document for its part confirms that Caxton was not resident in Bruges at this time, since the safeconduct was for a journey to go there.

[1] Thielemans 1966 pp. 262, 371: Lille, Archives départementales du Nord B 17674 and B 2030 fol. 247.

Caxton also appears in a lawsuit referred to in four documents.[1] The details of the suit, which this time was conducted in England, are not clear, though it extended over the years 1453–5. The suit is of interest in that it shows that Caxton was now an active merchant with goods in both England and Flanders. Of particular importance is the information that John Harow, one of Robert Large's apprentices, was standing surety for Caxton, since this shows that Large's former fellow-apprentices helped one another. Finally, it should be mentioned that the business was completed at Ghent. Caxton, like his fellow mercers, travelled round the various markets in the Low Countries in order to buy and sell his wares.

Caxton was now a successful businessman who had acquired wealth and prestige. The growth of his prestige can be traced in his election to the Governorship of the English Nation at Bruges and in the increasing role he played in international politics. The growth in wealth may be assumed from his appointment as Governor, since merchants honoured only those of their own number who were successful. Today we should not expect an unsuccessful businessman to be elected Lord Mayor of London; and the same was no doubt true then of the governorship of the English Nation. The year in which Caxton became Governor is not clear, but may have been 1462. In that year his predecessor in the office, William Obray (or Overey), was dismissed, apparently for accepting a bribe from the rulers of Antwerp to show special favour to that town. How Obray was to fulfil his part of the bargain is unknown, but the attempted bribery underlines the importance of the English merchants to the prosperity of the towns in Brabant and Flanders. Further, that Caxton was elected Governor after an incident of this nature indicates that his colleagues thought him of sufficient probity not to succumb to the same temptation. This does not mean that he received no gifts from the towns in the Low Countries. Several of their accounts record payment for some gift, usually a barrel or two of wine, to him. They may have been granted to make his stay in the towns more agreeable, and they were perhaps treated as part of the town's hospitality. He incurred no dishonour in accepting such gifts, which were commonly made at this time, and there can be no question of bribery.

In addition to what it tells us of his wealth and prestige, this appointment may be used to give further information about him. It was probably only about this time that he started to live permanently in

[1] Crotch 1928 Appendix I and XXI, and Blake, *Notes and Queries*, ccxii (1967), 86–87.

Bruges. Whereas before 1462 several documents record his presence in England, after that time the English documentary evidence refers only to the receipt of letters from or the despatch of letters to Caxton and to his activities beyond the sea on behalf of his fellow merchants. There is no record of any visit to England. Furthermore, as a result of his position he was often chosen as one of the English negotiators in Anglo-Burgundian talks. Since commercial relations between the two countries were strained in the 1460s, there were many, often fruitless, discussions. Nevertheless, as a result of them Caxton came into contact with many of the leading men in England and the Low Countries. He could use the knowledge of the nobility and their tastes to supply them with the luxuries they sought after such as books. Since the English emulated Burgundian taste, he was ideally placed to act as a middleman. His trade in manuscripts may thus date from this period of his business life, particularly because, as we shall see, the cloth trade suffered considerable restrictions at this time.

Caxton's appointment as Governor also suggests that he was a Yorkist. Edward IV had been on the throne only a short time when Caxton became Governor, and it would have been tactless of the merchant adventurers to elect a man with Lancastrian leanings. It is doubtful whether the Governor could have been politically neutral, for he would have to negotiate frequently on Edward's behalf. As it happens, the mercers had tended to support the Yorkists. Thus John Harow, who is probably to be identified with Caxton's old fellow-apprentice and business-partner, took an active part in the Yorkist siege of the Tower of London in 1460 and was beheaded after fighting for the Duke of York at the Battle of Wakefield. Another London mercer, William Cantelowe, was made a Knight of the Bath at Edward's coronation, which he had no doubt helped to bring about, and later two chronicles report that it was he who in 1467 captured Henry VI for Edward. The merchant adventurers, like the mercers in London, also favoured the Yorkist party, for the Lancastrians had tended to look to France rather than to Burgundy for support, particularly after Henry VI's marriage to Margaret of Anjou. When Edward IV had gained the throne with the consequent dispersal of the Lancastrians, one of these, the Duke of Somerset, found refuge at the Burgundian court, where Charles the Bold sided with the Lancastrians on account of his family connexions. This protection excited the animosity of the English merchants, with the result that street brawls between these merchants and the Duke's men broke out.

When Caxton became Governor of the English Nation at Bruges, he was forced to play some part in international politics. Though during his governorship he took part in the discussions with the Hanseatic League, for the most part he was involved in the diplomatic manoeuvrings among England, France and Burgundy. A few words on the relationships of these three powers are necessary. The duchy of Burgundy, under Philip the Good till 1467 and then under his son Charles the Bold, owed allegiance to France for its French possessions, but its rulers behaved like independent princes. Naturally this state of affairs was one that was distasteful to Louis XI, King of France (1461–83), who used all his diplomatic subtlety to bring about the destruction of the Dukes. For this purpose he was willing to enter into an alliance with the English. But not only was England closely connected by trade to the Flemish possessions of the Dukes of Burgundy, but also France was her traditional enemy, which meant that the English tended to look to Burgundy for support in their policy of trying to hold on to their own possessions in France or even to regain lost ones. For their part, the Burgundians wanted to preserve their independence of the King of France, but because of the propinquity of the two countries, and the theoretical allegiance owed to France, the Dukes were often forced to seek some form of rapprochement with Louis. However, although the Dukes valued the trade with England, they also wanted to protect their own industries from English competition: hence import restrictions were often raised against English cloth. This sketch provides the background of the political situation in the 1460s, but throughout the decade the situation was fluid with a multitude of proposals and counterproposals for alliances.

When Caxton took over the governorship in 1462, there was a commercial agreement in force between England and Burgundy. So apart from piracy, both official and unofficial, trade was carried on without too much hindrance. The English were as worried by the imports from Burgundy as the Flemings were by those from England. So the parliament of 1463 persuaded Edward to introduce protectionist duties against specified imports from the Low Countries. However, the English merchants wanted to continue their trade with Flanders, and shortly before the commercial treaty between the two countries was due to expire on 1 November 1464, they sent a sub-sheriff of London to Edward to remind him to take the necessary steps to renew it. The King then appointed William Caxton and Richard Whetehill, Lieutenant of Guines and a servant to the Earl of Warwick, as his ambassadors. They met their counterparts in October and an agreement was signed on the twenty-seventh of that month, whereby trade between the two countries was to be carried on as usual for the following year. But the previous day Philip, upon the insistence of his own merchants and in retaliation against the English parliament's restrictions of 1463, banned the import of English cloth.

The ban caused considerable anger among the English merchants, whose answer was to leave Flanders in a body and settle in Utrecht. Caxton, who had no doubt striven to prevent the ban, led the exodus. The town of Utrecht was only too willing to welcome the English merchants and granted them all the privileges enjoyed there by the Hanseatic League. Since these terms were ratified on 20 November 1464 the English merchants appear to have vacated Flanders with considerable expedition, though ratification could have been made before their departure. Utrecht also allowed the English to hold a fair where they could sell their cloth. The first of these markets was held in January and February 1465. It is not certain how long Caxton or his fellow merchants remained in their new home. The privileges were renewed by Utrecht annually up to and including 1467, so that most of the English merchants may have returned to Flanders in late 1467 or early 1468.[1] Caxton, however, returned to Flanders earlier than this, for he was present at many of the negotiations between England and Burgundy. The extension of the commercial treaty between England and Burgundy signed in October 1464 lasted only one year, and once again the merchants had to remind Edward of its impending lapse. The King wanted them to make their own treaty with Burgundy, but they shrank from such a bold departure from precedent. All this information was relayed by letter to Caxton, who was presumably in or near Bruges. Not long afterwards the treaty was renewed for another year, though the ban on cloth was not lifted. A period of intense diplomatic activity followed, much of it at or near St Omer. Letters to and from Caxton crossed the Channel frequently, and some record of them is to be found in the Acts of Court of the Mercers' Company. Caxton probably attended most of the negotiations as the representative of the English merchants overseas, though his presence cannot always be proved. These negotiations dragged on inconclusively for several years until finally in November 1467 a commercial treaty for thirty years was signed. It was ratified by the new Duke, Charles, in February of the following year. Many privileges were restored to

[1] Stein, *Hansische Geschichtsblätter* (1899), 179–89.

the English by this treaty, but the ban on English cloth was not lifted despite the marriage alliance which had also been arranged by the negotiators. Charles, who had begun to fear that he might be out-manoeuvred by Louis in his dealings with the English, had agreed in despite of his Lancastrian sympathies to accept Margaret, Edward IV's sister, as his third wife. The English hoped that this marriage would lead to concessions from Charles; but they had to be satisfied with promises of further negotiations. Caxton was to attend these later diets as one of the English ambassadors.

The marriage between Charles and Margaret which took place in 1468 provided an occasion for a magnificent display. The Burgundian court was noted for its extravagance, and this was a ceremony that called for pageants, tournaments and all the concomitants of chivalry. The bride arrived from England at Sluys on 25 June and made her way to Damme, the foreport of Bruges. The marriage took place in the magnificent stadthuis at Damme, which is still standing. After the marriage the couple made a triumphal entry into Bruges. Fountains flowed with wine. Pageants of great splendour with feasting and tournaments continued for nine days. We may assume that Caxton as Governor and one of the English negotiators attended these cele-brations, and he also met members of the English nobility who were present. This and similar events confirmed that taste for chivalry which he had developed and which was to find expression in his printed books —a taste he shared with many of his contemporaries.

Although the new treaty with Burgundy and the marriage of Charles and Margaret allowed the English to return to Flanders, there were still many difficulties in the way of their trade, particularly the ban on cloth. Yet while this ban was in force Caxton spent several years in Flanders. Presumably in these years either he gave up this trade in favour of other goods, or else he let factors at Utrecht carry on trade in his name. He would naturally have continued as a merchant, but the negotiations in which he was constantly involved would not have allowed him much time to attend to business himself. Possibly the difficulties which the English merchants encountered in these years encouraged him to give up the cloth trade altogether and to rely on other forms of merchandise. The development of the printing press presented him with an opportunity to diversify his business, in which he could use his knowledge of Burgundian taste and of economic matters to good advantage. The troubles which the English were having with the Hanseatic League may have added another inducement to him to change his business, since it was becoming increasingly difficult to trade with the Hanseatic towns other than Cologne, which remained friendly towards England. It was in that town that Caxton was to learn how to print.

The dispute between Edward and the Hanseatic League was largely of the former's making, for on his accession Edward had refused to confirm its privileges in England. It was only after pleas on their behalf from the King of Poland and the Emperor that he agreed to grant a temporary extension. The reasons for Edward's actions may be ascribed to the English merchants' envy of the privileges enjoyed by the League, his unwillingness to honour the debts incurred by his predecessor, and his preference for Italian merchants. The Hanseatic League, which was a loose confederation of merchant towns stretching over most of north-western Europe and beyond, reacted slowly because it took time for them to prepare concerted action. Furthermore, opinion as to what action to take was divided, since Cologne and the towns in Holland, which had close trading ties with England, preferred conciliation, whereas other towns further away insisted on Edward's complete capitulation. At first the controversy led to no more than a series of meetings or attempted meetings, while Edward granted continual temporary renewals of the Hanseatic privileges. Nevertheless, the failure to come to any settlement led to a consistent deterioration in the relationship. Matters came to a head in 1468. As the result of an unfounded rumour that the League had seized four English ships in the Øresund, Edward closed the Steelyard, its headquarters in London, imprisoned the Hansards there, and fined them £20,000. The men of Cologne, however, were soon released from captivity and were allowed to continue their trade with England under the former privileges enjoyed by the whole League. In January 1469 London's Common Council received a letter from Caxton about the Hanseatic League. We do not know what this letter contained, but it reveals that he was taking some hand in the negotiations to break the deadlock. His participation was natural, for many cities in the Low Countries either belonged to the League or had communities of Hanseatic merchants. The Duke of Burgundy had himself been trying to arbitrate between the disputants. Caxton was thus well placed to negotiate. Indeed, later in the year he was one of the ambassadors nominated to treat with the Duke over the ban on English cloth; but the same embassy was also empowered to treat with the Hansards if they should send a delegation. Cologne also tried to mediate between the two sides, for though a member of the League she was still trading with England. It may be that Caxton became friendly with the merchants from Cologne at this time. Unfortunately the troubles that broke out in England in the summer of 1469 made it clear that Edward would be unable to ratify any decisions his embassy came to, so no progress was made. Inevitably, therefore, the League retaliated against Edward's actions of 1468 by prohibiting the sale of English cloth in Hanseatic towns and by expelling Cologne from the League in 1470. Further negotiation then became impossible because the troubles in England took a turn for the worse, leading ultimately to Edward's flight to the Low Countries in 1470. As we shall see, these events had their influence on Caxton's project of learning how to print.

Although this chapter has covered a long period in Caxton's life rather cursorily, it is not to be inferred that it was an unimportant phase in his career. The briefness of the story is occasioned by the paucity of sources; it is difficult to glean much general information from his own writings about this part of his life. In this period Caxton learned how to finance projects and he acquired considerable wealth. Both were necessary for the successful completion of his venture into printing: the capital he used to buy a press and other necessary equipment, the financial knowledge to ensure that the project remained economically viable. While on the continent he also made those contacts which were so necessary for him. He met the Bruges booksellers who could provide him with wares, members of the Burgundian upper classes who set the pace in fashion, and members of the English aristocracy who would be among his future clientele for books. At the same time he remained a merchant with important connexions among the London mercers. These connexions would always enable him to raise money when necessary, to import material from the continent for his press, and to distribute his own goods. By 1469 he was both a seasoned merchant and negotiator. His decision to take up printing cannot have been lightly made and was not intended to provide him with a hobby during a kind of semi-retirement. The printing press was a form of economic speculation or investment. The project could fail; but Caxton must have felt that he had sufficient financial ability to make it a success. In this events were to prove him correct.

3

THE PRINTING PRESS

Caxton resigned from the governorship of the English merchant adventurers in order to devote his time to printing. This did not mean that he cut himself off from his former colleagues or that he necessarily gave up his business in cloth and general merchandise. He remained a mercer and merchant adventurer; and a man who had been Governor would have continued to exercise considerable influence on the affairs of the English community in Bruges. The change to publishing and bookselling involved an expansion of one part of his business and a contraction of the other part, the general merchandising: it did not amount to a complete break with what had gone before. This is a point to remember in following Caxton's later history, for from now I shall be concerned with tracing the development of his translating and printing activities.

The most important source for Caxton's first translation and printed book is naturally the *History of Troy* itself, in which he included a prologue and several epilogues dealing with the history of the translation. These reveal that the translation was commenced in Bruges on 1 March 1469[1] [2]. After he had completed only five or six quires, Caxton fell into despair that he would ever finish the task because of his faulty command of English. He therefore put it aside thinking never to take it up again. Two years later, however, he showed what he had translated to Margaret of Burgundy, who ordered him to finish the translation and to improve his style [4–5]. He continued his translation in Ghent [6] and finished it in Cologne on 19 September 1471 [2]. After his return to Bruges he set up the translation in type, for he had promised copies to various people. The date at which he finished printing the book is not stated, though he does say he defrayed the printing costs himself [7]. He also gave a few details about the book he was translating. The French version had been translated from Latin into French by Raoul Lefèvre in 1464 at the command of Philip, Duke of Burgundy [2], though Caxton does not say how he had managed to

[1] Caxton gives the date as 1468. But as he, like his contemporaries, reckoned his years from Easter, his 1 March 1468 is our 1 March 1469.

get a copy of this book, which itself presumably remained in the ducal library, only five years after it had been made. Several questions arise from this information. Firstly, what was Caxton's relationship to Margaret of Burgundy? Secondly, what is the relationship between the translation and the printed book? Was the translation made to be printed; or were the translation and printing originally independent projects? Finally, how did Caxton learn the art of printing?

It has always been assumed that Caxton relinquished the governorship of the merchant adventurers in order to enter the service of Margaret of Burgundy. He has been described either as Margaret's private secretary or her librarian. The explanations for his move have included, among others, that he wished to get married, and that he wanted to gratify his scholarly interest in books.[1] There is, however, no evidence for any of these hypotheses, just as there is insufficient proof that he was ever in Margaret's service.

Three reasons have been offered to justify that suggestion. Firstly, he refers to Margaret as 'my ... redoubtyd lady' [6] as well as employing many similar terms. Secondly, he received a yearly fee from her [5]. Finally, he describes himself as 'a servant unto her sayde grace' [5]. The first point clearly carries little weight; the expression is a polite form that any member of the middle classes might use when addressing someone of a higher station. Caxton used this or a similar apostrophe in all his prologues and epilogues. Earl Rivers is 'my lord' [28] or even 'my special lorde' [32], and the young Prince of Wales is 'my moost redoubted yong lorde' [34]. Margaret, Duchess of Somerset, is 'my redoubted lady' [104]. Other fifteenth-century writers such as Lydgate refer to their patrons in identical words. The expression may indicate that Margaret was Caxton's patron; it certainly does not prove that she was his employer.

The second point, that he received a yearly fee from Margaret, is equally inconclusive. This fee was not an annual salary; it had more the nature of an annual gift granted as a token of respect, as a parallel from Caxton's later life shows. He started to translate the *Golden Legend*, but for various reasons he was tempted to discontinue it, just as he had the *History of Troy*. As Margaret had encouraged him to continue with the *History of Troy*, so the Earl of Arundel urged him to finish the *Golden Legend*. As an inducement the Earl offered him 'a yerely fee' [70] of a buck in summer and a doe in winter. Margaret's fee may have been of

[1] See for example Plomer 1925 p. 47 ff., and Hittmair 1934 p. 32.

the same type, or even a cash payment. It was a mark of favour given to encourage him to complete his work and to lead him to hope for further favours. The 'fee' does not prove that he was in the service of Margaret at this time any more than the later fee proves that he was then in the service of the Earl of Arundel. The fee was part of the system of patronage and had nothing to do with service.

The final detail, Caxton's statement that he was 'a servant unto her sayde grace' [5], is similarly inconclusive. The two usages of the word *servant* commonest at this time indicate firstly a gentleman's sub-servience and humility to his lady, and secondly the respect owed by a member of a lower class to a member of the nobility.[1] Caxton used the word in the latter sense. Just as he called Margaret his redoubted lady, so he called himself her servant; these are the obverse and reverse of the same coin. They indicate social position, not an employer-employee relationship. Caxton referred to himself as the servant of many people—and he certainly cannot have been in the employment of all of them. Thus the *Game of Chess* is dedicated to the Duke of Clarence 'by hym that is your most humble servant' [16]. Caxton is the 'humble servaunt' [105] of Margaret, Duchess of Somerset. In some prologues *servant* is linked in a doublet with *subject*, a connexion which confirms that Caxton understood the word to imply feudal respect. The Prince of Wales is asked to accept *Jason* from 'his humble subgiett & servaunte' [34]. Caxton is the 'moost humble subget and litil servant' [44] of Edward IV and the 'most indigne, humble subgette and lytel servaunt' [104] of Henry VII. The use of *servant* in these examples is no different from its use in the *History of Troy;* he often uses *servant* and *redoubted lady* (or *lord*) in the same prologue. In neither case can the expression be taken as proof that he was in the service of Margaret of Burgundy in the sense that he was a paid servant in her household. Margaret was his patron, not his employer. She gave him encourage-ment and some form of financial assistance; but otherwise he continued to provide for himself from the profits of his trading.

Why Caxton should have wanted the patronage of Margaret of Burgundy is easily explained. Margaret was the sister of Edward IV of England and her marriage to Duke Charles of Burgundy was a political one to strengthen the Anglo-Burgundian alliance. Because of her position she became the focal point for promoting English interests in the Low Countries. Caxton, as Governor of the English Nation at Bruges, would have come into contact with her over political

[1] *The Oxford English Dictionary*, s.v. *Servant*, sb. 4.

and commercial matters. With regard to his personal ambitions, he would have seen her as the leading lady in Burgundy and a member of the English royal house, and desired her patronage as the most accessible member of the English nobility and so able to introduce him into court circles in England through her recommendation. There were also many Englishmen at Margaret's court, including many members of the aristocracy. By becoming one of Margaret's protégés Caxton could further his acquaintance with them. He may already have provided some of them with books or other wares, but he would be able to use Margaret's patronage to extend such operations. He may indeed have sold books to Margaret herself, for we know she was interested in literary matters. There were several English books in the Burgundian ducal library which probably entered it through her. She also commissioned many translators and writers to make books for her (cf. plate 3). David Aubert executed several orders for her, and her almoner Nicholas Finet made the translation, *Benois seront les miséricordieux*, at her command.[1] She was particularly fond of devotional works, especially when they were sumptuously illustrated and bound. Many of these books were made for her at Ghent, where Caxton continued his own translation. In view of Margaret's tastes it would have been natural for Caxton, the Governor of the English Nation, to provide her with manuscripts either by way of trade or as presents to win her favour, and to introduce to her the local craftsmen who prepared many of the luxurious volumes so common in the Low Countries. One can imagine it was on an occasion of this sort that he first raised the matter of his own translation. It would be a natural continuation of the subject of books and booksellers. It is impossible to know what took place at that interview, particularly as it was customary for writers to inflate the part played by their patrons in the genesis of their works. One thing is certain: Margaret offered him her protection and some form of financial assistance if he continued his translation. She may also have encouraged him to use a more courtly style and she may have approved his intention to print the translation. In order to evaluate these two possibilities we must consider how and why the translation came about.

In his prologue to the *History of Troy* Caxton informs us that Margaret heard of the project of the translation only in 1471, two years after he had started it. He had begun translating in 1469 and then given it up. The reason, according to Caxton, was his incompetence as a

[1] For a biography of Margaret see Hommel 1959.

translator and his lack of command of English. It is not a convincing one, for in the centre of the European book trade he could probably have found someone else to do it for him if he had just wanted a translation. He evidently wanted to make the translation himself and was prevented from completing it for two years. Yet later, when he resumed his translation, he finished it very quickly, which in view of the length of the book indicates that his command of the two languages involved was not so imperfect as he alleged. We must look for a more plausible explanation of this break in his plans. Before doing that, we must decide whether the *History of Troy* was his first translation and whether it was made to be printed.

It has been suggested that Caxton was interested in literary matters from an early age and that this interest had led him to make translations long before he started the *History of Troy*.[1] Two of his printed books, *Reynard the Fox* and the *Vocabulary*, have been attributed to this early phase of translation. This theory, however, finds no support in the available evidence. *Reynard the Fox* is a translation of a Dutch version printed at Gouda in 1479, so that the translation was made immediately before it was printed in 1481.[2] The *Vocabulary* was almost certainly translated in 1465–6, as Grierson in a study of the coinage mentioned in it has suggested.[3] But both the method of translation and the linguistic details characteristic of it are very different from those in Caxton's known translations. So it is improbable that the *Vocabulary* was translated by Caxton. It may well have been made by another mercer or merchant adventurer, and the translation probably reached him only shortly before he set it up in 1480.[4] In the light of our present information the *History of Troy* was his first translation. Certainly one gets this impression from its prologue and epilogues. In them he compared his attempt at the translation of those first five or six quires with the running of 'blynde Bayard' [4]. Although this proverbial phrase is used by other writers,[5] it nevertheless gives the impression of a first attempt. Caxton did not use this expression again. Perhaps he thought it suitable only for his first work though he made repeated use of similar traditional phrases in his later books. Yet his

[1] Plomer 1925 p. 175.

[2] Blake, *Bulletin of the John Rylands Library*, xlvi (1963–4), 298–311.

[3] P. Grierson, 'The Date of the "Livre des Mestiers" and its Derivatives', *Revue Belge de Philologie et d'Histoire*, xxxv (1957), 783.

[4] N. F. Blake, 'The *Vocabulary in French and English* printed by William Caxton', *English Language Notes*, iii (1965–6), 7–15.

[5] E.g. *Canterbury Tales* G 1413, and Lydgate's *Troy-Book* II. 4730–5, V. 3506.

faulty command of English is never again used as an excuse. When at a later date he delayed the completion of the *Golden Legend*, he was deterred by its length, not by his own incompetence. When he translated *Eneydos*, he was worried about which of two styles to use, not by his incompetence in either of them. Consequently, although his phraseology in the *History of Troy* is traditional, it nevertheless makes it unlikely that he had made any translation before 1469. If he had been translating for some time, he ought to have acquired both experience and confidence by then; the prologue and epilogues do not lead one to think that he had.

If it was Caxton's first translation, the question naturally arises as to why he started to translate at all. He claimed that he did so to eschew sloth and idleness; but this is a traditional formula which means little or nothing. It is also difficult to accept that the translation was the scholarly hobby which a busy man used to occupy his leisure hours. If so, he would surely have made earlier translations. The conjunction of a first attempt at translation and a first attempt at printing can best be interpreted in my opinion to mean that the translation was made to be printed. In other words Caxton's decision to learn how to print may be dated to 1 March 1469, when he began the translation. It was part of the grand design of learning to print. Further lines of reasoning are opened up by this conclusion. It is not necessary to have a translation to learn how to print. Most of the early printers started by issuing Latin texts. Caxton could have done this or he could have printed a French book. All the books commissioned by Margaret of Burgundy were in French and it would thus hardly be for her sake that he produced a printed book in English. Similarly a translation does not need to be printed. He could easily have employed one of the many scribes in Bruges to make copies for him. The production of multiple copies of an English translation clearly indicates an intention to capture the English home market, for there cannot have been sufficient Englishmen at Margaret's court to create a demand which could be satisfied only by printing. This does not mean that Caxton at first planned to return to England, but it does suggest that he was familiar with the pattern of book distribution in England. It seems as though he intended to produce books in Bruges and then send them to England to be distributed. The books would be mainly for sale to courtiers and the richer merchants, as we shall see in the next chapter. That this was so may account for Caxton's decision to make the translation himself. There is no evidence that he could have found in Bruges translators who would be able to turn French texts into English, though as Bruges was an important centre for the production of manuscripts, it is not improbable. But the trouble with the work of a professional translator was that the English courtiers might have regarded it as uncourtly. We shall see that there were two styles in England, and that the court favoured the new style, which had been established by Chaucer. Caxton may have felt that a translation by an unknown professional scribe would not have the cachet of one made by a courtly translator and therefore would not have any appeal for the type of buyer he envisaged. Caxton, however, was Governor of the English Nation at Bruges and was acquainted with members of the nobility. His position was a guarantee that he was acquainted with the courtly style. Furthermore, Margaret of Burgundy was or became his patron, and in his prologue he laid particular emphasis on Margaret's comments on his style. He had stopped the translation on account of his own dissatisfaction with his style. Margaret, however, approved of it though she suggested some improvements. By stating this he paid a compliment to his patron while implying that his style had the *imprimatur* of one of the most fashionable ladies of the time. Who could deny that his style was courtly if Margaret approved it? Caxton's little story is a means of recommending his book to the purchasers — a publisher's 'blurb' — rather than a literal account of the translation's genesis.

If the book was not held up by Caxton's stylistic difficulties, why did he wait for two years to complete the translation? The answer to this question is not difficult if we accept that he intended to produce books for the English market. On 1 March 1469 it seemed as though conditions in England were ideal for the introduction of English printed books. Despite intermittent squabbles, the Yorkist monarchy was well established. Although he had as yet no male heir, Edward IV had been on the throne for some time and had brought relative stability to English political life. In July 1468 his sister, Margaret, had married the most illustrious and richest ruler in Europe, Charles of Burgundy, a match which opened up prospects of better trade relations between the two countries. Much of the old aristocracy still remained and a new one had been created; and both could provide potential clients for the trade Caxton had in mind. So on 1 March he started his translation. Then suddenly in July occurred the breach between the Earl of Warwick and Edward. The King was captured by the Earl who was, however, too weak to detain him for long. The kingdom was plunged into chaos once more, and Caxton decided to postpone his project. Edward's position took a turn for the worse in 1470 when he had to flee from England taking with him only what he had on at the time. He took refuge in the Low Countries, first with Louis of Bruges, Seigneur de la Gruthuyse, and then with Duke Charles. With Charles's help Edward returned to England in March 1471 where he began the task of regaining his kingdom. He accomplished this by winning two important battles: Barnet (14 April) saw the defeat and death of Warwick, and Tewkesbury (4 May) resulted in the rout of the Lancastrians and the death of Henry VI's son, Prince Edward of Lancaster. Fauconberg's attack on London in support of Henry VI failed and that unfortunate King was murdered on 21 May. Edward's position was secure again and his enemies had been dispersed. Men could once more turn their attention to peaceful pursuits. Caxton, who had been waiting to see what the outcome of the struggle would be, resumed his translation. This resumption may be tentatively dated to June 1471, so that the two years in which he put his project aside were from approximately July 1469 to June 1471.

The following is a summary of the results so far elicited about the early history of Caxton's project. In 1469 or earlier he decided, either on his own initiative or through the urging of friends, to learn how to print and by using this knowledge to produce books in English for sale in England to the nobler classes. Having acquired a copy of the French version of the *History of Troy*, he started to translate it on 1 March 1469 with the intention of printing the finished translation. The outbreak of civil hostilities in England led him to postpone his plan. When after two years Edward IV was safely re-established in England he resumed his project, but this time he took the precaution of enlisting the patronage of Margaret of Burgundy. She was probably not involved in the project at an earlier stage. Caxton implies in his prologue that he approached her only at the end of his two-year wait. As her marriage with Charles had taken place only in the July preceding the start of the translation, it is improbable that she would have been supporting a project so early in her new life. Nevertheless her arrival and marriage had created a new situation, which Caxton turned to his advantage. When he re-started his project in 1471, Margaret gave her general protection and some financial assistance, though her help went no further than that. With the assurance of her patronage Caxton quickly finished his translation and went to Cologne to learn the art of printing. This visit with all its implications will be our next concern, but first it is desirable to clarify two smaller points. Did Caxton make the decision to print by himself? In what ways did this decision affect his life?

As to the first point it is impossible to come to a decision. There is no evidence that Margaret or any other patron suggested the printing venture to him, and since Caxton claimed that he had paid for the cost of setting up the *History of Troy* in print himself, it is likely that the establishment of the press was undertaken on his own initiative. Another possibility is that several merchant adventurers with Caxton at their head embarked on the project. Certainly he would have discussed it with some of them, such as, for example, his friend, William Pratt. We shall see later that mercers contributed to the cost of individual books and so were also possibly involved at an earlier stage. Unfortunately we know nothing about the financial arrangements for the press so that we are unable to say who was involved. But there is no reason to withhold from Caxton the principal credit not only for the initiation but also for the successful completion of the project, even though others may have taken part in the venture.

Caxton was Governor of the English Nation at Bruges when he started translating on 1 March 1469. It has been shown above that he did not relinquish this post in order to enter Margaret's service, and presumably there was no need for him to resign to make his translation. Anyway the records of the town of Middelburg show that he was still Governor in 1470, for the town gave three quarts of wine during that year to 'Willem Caxstoen, meester van der Ingelsche nacie'.[1] While he was making his translation and preparing for his journey to Cologne he continued his normal life trading and acting as Governor. There is no evidence as to the exact date on which he resigned the governorship. He was succeeded in the office by another mercer, John Pickering, who was certainly Governor in 1474 and may have been so already in 1473, for in that year he was taking part in the negotiations with Burgundy for a commercial treaty.[2] It may be suggested that Caxton gave up the governorship when he left for Cologne sometime in 1471. Although the Governor was frequently away from Bruges on business of one kind or another, Caxton may have realized that he might be in Cologne for some considerable time and that it would be more sensible for another to take over the office of Governor. He was in Cologne by

[1] Crotch 1928 p. cxxxviii.
[2] Lyell and Watney 1936 pp. 72–73.

17 July so we can assume that he had relinquished his office by July 1471.

Although Caxton said that he finished his translation of the *History of Troy* in Cologne, he made no reference to learning how to print there. For many years it was doubted whether he had learned the art there, for the only evidence was an ambiguous statement to that effect by Wynkyn de Worde in his edition of the English translation of *De proprietatibus rerum*. But in 1923 Colonel Birch found Caxton's name in the Cologne Register of Aliens.[1] He was given permission to reside in Cologne from 17 July 1471. This permission was renewed three times, the last time being for six months from 19 June 1472, so that he presumably had an unbroken stay in Cologne from July 1471 until about November or December 1472. This evidence proved only that he was in Cologne for about eighteen months. It did not prove that he learned to print there. This discovery, however, led to a reassessment of the evidence found in Wynkyn's *De proprietatibus rerum*. Wynkyn's verse about Caxton states:

> And also of your charyte call to remembraunce
> The soule of William Caxton, first prynter of this boke
> In Laten tonge at Coleyn, hymself to avaunce,
> That every well disposyd man may theron loke.[2]

This verse can be punctuated and interpreted in several ways. The most likely interpretation is that Caxton took part in the printing of a Latin edition of *De proprietatibus rerum* in Cologne. There is a Latin text of this work which was printed there about this time,[3] so that there is no difficulty in accepting that he was present when the work went through the press. There is no need to assume that he printed it himself or that he was in any sense responsible for the edition, though he may have made some financial contribution. He would, however, have learned the art of printing in the office in which the book was printed while it was going through the press. He would also, it is fair to assume, have acquired his press, type and other necessary equipment, including even perhaps his future foreman, Wynkyn de Worde, through the good offices of the owner of the press. It is the type he

[1] *The Library*, 4th series iv (1923–4), 50–52; also Thomas 1928.

[2] Wynkyn's edition is dated to 1495, and the verse appears on fol. 005^r; see Duff 1917 No 40. I have modernized the punctuation.

[3] *Catalogue of Books Printed in the XVth Century now in the British Museum* (London, repr. 1963), I. 234–5.

used for his first book which provides the final proof that Caxton learned to print in Cologne. This type was made by Johannes Veldener, who was at first a typecutter and supplier of type based at Cologne, but later acted as a printer-publisher in Louvain. Veldener supplied several printers in Cologne with type (the *De proprietatibus rerum* was printed with type supplied by him), and he doubtless supplied Caxton with his when he was there. He was later to supply Caxton with his second type, when he himself was in Louvain and Caxton in Bruges.[1] The combination of these factors makes it quite clear that Caxton learned to print in Cologne and brought back with him from there sufficient equipment to set up a press in Bruges.

Cologne, with a press dating from about 1465, was the town nearest to Bruges which had a press at that time, and Caxton had little choice where to go. In many ways Cologne had become the capital of the Low Countries. It contained an important archbishopric and university, in which many students from the Low Countries were matriculated. In educational and religious matters there was considerable intercourse between Cologne and the towns of the Low Countries. There was also a flourishing trade, which embraced England as well. Much of the trade between England and Cologne passed through towns like Bruges or down the Rhine. The Cologne merchants were well established in London, and during the trouble which Edward IV had with the Hanseatic League in 1468 they made a separate agreement with the King. The Cologne merchants had especially close connexions with England which they were loth to see broken. Among items that they imported were books; and by the fifteenth century they had established bookshops in England. Furthermore, the start of printing in both Oxford and Cambridge came through the initiative of men from Cologne.[2] It is therefore hardly surprising that Caxton should have gone there; it was the centre from which printing reached many parts of north-western Europe and to which many from the Low Countries went to learn the art.

We do not know how Caxton acquired the secrets of the press. He appears to have been a shrewd businessman who would have made careful plans to ensure the successful completion of his project. One cannot imagine that when he arrived in Cologne he went knocking on

---

[1] Hellinga 1966 i. 17–24; *Catalogue of Books Printed in the XVth Century now in the British Museum* (London, 1962), IX. ii.

[2] Juchhoff 1960 pp. 46–49.

printers' doors. He would have made arrangements before he left Bruges, which may have been made as early as 1469, for he intended to print the translation he began then. Not long after he took up the translation again in 1471 he was on his way to Cologne, which suggests that plans had already been laid. Yet although there were several presses in operation in Cologne by this time, it cannot have been an easy matter to acquire the secrets of the business, even if the heyday of secrecy was past. The task demanded capital and influence.

This is not the place to enter into a discussion of the early history of printing in Cologne, but it is important to know a little about it.[1] Ulrich Zell, the first printer in Cologne, was matriculated in the university on 17 June 1464, though he may not have started printing till later. He had connexions with the Mainz printers and used a type which was based on the scribal habits found along the middle Rhine. At that time it demanded relatively little capital to buy a press and type; the greatest expense a printer faced was the purchase of paper. Printing involves the production of a large number of copies, which means a large investment in paper, before a single copy can be sold. Since a large number of copies were produced, it was necessary to know how to distribute them as the local demand would quickly become satisfied. But many of the early printers were artisans who did not have the necessary ability or experience in finance and merchandizing; Zell was no exception. These attributes, however, were to be found among the merchants and to a lesser extent among some religious orders. The merchants had the necessary capital, they imported the paper, and they knew how to distribute the finished goods along the European trade routes. It was not long therefore before merchants took over control of the presses, and the division of labour between printer and publisher appeared. The printer remained an artisan, the publishing was done by an entrepreneur. The merchants provided the capital and paper and farmed out the work to the printers. Zell seems to have succumbed early to some such partnership. The expertise and capital which these entrepreneurs possessed could also be found in some religious orders. These may have encouraged the spread of printing, as the case of Arnold Therhoeren suggests. Arnold, a priest from the diocese of Utrecht who matriculated in Cologne University on 4 May 1468, went to Cologne to learn printing from Zell. His books were

[1] See particularly Corsten, *Jahrbuch des Kölnischen Geschichtsvereins*, xxix-xxx (1957), 1–98.

printed in a type based on a Netherlandish script related to the script used by the Brothers of the Common Life. This script was in common use in the Netherlands and North Germany, including Cologne, where the Brothers had a convent with a large library. The script used by Arnold and his priestly calling suggest that a religious order may have played some part in the establishment of his press. The type, probably cut by Veldener, is affiliated among others to that used in the *De proprietatibus rerum* and to the first types of both Veldener and Caxton. Veldener also supplied the type for the first press of the Brothers at Brussels.

It is a reasonable assumption that Caxton learned the art of printing either through a Cologne merchant or through a religious order. The former seems at first to be the more likely solution. The capitalist entrepreneurs quickly established a dominant position over the presses in Cologne. As a merchant Caxton was probably familiar with many of his opposite numbers from Cologne; they traded in the same goods. It would have been easy for him to come to some arrangement with one of them over some other piece of business, and he could have paid for the knowledge if necessary. On the other hand, a Cologne merchant might have been worried about the competition which a press in the Low Countries or England, both of which were supplied with books from Cologne, might bring.

At the end of the last century Madden suggested that the convent of the Brothers of the Common Life at Weidenbach in Cologne was the centre at which many of the Cologne incunabula were printed.[1] Yet Madden claimed so much for the Brothers that his view was easily refuted,[2] with the result that the contribution of the religious orders to printing has subsequently been somewhat undervalued. Corsten, however, has recently done something to restore the balance by showing that the Brothers of the Common Life, the Carthusians and the Crutched Friars all had important houses in Cologne where an interest was taken in printing.[3] The first of these orders, which was founded at the end of the fourteenth century by Gerard Groote in the Low Countries, from where it spread to North Germany, is the most interesting as far as Caxton is concerned. This order of communities of laybrothers was devoted to education and the reproduction of books.

[1] J. P. A. Madden, *Lettres d'un Bibliographe* (Paris and Versailles, 1868–78), *passim*.

[2] Voulliéme 1903 pp. iv–v.

[3] Corsten, *op. cit.*

Their books were written in a standardized script.[1] The Brothers
naturally took an interest in printing soon after its invention, and
several houses had presses in the fifteenth century. There is no evidence associating Caxton with the Brothers, but if he did have dealings
in manuscripts before he turned to printing, he may well at that time
have sold volumes written by them. The press from which he learned
printing in Cologne used a type based on the Brothers' script, the
printer Arnold Therhoeren, who was a priest and introduced this
script into Cologne printing, came from the Netherlands and may
have been encouraged in his printing enterprise by the Brothers, and
the typecutter Johannes Veldener supplied type to the Brothers. This
evidence is circumstantial. However, Caxton himself was a man of
strong religious convictions and when in Ghent he had stayed with the
Benedictines.[2] When he took up his translation of the *History of Troy*
again in 1471, he was in Ghent for a little time before going to Cologne.
It would be a possible, but by no means a necessary, inference that in
Ghent he made the final arrangements for his trip to Cologne and that
he received help from the religious orders there. This is speculation.
As already stated, there is no proof that Caxton made use of an order,
such as the Brothers of the Common Life, any more than there is any
evidence that he learned printing from a Cologne merchant. The state
of printing in Cologne in the fifteenth century certainly suggests that
he used one of these two channels.

When in Cologne Caxton learned the techniques of printing:
how to put type in a composing stick, how to ink the formes, how to
work the press and how to handle the paper, for the success of his
printing venture could be guaranteed only by his own technical
knowledge. He would have to be able to train his apprentices and work
the machines. Normally he would not have interfered in the actual
printing operations, and it is not right to think of Caxton as a printer.
He was the publisher and entrepreneur. He provided the capital, chose
the books and distributed them, leaving the printing to others. The
bulk of this work would have fallen to Wynkyn de Worde, who was
Caxton's principal assistant and who accompanied his master to
England in 1476. We do not know when Caxton recruited him, but as
Wynkyn was a native of Wörth in Alsace, he would have gone to
Cologne rather than the Low Countries to look for work. Caxton

---

[1] See also L. M. J. Delaissé, *A Century of Dutch Manuscript Illumination* (Berkeley
and Cambridge, 1968).

[2] Infra p. 129.

would want a helper to attend to the press from the beginning, and it would have been easier to acquire a trained assistant in Cologne than to train one on his return to Bruges. If he had recruited labour in Bruges, we would expect such a helper to be an Englishman or a local inhabitant rather than a native of Wörth. The drawback in thinking that Wynkyn may have been recruited in Cologne is his age. He died in 1535, so that if he was twenty by 1472, he would have been over eighty at his death. However, Caxton himself lived to a ripe old age; and since Wynkyn was in Caxton's employment by 1476, the difference of four years (1472–6) seems unimportant. We may assume then that Wynkyn joined Caxton in Cologne. Although Wynkyn will not be mentioned frequently in the ensuing pages, his faithful, continuous service was an important feature in the successful running of the press. Caxton recognized this by leaving the business to him on his own death.[1]

Together with his assistant and the materials for his press Caxton left Cologne in late 1472. There is no particular evidence that he returned to Bruges, but since this was his former home and since he was there later on, it may be taken as certain that it was in Bruges that he printed his books. The first book he printed, and the first book to appear in English, was his own translation of the *History of Troy*. Just as it contains no evidence as to the place of printing, so it gives no information as to the year in which the printing was finished. It probably appeared in late 1473 or early 1474. The earlier date may be preferred if we assume that Caxton would want to complete his project as soon as possible. Although the *History of Troy* is a large work, he could have set up the press and printed the edition within eight or nine months. As he left Cologne late in 1472, the book could have appeared in the latter half of the following year, which would leave two and a half years in which to place the publication of the other books issued in Bruges. In all he printed six or seven volumes before returning to England. These include his two translations, the *History of Troy* and the allegorized *Game of Chess*, and four works in French, including the French original of the *History of Troy*. The doubtful volume, which may have been printed in Bruges or Westminster, is a pamphlet entitled *Propositio*, a sermon delivered by the Bishop of Lincoln in Burgundy. This selection of texts printed has important implications.

[1] For a modern, if not thorough, account of Wynkyn de Worde see Moran 1960.

As we saw above, Caxton printed an English translation to capture the English market, and consequently used the patronage of Margaret of Burgundy, Edward IV's sister. It was as a continuation of this policy that he dedicated the *Game of Chess* in March 1475 to George, Duke of Clarence, who was, as Caxton carefully pointed out, the 'oldest broder of Kynge Edward' [10]. There can be little doubt that Margaret recommended Caxton to her brother George; he was her favourite brother, and Caxton was not acquainted with him previously, for he described himself as 'your humble and unknowen servant' [12]. Caxton had seized the opportune marriage of Margaret to Charles of Burgundy to enlist her as the patron of his first translation. But though her name guaranteed the book's courtly character, it failed to help its distribution in England. Caxton evidently wanted a patron who would recommend his work to his friends and even possibly help the printer set up his press in England. The choice was unfortunate. The Duke of Clarence had been involved in Warwick's rebellion of 1470–1, and although pardoned he had never completely regained the royal favour. He died finally in the Tower in 1478—according to popular report in a butt of Malmsey wine. Furthermore, he lacked any great ability or strength of character, and he apparently took little or no interest in literary matters. He was of no help to Caxton who had to look elsewhere for more reliable patronage.

Apart from his two translations, Caxton printed four books in French while in Bruges. These books can hardly have been designed for the English market, for one of them, the *History of Troy*, was already available in Caxton's English translation. Three considerations may account for this deflection from the original plan. Probably Caxton found it more difficult to distribute English books from Bruges than he had anticipated. It would after all demand a more extensive organization to dispose of two hundred or more copies of the same work[1] than it had done to dispose of individual manuscripts. This difficulty was no doubt a contributory, if not the principal, factor in his return to England in 1476. Secondly, he entered into some form of association with Colard Mansion, a scribe and bookseller in Bruges, who may have recommended the printing of books in French, as more popular in Bruges than English books. Finally, Caxton may not have had the necessary time to make sufficient translations to keep the

---

[1] We do not know how many copies were printed in editions of incunabula; and the number doubtless varied according to the size of the book and its contents. See further Febvre and Martin 1958–9 pp. 327–36.

press busy. The latter two points should be considered in more detail.

It was for many years held that Mansion was the first printer in Bruges and that he instructed Caxton in the art, so that some or all of the French books printed by Caxton have also been attributed to Mansion's press at various times. But Sheppard has proved that it was Caxton who taught Mansion how to print and that the latter started to print on his own behalf only about 1474.[1] The details of this dispute are of little relevance here, but Mansion is an important character in our story. A skilful copyist and bookseller, he appears in the records in 1450 when he sold 'ung volume couvert de velours bleu' to Duke Philip the Good of Burgundy. Mansion also provided Louis of Bruges with manuscripts, to whom he refers in his works three times as his 'compère'. Mansion was also a translator of Latin works into French, three of his translations being extant. He was a member of the Guild of St John the Evangelist, the corporation of the booksellers in Bruges, and in 1472–3 he was its dean. It is only natural, therefore, that he, like Caxton, should have wished to develop his business by learning to print, though even after he started printing he continued to produce handwritten manuscripts.

Unfortunately, we do not know when Mansion and Caxton started to work together. If Caxton was a seller of manuscripts earlier in his life, he would almost certainly have come across Mansion long before he embarked on his translation in 1469. Indeed, since Mansion supplied books to both Duke Philip and Louis of Bruges, it might well have been through his agency that Caxton acquired a copy of the French *History of Troy*, a work which was to be found in both those noblemen's libraries. It is also quite possible that Caxton not only taught Mansion how to print, but also entered into a partnership with him, just as Caxton may have formed a partnership with some Cologne merchant. A business association with Mansion would have provided Caxton with further capital and books, with a partner to run the press while he was away on business, and with an established retail outlet for his French books. Mansion would know what was fashionable and could advise on what to print. He may indeed have continued to supply Caxton with books and manuscripts after the latter's return to England. So it is possible that the four French books attributed to Caxton which were printed without date, place or printer's name were published by Caxton and Mansion in partnership. The evidence for

[1] *Signature*, New Series xv (1952), 28–39.

the relationship between the two, which is largely typographical, is scanty; but it is nevertheless important as it gives us one of those rare glimpses in which we can see Caxton's association with the book-sellers in Bruges.

When Caxton returned to Bruges from Cologne he was no longer Governor of the English community there, but he was a respected, wealthy and powerful member of it. While in Cologne he had acquired a pardon for all offences.[1] Since similar pardons were issued to many dignitaries at this time, it probably signifies only that he wished to cover himself against possible accusations which might have arisen from the aftermath of Warwick's rebellion of 1470-1. After all, Warwick and Clarence had sailed from France to oust Edward, and Caxton might have felt that the proximity of Bruges to France and his position as Governor might arouse suspicions. Despite his marriage, Charles of Burgundy had Lancastrian leanings and his court harboured English exiles. The pardon may, however, simply be an expression of Caxton's caution. Certainly he did not suffer any disfavour, for he was employed on various diplomatic missions after his return to Bruges. These missions included negotiations for commercial treaties with Burgundy and the Hanseatic League and arrangements to provide shipping for Edward's expedition to France, an oblique reference to which is found in the epilogue to the *Game of Chess*.[2] He was still sufficiently important to witness an important document on behalf of the English community,[3] and in some documents in which we can trace his activities he is referred to as the factor of the English king.

These missions were difficult and involved considerable travelling, and while engaged on them Caxton would have had little time for translation or for the supervision of the press. He was indeed living a life which hardly differed from the one he had led as Governor. While exercising a general supervision over his business, he left the daily running of it to his employees and business associates. He travelled the country for the benefit of his fellow merchants and in the cause of Edward IV. As yet, little had changed in his life: his business had been extended by the inclusion of the press, and when he had time he did some translation; otherwise he was still an important English merchant in Bruges.

[1] Crotch 1928 pp. cxxxix-cxl.
[2] The phrase 'in conquerynge his rightfull enheritaunce' [16] must refer to this expedition.
[3] Crotch 1928 pp. cxlii-cxliv.

4

CHOICE OF TEXTS

The last chapter was devoted to the establishment of Caxton's press and its early history. In Bruges he printed the two English books he had translated and several French ones, though this activity was a prelude to the transfer of the press to England. The following chapter will trace the fortunes of the press at Westminster. This present chapter will consider why Caxton published the books he did and how he made the choice of texts to print. This discussion is placed here because a knowledge of how he chose books to publish illuminates many of his actions and contributes to a fuller understanding of the later history of the press.

Previous commentators have concentrated their attention on two interrelated aspects of his publishing activities: to what extent he printed his books under patronage and whether the books he published were popular or not.[1] Their conclusions have in turn led to a dispute as to whether Caxton followed or educated public taste. Unfortunately the controversy has been clouded by a desire on the part of some scholars to vindicate his literary reputation and independent taste, as though the publication of a book by him under patronage or because it was popular detracted from his merits as a printer or as a man of letters. There is no reason why it should be considered shameful to print a book under patronage. The custom was widespread in the fifteenth century and Caxton naturally followed it. A patron's name gave a book a certain distinction and recommended it to possible purchasers, though the patron often gave little financial assistance to the printer or author. A patron often had little to do with the book, as was the case with the *Game of Chess*. The Duke of Clarence had never met the printer, had probably never read the book dedicated to him, and certainly gave the printer no remuneration. But his name indicated that the book was considered suitable for princes. Other patrons took a more active interest in literary matters: they suggested titles to

[1] See for example Lathrop, *The Library*, 4th Series iii (1922–3), 69–96, and Sands, *Papers of the American Bibliographical Society*, li (1957), 312–18.

1　The Merchant

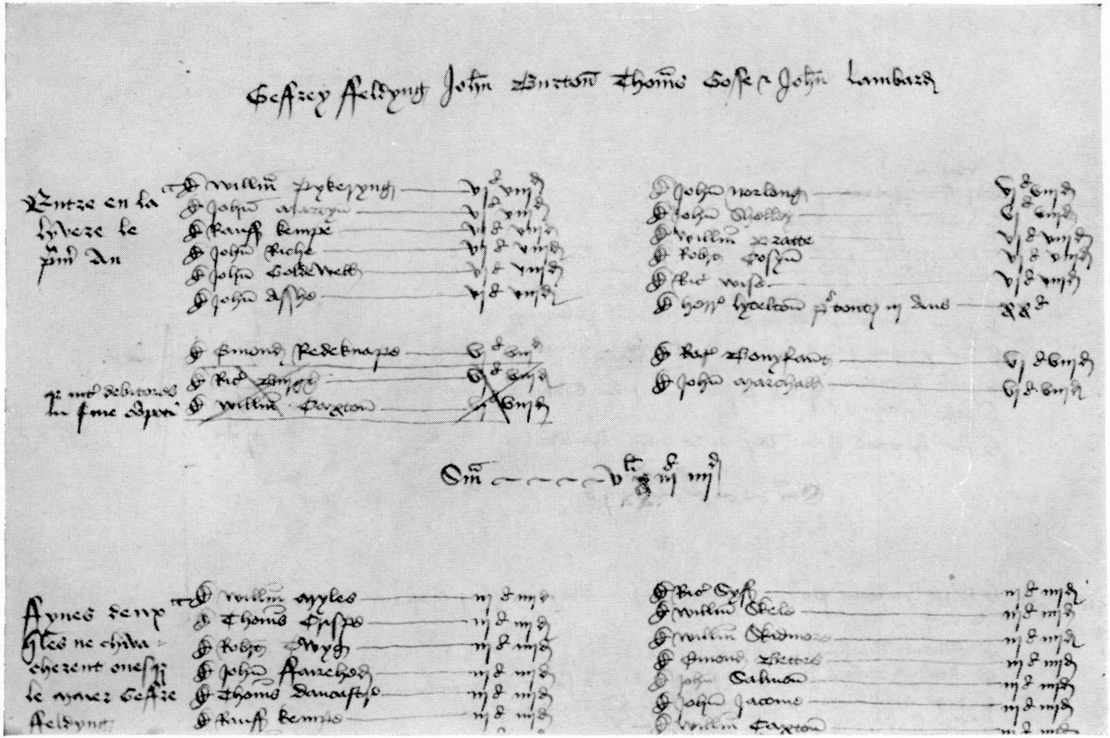

2 The Livery Payment

the printer and were liberal in their rewards to him, though their gifts of money were perhaps less important to him than the appeal their names gave to his books. Patronage was thus a part of the system of publication at that time; but we should not let it dominate our attitude to Caxton's literary accomplishments: he himself chose many of the books printed under patronage.

The controversy about Caxton and patronage has served to show that the types of book he printed were popular, though it has done nothing to explain how he chose individual titles, for scholars have divided his output into broad categories such as history, romance and satire, and then proved that such categories made up the favourite reading matter of the fifteenth century. But sufficient examples from these broad categories could be produced from most periods of English literature to prove that these genres were popular with the English public of any time. Has history ever been unpopular? The categories are too broad and they provide us with no insight into why he chose the individual titles in any group; and this is the important question. A parallel could be provided from modern times: today the novel is a popular genre, but this does not mean that every novel written is published. It is necessary to look a little deeper than the popularity of certain broad literary genres in order to find out why particular books were published.

The material printed by Caxton falls into two categories which may be termed the courtly and the practical. As the second group is not an extensive one, I shall deal with it first. By 'practical' I mean that either the work was paid for by a particular client on a commercial basis, as the indulgences were, or else the printed work was directed at a specialist market. The *Statutes* was produced for sale to lawyers, we may assume, and would not have had much appeal to a wider market. The range of material in this practical group consists of the law books; phrase books like the *Vocabulary*, which may have been used by merchants as well as by schoolboys; religious books like the psalter, books of hours and other works specifically for the use of the clergy such as *Directorium Sacerdotum*; and possibly some of the humanist writings in Latin which appear to have been seen through the press by the authors, as was the case with the *Nova Rhetorica* of Lorenzo Guglielmo Traversagni. With some religious books it is difficult to draw a precise line between courtly and practical, for the nobility had books of this type in their libraries for use in their private chapels. Thus the sole extant copy of Caxton's *Psalter* printed about 1480 once

C

belonged to Queen Mary I,[1] and the Dukes of Burgundy had many service books in their magnificent library. Some religious works may thus have appealed to both a specialist and a more general market. However, it is the time at which many of them were printed which suggests that Caxton intended them for the more specialized market. Books in the practical group were printed either to keep the presses working or when political conditions made the publication of courtly books too speculative. The smaller pieces were printed as soon as the press was set up in England, as Robert Copland informs us, or between the printing of longer works. Many of the religious works and the *Statutes* were produced at a time when no courtly works were appearing, namely the years following the succession of Henry VII. The reason for this, as we shall see, was the collapse of the House of York with which Caxton had been so closely associated. His position was delicate at that time since many of his old patrons had been killed or had fallen from power. In order to keep his presses busy he turned to works of a different nature for a different market. When his position improved again and he found new patrons, he returned to the production of courtly literature. Since the technical religious books were produced at this difficult time in politics, it suggests that they were not designed for the court. How exactly Caxton chose the books in this practical group is difficult to decide. Some were paid for on a commercial basis; some may have been brought to him by interested parties, such as the translator, for the *Vocabulary* was translated by another merchant;[2] and with others Caxton may have consulted mercers from London or the monks at Westminster, for he seems to have been on friendly terms with the Abbots. The ultimate choice may well often have been rather arbitrary—as it is in modern publishing—depending upon what was available at any given time.

The bulk of Caxton's production falls within the category I have called 'courtly'. This can be subdivided into three main groups: translations made by Caxton, works of the English poets, and prose works in English. I shall deal with each group in this order.

In the last chapter I traced the steps leading up to the translation and publication of the *History of Troy*. The prologue and epilogues of that work contain many revealing statements about Caxton's intentions as a publisher. One day during an idle moment he glanced at a story

[1] de Ricci 1909 p. 86.
[2] N. F. Blake, 'The *Vocabulary in French and English* printed by William Caxton', *English Language Notes*, iii (1965–6), 7–15.

about Troy in French. He was captivated by the strange and exotic tales, though the story of Troy was popular throughout the Middle Ages, and by the book's elegant and 'compendious' [pithy] style. This version had been recently compiled for Duke Philip of Burgundy, and the recent date of composition meant that there was as yet no English translation, though Caxton does mention Lydgate's poetic version of the Troy narrative. So Caxton decided to attempt an English translation. Similar ideas recur throughout his prologues and epilogues. For example, he mentions the strange and exotic stories in the *Siege of Jerusalem* and the *Polychronicon*, the novelty of *Jason*, and the style of the original French version of *Eneydos* in much the same words as he uses about the *History of Troy*. They give us some idea of what Caxton was looking for: a book written for an important member of the European aristocracy in an elegant style, preferably not too long ago. Such a book would naturally have an appeal to a courtly audience.

While the preceding paragraph helps to clarify Caxton's tastes and his reasons for choosing particular books, it does not explain why he bothered to make translations at all. Of the three groups of his 'courtly' work, translations, English poetic works and prose works in English, the first is the largest, and presumably he considered it the most important. Yet he could have confined his attention to works in English. The reason for this preference lies in the great prestige attached to French, particularly Burgundian-French, literature. The Burgundian court was the most cultured and fashionable in northern Europe and it set the pace in all matters of taste and fashion. The Dukes attracted artists of various kinds to work for them, and what they did tended to be imitated in other courts in the north of Europe. This applies as much to literature as to any other art form. This prestige of the Burgundian court is the reason for Caxton's emphasizing that the French version of the *History of Troy* was made for Duke Philip the Good and his own translation under the patronage of Margaret of Burgundy. The book was acceptable at the most fashionable court in Europe and therefore would be suitable for English gentlemen, many of whom aped the fashions set in Burgundy. Similarly, *Jason* was written by Raoul Lefèvre who had been Duke Philip's secretary, and it had particular associations with Burgundy since the Golden Fleece was the Burgundian order of chivalry. The French original of Caxton's *Cordial* was translated from Latin by Jean Mielot, Duke Philip's secretary, and of his *Feats of Arms* by Christine de Pisan, a writer popular at the Burgundian and the French courts, who had dedicated many of her works to the Dukes. Two of Caxton's translations, *Art of Dieing* and *Ovid's Metamorphoses*, show a close affinity with the French versions printed by Colard Mansion, Caxton's printing partner in Bruges. In addition to the works composed for the Burgundian court, some of the manuscripts which Caxton used for his translations were produced in the Low Countries or were in the ducal library. The manuscript he used for the translation of the *Mirror of the World*, Royal 19 A IX, was copied in Bruges in 1464. The original work had been composed almost a couple of centuries earlier, but it was revised, rewritten and illuminated in 1464. The French manuscript closest to Caxton's translation of the *Knight of the Tower* was formerly in the ducal library and is now Brussels MS 9308. It is quite likely that other French manuscripts he used also had a Burgundian connexion, but as so few of his translations have been fully edited, we cannot yet identify the ones he used.

It is hardly surprising that Caxton should have followed Burgundian literary taste, having lived within the territory of the Dukes of Burgundy for so many years. By the time he returned to England he was in late middle age and his tastes were no doubt already formed. During his stay in the Low Countries he may have become acquainted with the two important secular libraries in Burgundy, one belonging to the Dukes themselves and the other to Louis of Bruges, Seigneur de la Gruthuyse, for he had business associations with some of the booksellers who provided books for them. He would almost certainly have accepted these libraries as the ideal to be followed by any collector. In this he was not alone. When Edward IV fled to the Low Countries in 1470 he stayed with Louis of Bruges and was greatly impressed by his host's library. When Edward returned to England he extended his own library to make it more fashionable by buying foreign manuscripts, though even before this time he had bought books produced in Bruges.[1] Furthermore, the ties between England and Burgundy were of long standing, and they had recently been strengthened by the marriage of Edward IV's sister to Duke Charles. Edward IV's queen, Elizabeth Woodville, had Burgundian family connexions, and Jacques of Luxembourg with a hundred Burgundian knights had attended her coronation. Tournaments between English and Burgundian knights were arranged, like the famous one between Earl Rivers and the Bastard of Burgundy. In chivalry and courtly behaviour

[1] Byles 1926 p. xviii.

England looked to Burgundy for a lead. The longstanding commercial connexion between the two countries is, as we know, the reason for Caxton's own residence in the Low Countries. As part of his trade he may have had a hand in supplying these manuscripts to the English market. If he had imported French texts into England, he would also have been in a position to sell English translations because he would know what was being read and by whom. His knowledge of Burgundian literary fashion would be put to good use to provide English buyers with what they wanted: fashionable literature in their own language. As the stories were translated and then printed, he would have been able to sell more copies while still providing the same sort of literature. Other merchants were selling Burgundian manuscripts in England, but only Caxton was able to provide cheap, plentiful translations of that literature. Other booksellers in England were able to provide their customers with English literature, but only Caxton could provide them with literature which was in their own language but which was also the courtly reading of the Burgundian court. He had a great advantage over any would-be competitors.

It is not possible here to make an exhaustive comparison between Burgundian literary taste and Caxton's output. Inventories of the ducal library are extant, however, and give some indication of its contents.[1] An important characteristic of the library was that it was essentially a vernacular one. The Dukes preferred to read books in French. Whatever classical or patristic literature there was, and it was not very much, was written in French. And the Dukes employed various secretaries to translate Latin works into French; we have already met Raoul Lefèvre and Jean Mielot in this capacity. If the Dukes of Burgundy employed secretaries to translate works into French, why should Caxton not translate the books into English for the English aristocracy? The vernacular character of the ducal library may also explain why Caxton printed few texts in Latin, for not all libraries at this time contained books in the vernacular. Charles, Duke of Orleans, the poet and patron of Villon who died in 1465 after spending much of his life in England, had an extensive library, the two largest sections of which were theological texts, especially works of the fathers, and classical texts, including works by such authors as Horace,

[1] J. Barrois, *Bibliothèque protypographique, ou Librairies des fils du roi Jean, Charles V, Jean de Berri, Philippe le Bon et les siens* (Paris, 1830), and G. Doutrepont, *Inventaire de la 'librairie' de Philippe le Bon (1420)* (Brussels, 1906).

Juvenal and Terence.[1] These books were in Latin for the most part; and many of them came from England. This library differed from that of the Dukes of Burgundy not only in the language in which the books were written, but also in the contents of the books. The Burgundian library contained few theological and classical works. The inventory for 1467 divided the library into the following categories: *Bonnes Meurs; Etiques et Politiques; Chapelle; Librarie meslée; Livres de Gestes; Livres de Ballades et d'Amours; Croniques de France; Oultre-Mer; Médecine et Astrologie; Livres non parfaits.* The last category is that of books which were incomplete at the time of the inventory. Apart from the service books which belonged to the chapel, the library contained books of the courtly type, books which combined romance with edification. If a comparison of this list is made with modern categorizations of Caxton's output,[2] the two will be seen to agree closely. Where they differ, it is where Caxton has substituted English books for French ones: he published chronicles of England rather than those of France, and he printed works by the English poets, not *Livres de Ballades et d'Amours.* There is, however, a general similarity in tone between his printed works and the ducal library. This does not mean that he had a list of the contents of the ducal library which he followed in his publishing enterprises. It does prove that he followed Burgundian literary taste, itself best represented by the ducal library.

The second group of Caxton's courtly output consists of the writings of the English poets. He did not print all types of poetry: he confined his publishing to the works of the courtly poets. The alliterative style had ceased to be fashionable at court, where the prevailing taste was Chaucerian. It is not possible to tell whether Caxton was acquainted with the northern alliterative poems, but someone so closely associated with the distribution of books as he was would surely know of the existence of *Piers Plowman.* Many manuscripts of this work were copied in the fifteenth century, some of them in London. Whether Caxton knew *Piers Plowman* or not, he would not have printed a work written in a popular, rather than the fashionable, style. He confined himself to the court poets; Langland was not one of them. The major poets whose work Caxton printed were Chaucer, Gower and Lydgate. In the fifteenth and sixteenth centuries they were regarded as the three

[1] P. Champion, *La librairie de Charles d'Orléans* (Paris, 1910).
[2] As in the articles by Lathrop and Sands mentioned above.

poets who had established the courtly style, for which they were constantly praised. These poets had written for courtly patrons and had based their work on fashionable foreign models. Their poetry was thus not far removed in tone and emphasis from Caxton's translations, likewise written under patronage and modelled on foreign works. The major difference—Chaucer's superiority apart—is that the poems were composed in a more elevated language than Caxton could command, though it is one which he emulated. But this is a difference of degree, not of kind. Furthermore, the works of these poets were read in court circles and were produced in magnificent manuscripts for wealthy customers by the bookshops devoted to supplying this kind of need. The existence of these bookshops must have encouraged Caxton to print these poets for sale to his clients; it would confirm that they were popular. He did not of course print the complete works of these poets, perhaps because they were not all in his possession, though he did produce, for example, the *Canterbury Tales* and the *Confessio Amantis*. The other poets printed by Caxton belong to this new stylistic tradition. Benedict Burgh was Lydgate's pupil and completed some of his work; the *Court of Sapience* was often attributed to Lydgate himself; and the poet of the *Book of Courtesy* looks back to Chaucer, Lydgate and Gower as the three great poets, and in this way reveals his poetic allegiance. All the poems use stanza or couplet, a markedly French vocabulary and many rhetorical devices.

The final group of his courtly output is that of the prose works in English. The feature of this group is that it also largely consists of translations. In this respect it differs little from the previous ones. There is a further similarity in that these translations include those made by English poets, like Chaucer's *Boethius* and Lydgate's *Pilgrimage of the Soul*; those made by members of the nobility, like Earl Rivers's *Dicts or Sayings*, the Earl of Worcester's *Declamation of Noblesse* and Sir Thomas Malory's *Morte Darthur*; and those made under patronage, like Trevisa's *Polychronicon* for Lord Berkeley, and *Of Old Age* for Sir John Fastolf. Most of the translations had been made recently, the two oldest being those by Trevisa and Chaucer, which were made about a century earlier. They were all part of the new courtly stylistic tradition which tried to raise the standard of English by the use of foreign models. Although a great deal of native English prose had been written before and during the fifteenth century, Caxton did not print it. He must have been acquainted with some of these writings, for they were well known at the time and some of them were later to be printed by his successor, Wynkyn de Worde. The choice not to print such works was no doubt deliberate, and the crucial factor which led to their rejection was that they were not fashionable. Caxton wanted to publish only what would appeal to his clients at court. Only one prose work of this sort was not a translation, the *Chronicles of England*, and this originated as a translation from a French book, though it had since been considerably modified. Contemporary foreign models, such as the *Croniques de France*, were plentiful and popular. Furthermore, the *Chronicles of England* does not form part of the alliterative tradition; it was a book closely associated with London, and otherwise not very different in style and tone from the others he published. One manuscript associates it with Lydgate.

Once Caxton had decided on the sort of book he would publish, did he have any method for selecting individual titles? Did he have any programme to which he adhered? The evidence suggests that for the most part he did not. It is difficult to trace any order in what he printed; his output was regulated by what he had available at the time and by political conditions. However, a few tendencies can be discerned. The earliest years of the press in England are marked by a high proportion of English poetry. Few translations were printed and most of those were made by others. Caxton himself translated only *Jason* (1477) in this period. It is not difficult to understand why Caxton did little translation at first. It would have taken him some time and effort to establish his press and to make it known to his clientele. Quite apart from political missions he performed for Edward IV, this would give him little opportunity to settle down to make translations himself. Then, many of the poetic works he published in these years are slight. Poems like *Horse, Sheep and Goose*, *Cato*, the *Parliament of Fowls* and the *Temple of Glass* could be run off quickly to get some financial return without too long a delay. Many of the books he translated were large, and it would demand considerable financial resources and patience to make them successful commercial ventures. He may well have learned this lesson in Bruges, where he had started by printing an extensive work, the *History of Troy*, which may have put a considerable strain upon his financial resources. Furthermore, the works he first printed in England were of known popularity, for they were being produced by the commercial bookshops, or they were translations by such people as Earl Rivers and Chaucer, whose names guaranteed a steady sale. Caxton was no doubt a cautious man; his policy was to establish himself by printing accepted works and shorter pieces. Furthermore, the works of the English poets he printed would offer his public a wide selection of texts, and each piece would act as an advertisement for the others. They would amount almost to a publisher's series of texts. It is notable, for example, that the works of Chaucer were printed in two groups, one about 1478 and the other about 1484. The *Canterbury Tales* forms the major item in each group, supported in the first instance by *Anelida and Arcite*, *The Complaint of Chaucer to his Purse* and *Boethius*, and in the second by the *House of Fame* and *Troilus and Criseyde*. In his first years in England Caxton produced a comprehensive list of English poems set off by a number of translations, a mixture of the established and the new. Though not usually his own, these translations were of the same sort of texts that attracted Caxton. In this way he could see how translations sold. Later when the press was well-established and he had more time to himself, he extended his translating activities, no doubt in the knowledge that such versions were well received. This extra time that he had to devote to translation arose in some instances through political events, as was the case in 1483–85. Those years are notable for a considerable number of his translations. And after 1485, as we have seen, he had to turn to religious works for a time before he could recommence his translation activities. To some extent, therefore, Caxton was guided by commercial considerations and political events in the choice of his texts.

The choice of individual titles was perhaps arbitrary. In only one case does Caxton mention that he took active steps to acquire a particular manuscript to print it. He said of the text in question, *Of Old Age*, that he had not seen another copy of it, but he did not say how he knew of its existence or how he managed to get hold of the manuscript. Why he should have gone to this trouble is not clear, though perhaps his exertions were not so great as he makes them appear. *Of Old Age* was printed with *Of Friendship* and the *Declamation of Noblesse*, both translated by the Earl of Worcester. Caxton evidently felt that the three treatises would complement one another, for *Of Old Age* and *Of Friendship* are translations of Ciceronian texts. The three works appeared in one volume. However, his edition is unusual in that *Of Old Age* has one set of signatures while the remaining two treatises share another. This suggests that he had intended to publish the two Worcester translations by themselves, and had them set up. Then he discovered the existence of the translation, *Of Old Age*, thought it would be a suitable companion piece for the other two, acquired it by some means, and printed it as part of the common volume. Since he acquired this treatise later than the other two, he gave it a new set of signatures. If this reasoning is correct, it would mean that rather unusual circumstances combined to make him go out of his way to get hold of the manuscript. As he never refers to difficulties in obtaining a copy of any other book, presumably he did not go out of his way to look for books to print.

For his other books the example of *Eneydos* is instructive. In his prologue to that work Caxton wrote that he was sitting in his 'studye' when he picked up a copy of the French *Eneydos*, which he proceeded to read. Those who think of Caxton as a scholar have understood this study to be the equivalent of a modern scholar's workroom with its many books diligently collected by the owner. I prefer to think of it as his workroom in the printing shop. It may be thought of after the model of the shop in the woodcut of Death and the Printers (see plate 5). On the left hand side of the picture we see Death leading off the compositor and the two pressmen. On the right in a kind of cubicle built into the main room we see a man behind the counter with books both on the counter and on shelves behind him. This was no doubt the masterprinter selling his finished products. Caxton's shop may have had a similar arrangement. He would have attended to his customers personally, for we know he had long conversations with them, and he would have had the books to sell at hand—not only his own books but also manuscripts and other printed books. In other words he ran an ordinary bookshop, in which his own printed books formed the principal, but by no means the only, items for sale. From his stock he would have sold to his noble customers the books he had printed, manuscripts of works of the same type, and even books printed abroad.

That Caxton was a bookseller of this type has not always been appreciated earlier, and it is necessary to explain why I think he was. I have already shown in an earlier chapter that he had dealings in manuscripts while in Bruges, and his establishment as a bookseller at Westminster would be a logical continuation of that activity. When he set up his press at Westminster he would want some method of distribution for his books. However, one of his reasons for settling at Westminster was to be near the court, for he intended to sell his books to the courtiers, whose gifts to him and orders for translations confirm that he was personally acquainted with many of them. If so, he would hardly have entrusted the sale of his books to anyone less favourably placed than himself. He would use his position to dispose of his own books through his personal contacts. Furthermore, the distinction which we make today between books and manuscripts was not so clear then. Books were printed to look like manuscripts, and they were often illuminated and rubricated in the same way. Where a book was printed on vellum, the difference between it and a manuscript would have been even smaller. So it would be natural for anyone dealing in books to handle manuscripts as well. Many manuscripts passed through Caxton's hands for his translating activities alone, and when he finished with a manuscript, he would presumably dispose of it in the same way as his printed books—by selling it to one of his noble customers. Then there is the information which Caxton gives in his prologues and epilogues that many members of the court visited his shop and held conversations with him on various literary matters. He implies that these conversations were not infrequent. Yet if he was only a printer and seller of his own printed books, there would have been little reason for his clients to drop in frequently. However quickly he worked, there would never have been much new to report, particularly when the presses were engaged in printing the larger volumes. But if he was a bookseller with a modest stock of manuscripts as well as printed books, his clients would come periodically to look over the new stock and to suggest what titles they would like to acquire. From such enquiries wider conversations on literature would develop almost spontaneously. And if Caxton had any business sense at all, he would want to make use of the information gained from these talks, and that could best be done by selling manuscripts as well as books. Finally, it might be suggested that his commercial experience would have led him to cushion the risks of a new venture like printing by the sale of other books and manuscripts. Whenever the press entered a lean phase, he could always fall back on his booktrade. Experience might well have told him that this was a reliable, if not a spectacular, business.

That Caxton sold books at his shop is proved by his advertisement for his edition of the *Ordinale*, in which would-be customers are invited to come to the shop at the sign of the Red Pale (see plate 8). We know also that he had a missal after the Sarum usage printed in Paris by Guillaume Maynyal, but with his own device included. He would not have done this unless he were a distributor of books, which were sold at his premises. The copy of Caxton's *Polychronicon* which belonged to Mark Cephas Tutet and was disposed of at his sale in 1786 contained the inscription 'Presens liber pertinet ad Willelmum Purde emptus a Willelmo Caxton, regis impressor [*sic*] vicessimo

Novembris anno Regis Edwardi quarti vicessimo secundo' [i.e. 20 November 1482].[1] Unfortunately the book is no longer extant, but there seems no reason to doubt the validity of the inscription, which confirms that Caxton was selling books from his own premises. These pieces of evidence reveal that he was selling his own books at least. A detail from *Blanchardin and Eglantine* shows that he also sold manuscripts. In the prologue to that work he states that Margaret, the mother of Henry VII, gave him her French copy of the text with a request to translate it into English. This French version he had himself sold to Margaret at an earlier date. This is an unambiguous example of his activities as a seller of manuscripts. It is also now known that Caxton imported books in large quantities.[2] The majority of these were no doubt books printed on the continent for in 1488 he imported over a thousand volumes, though there may well have been some manuscripts among them. His bookselling projects appear to have been extensive, and it may well be that his printing business was only a part of a much larger commercial undertaking. How many books and manuscripts passed through his shop it is no longer possible to tell. It is clear enough, though, that many printed books reached him very quickly from the continent. For example, *Reynard the Fox* and *Charles the Great* had been translated and printed within two years of their publication on the continent. No evidence remains to tell whether he maintained an agent or factor on the continent as some have suggested,[3] though there is nothing improbable in the idea. In any case he maintained close links with his mercer colleagues, who no doubt kept him informed about what was going on over the Channel. All this evidence points to the conclusion that Caxton was a large distributor of books and manuscripts in England. Other evidence which shows that he had a knowledge of the booktrade points in the same direction. There cannot have been many people who knew that *Of Old Age* was available in an English translation; and his acquisition of it suggests he knew the workings of the trade. Similarly, he appears to have known which books were to be found in England, for he frequently mentions in his prologues and epilogues whether a certain title was available in English or not. These details confirm that Caxton was actively engaged in the book trade and that he had a shrewd idea of what was circulating.

If Caxton was a bookseller, as I have suggested, it is probable that

[1] Blades 1863 ii. 128.

[2] Kerling, *The Book Collector*, iv (1955), 190–9.

[3] H. W. Davies, *Devices of the Early Printers 1457–1560* (London, 1935), p. 139.

when he selected *Eneydos* for translation, he did so from among the books he had for sale in his 'study'. Whether the choice was quite as fortuitous as Caxton makes out is uncertain; he might have earmarked it for translation as soon as it entered his stock. His choice of texts was fortuitous to the extent that he chose books from the titles in his shop. The majority of these are likely to have belonged to the general category of courtly literature I have described above, for they would be for sale to courtiers and the richer merchants. Often the books he chose to print were presumably recent additions to his stock. In many of his prologues and epilogues he mentions that the particular text he is translating had come 'of late' into his hands. This expression is found in other writers besides Caxton, often indeed in his French originals, so that it may have been a traditional one which he copied. Nevertheless, many of his texts were probably recent arrivals and had that novelty he regarded as so important. It is perhaps unlikely that he would have set to work on a manuscript which he had been unable to sell. Sometimes the sale of a manuscript might have prompted him to prepare a printed edition. In 1480 Caxton issued the *Description of Britain*, which contains only the geographical sections of *Polychronicon*. Two years later he printed the complete *Polychronicon*. There is evidence that he used two manuscripts to set up the *Description of Britain*, but only one for *Polychronicon*;[1] this suggests that in the meantime he had sold one of the manuscripts and realized from that sale that the whole book was marketable. The text of some of his editions suggests that Caxton printed his books from manuscripts or books in stock. His first printed edition of Mirk's *Festial* is defective at the beginning and the end, a feature best accounted for by the incompleteness of the manuscript from which it was set up.[2] If so, this would in turn suggest that Caxton printed what he had available, perhaps without bothering to find a complete manuscript. He may not even have realized that his manuscript did not contain the complete text. When the second edition of the *Festial* was printed, it was set up from the St Albans edition and not from Caxton's first edition. He had evidently acquired a copy of this edition in the meantime, and realizing the defective state of his own text reprinted that edition. He was willing to print a complete text if he had one available, but he was not prepared to go to the trouble to find one. His attitude to Chaucerian texts was no different, as we shall see in a later chapter. Someone at the centre of the booktrade could

[1] Cawley, *London Medieval Studies*, i (1937–9), 463–82.
[2] Blades 1882 p. 264.

probably have acquired a complete manuscript without much difficulty if he had wanted to, but Caxton was satisfied to print the volume he had.

It is time now to summarize how I think Caxton set about choosing his texts. He owned a bookshop in which he kept books and manuscripts principally destined for courtiers and the richer merchants. Many would be in the courtly style and Burgundian in taste. Some were in French and were no doubt shipped direct to Caxton from Bruges and other continental book centres. When deciding what to print, he would have let his choice be governed by the following considerations. Firstly, the book would normally be in his stock; it was exceptional for him to make special efforts to acquire a manuscript. To this extent his choice was arbitrary. However, since his stock presumably consisted of books of the type I have just described, the books he printed, or translated and printed, would belong to certain well-defined genres. Within these genres he no doubt pleased himself as to which title he printed, since all the titles in those genres would have an appeal for his customers. Secondly, when he was asked to print a book, it was by the people who were his customers. Since he was selling to them the sort of books that they would ask him to print, as happened with *Blanchardin and Eglantine*, they would ask him for a title which belonged to the genres he stocked. The type of book would be the same as the ones Caxton printed on his own initiative, though he might never himself have printed that particular title. Viewed in this way, patronage becomes a less important feature in his choice of books. Finally, he may have been influenced by particular circumstances which may be most fairly characterized as extra-literary: by the prevailing political conditions, by what had recently arrived, by what he had recently sold, or by how many copies of a particular work he had. His literary criteria were not so much governed by the particular excellences of a given text as by the particular stylistic tradition to which it belonged. His books were in the new courtly fashion set by Chaucer in England and exemplified abroad by Burgundian literature. In this Caxton accepted the fashionable views current at his time. His texts reflect the taste of the court at the end of the fifteenth century, though this need not imply that he was not convinced of the superior literary excellence of the courtly style. A man is not necessarily a slavish imitator merely because his tastes are in line with the prevailing ones of his time.

5

WESTMINSTER AND
THE COURT

The first known item to be printed in England is an indulgence which must be dated prior to 13 December 1476, since that date has been entered by hand in the surviving copy. It is printed in Caxton's type 2 with six letters in his type 3.[1] This indulgence provides us with a date by which Caxton had returned to England; he may have returned somewhat earlier in that year, for though the indulgence is the earliest extant printed item, it is by no means certain that it was the first thing Caxton printed on his return. Probably he returned some time during the summer of 1476. When he came to England to settle permanently, he brought his assistant, Wynkyn de Worde, his manuscripts and books, his press and the two sets of type known as his types 2 and 3. Type 1, which he had acquired in Cologne, was left behind, no doubt because the quality of its workmanship was poor. Types 2 and 3, like type 1, had been cut by Johannes Veldener, who was by this time a printer in Louvain. It may be assumed that Caxton had acquired these types while still in Bruges, for one of the French texts, *Cordial*, and Russell's *Propositio* were printed in type 2, though there is no evidence that he had used type 3 in Bruges. However, its use so soon after Caxton's return to England suggests that he brought it with him.

On his return Caxton settled in Westminster, and not in the city of London which had been his home. It was at one time thought that the hostility of the professional scribes and copyists had forced him to make his home outside London for, it was suggested, they were bitterly opposed to the introduction of this new art which threatened their livelihood. Although there may have been isolated cases of antagonism between scribe and printer, the history of printing makes it clear that the two co-operated, and often a printer had been or still remained a scribe. We saw in Chapter Three that this was true of the Brothers of

[1] Pollard, *The Library*, 4th Series ix (1928–9), 86–89.

the Common Life and of Colard Mansion. In England the earliest
press at Oxford is notable for a partnership between a printer and a
stationarius.[1] In general, relations between the old and the new art were
reasonably good. If Caxton had wished to avoid the hostility of the
professional scribes, he would hardly have rented a shop within the
precincts of Westminster Abbey, which also at this time housed an
important scriptorium. From the scanty evidence available it would
appear that he was on good terms with the Abbots and the scribes
there. He may even have worked together with them, for there is
evidence of co-operation between Caxton and William Ebesham, a
scribe attached to the Abbey.[2] It may also be imagined that he owed
some of his commissions, as for example the indulgence printed in
1476, to the good offices of the Abbot. Both the scribes and the
printer would profit from working together rather than in competition,
and we have no reason to think that they were not sufficiently astute to
realize this for themselves. In this connexion the evidence of Caxton's
Ovid's Metamorphoses may be taken into consideration. The second
part of the manuscript of this work was found recently and is now
happily reunited with the first part in the Pepys Library, Magdalene
College, Cambridge. The translation of *Ovid's Metamorphoses* survives
only in this manuscript; no printed copy has been found, so it is
questionable whether the translation was ever printed. The manuscript itself is professionally written and illuminated. Caxton evidently
found no difficulty in getting scribes to prepare manuscripts of his
work; and this manuscript may well be the sole extant example of a
wider co-operation.

Apart from the benefits of being associated with the Abbey, Caxton
chose to set up his press at Westminster in order to be near the court.
He printed books which would appeal to its members, from among
whom he sought to find his patrons. Most of the nobility would have
come to Westminster at one time or another, as would many litigants,
professional men and merchants. Their reasons for coming were
varied, but they were all potential customers. To a great extent,
therefore, the customers came to the bookshop, thus making it unnecessary for Caxton to distribute his books along normal trade
channels. If he had wanted to do this, he would have set up his shop in
London, at the focal point of the English trade routes. Most of the

[1] C. Clair, *A History of Printing in Britain* (London, 1965), pp. 112–13, and E. G.
Duff, *Early Printed Books* (London, 1893), pp. 147–55.
[2] Doyle, *Bulletin of the John Rylands Library*, xxxix (1956–7), 298–325.

continental presses at this time, particularly the successful ones, are placed in important commercial centres with good trade connexions. Caxton's press is unique in not being at such a centre, which suggests that the decision to settle at Westminster was deliberate. He may well have discovered that the type of book he wanted to print was not so conveniently distributed from London. While in Bruges he had printed the *History of Troy* and the *Game of Chess*, which were sent over to London for distribution. As we saw, the slow disposal of these books may have been one of the reasons behind his decision to return to England, and once back, to settle in Westminster rather than London. It was so much easier and cheaper for the printer to let the customer come to Westminster for his book than to send it from London to various parts of the country.

There is thus a very close connexion between the choice of books and the establishment of the press at Westminster, and this relationship is confirmed by the history of the press under Wynkyn de Worde, Caxton's assistant and successor. Although Wynkyn began by imitating his master in his choice of texts, he later changed to more popular works. When he did this, the location of the press at Westminster became a handicap. It was better to be near the centre of distribution, where he could more easily discover what was popular and from where these books once printed could more conveniently be distributed to other centres of population. Wynkyn therefore moved the press to Fleet Street in 1500. Nevertheless, other reasons have been advanced for Caxton's presence at Westminster. References have been found, for example, to various Caxtons living in the area at this time. Thus the Parish Accounts of St Margaret's, Westminster, refer to the burial of a William Caxton about 1478, and the monastic records refer to the institution of a Richard Caxston or Caston as a monk at Westminster in 1473.[1] It would be possible to imagine that William was the printer's father and Richard his cousin or some other relation. If so, their presence at Westminster would account for the printer's wish to settle there as well. There is no evidence, however, to prove that there was any relationship between these Caxtons and the printer. The propinquity of the court and Palace of Westminster is a sufficient reason for the establishment of the press in the Abbey precincts; there is no need to adduce doubtful ties of kinship.

That Caxton did settle at Westminster there can be no doubt since he tells us so in his advertisement (*c.* 1477) and since his name

[1] E. H. Pearce, *The Monks of Westminster* (Cambridge, 1916), p. 165.

occurs as the tenant of different shops in various Westminster Abbey muniments. His tenancy appears to be no different from many others entered in these muniments. There were many shops within the precincts of Westminster Abbey and Caxton at first rented only one. The existence of all these shops underlines the commercial attractions of the site, which was advantageously located close to the Palace of Westminster. Caxton was not the first merchant to tempt idle courtiers with his wares. Although we know from the prologues and epilogues that he was on good terms with some courtiers, there is no need to assume that his was the only shop in the precinct they visited. He was just another merchant trying to capitalize on the advantages of the site. In the Westminster Abbey muniments Caxton's name appears for the first time in the Sacrist's Roll for the year 1476-7. He paid a full year's rent, i.e. ten shillings, for a shop from some time in 1476 till Michaelmas 1477. His payment of the full rent confirms that he was in England before December 1476. He continued to pay the same rent for this shop till his death in 1491/2, when the shop was rented by Wynkyn de Worde. In the Sacrist's Roll for 1483-4, he rented another, presumably smaller, shop for two shillings and sixpence. In later years this shop remained empty so no rent was paid, though the accounts imply it was allocated to Caxton.[1] In 1486-7 and 1487-8 a third shop seems to have been allotted to him, though no rent was paid as it was empty. In 1488-9 Caxton rented only his original shop for the year for ten shillings, and another one, at fourpence, for the week that Parliament was sitting. In 1490-1 he rented two shops for the year, at ten and four shillings respectively. From the evidence of the Sacrist's Roll it would seem as though the business fluctuated. But it is not the only source available in the Abbey muniments for Caxton's stay at Westminster. The Prior's Account Book records that Caxton was renting two tenements in the Almonry from 1482-3. From it we learn further that he later added a loft and another room in the Almonry. The interrelation of these two sources has yet to be satisfactorily worked out. What seems certain is that Caxton started to rent a shop within the precincts of Westminster Abbey in 1476 and that as time passed, his business flourished so that he gradually extended his premises. Their exact location is disputed. Tanner has suggested that his first shop was situated by the chapterhouse and that it was only when he started renting his second shop that he had any premises in the

[1] Relevant extracts from the accounts are printed in Crotch 1928 pp. cl-clvii.

Almonry itself.[1] But Caxton in his advertisement, usually dated to 1477, asked his customers to come to the sign of the Red Pale in the Almonry (see plate 8). This implies that he rented a shop in the Almonry from the start and that later he merely took over shops near his first one, which would in any case have been the most practical step. Until a more satisfactory solution of the evidence in the Westminster Abbey muniments is proposed, we shall remain unable to decide the location of his shops; all that we can say is that these records indicate the general position within the precinct and confirm the successful development of the business. The entry which is particularly important is that recording the renting of a shop for the week Parliament was sitting. Caxton no doubt rented it to mount a special display of his books for the benefit of the members of Parliament; just as today publishers often arrange an exhibition of books at large congresses. That this display was for the benefit of his trade rather than to promote scholarship seems more than probable, particularly in view of the occasion. The Commons have never been noted for their scholarly interests. This book exhibition underlines the advantages of having the press at Westminster instead of London. It may have been the first one of its kind in the country, though it is possible that the advertisement of 1477 was printed for a similar occasion.

Though Caxton rented a shop continuously at Westminster after his return to England, it does not follow that he was engaged solely on his printing and bookselling activities from then on. His experience in negotiations, his former services for Edward IV, and his present propinquity to the court ensured that he would be employed on affairs of state from time to time. What those affairs were we today cannot tell, but payments made to him and recorded in the Issue Rolls of the Exchequer were presumably granted to cover expenses incurred in some form of state business.[2] Even Henry VII, or his officers, benefited from Caxton's advice and services in various matters, for several payments were made to him towards the end of his life. These payments were not frequent, and no doubt he was forced to withdraw increasingly from public life as he grew older. They are important, however, for they reveal that his way of life had not altered much as a result of his return to England. He was still a mercer, and his connexions with his merchant colleagues were probably as close as ever:

[1] Tanner, *The Library*, 5th Series xii (1957), 153–66. This is the best modern account of Caxton's stay at Westminster.

[2] Crotch 1928 pp. cxi, clvii–clviii.

some asked for books from him, and he no doubt met others on his visits to London to attend to his imports of books and paper. He may have used the services of his mercer friends to buy books and manuscripts abroad, though probably he also had an agent in Bruges. As late as 1487 a mercer of London, William Shore, entrusted Caxton and two others with all his goods and chattels.[1] Thus, although it might seem from his prologues and epilogues that his daily companions were solely knights and earls, he continued to keep company with mercers and other merchants. So there were no sharp breaks in Caxton's life, though there were changes. He was no longer in a good position to trade in cloth or general merchandise. This side of his business, which he may have started to run down in Bruges, would now be stopped. To compensate for this contraction, he would have expanded his book trade and possibly also his dealings in such commodities as paper. Translation and printing would have continually grown in importance for him—and it is this side of his business which I must now examine more closely.

When Caxton was in Bruges he had enjoyed the patronage of Margaret of Burgundy and had tried to arouse the interest of the Duke of Clarence. The latter attempt failed and he was forced to seek patronage elsewhere. He found it with the Woodville family, some of whose members were his firm supporters till the death of Edward IV. It is not possible now to say how Caxton became acquainted with the Woodvilles, though it is improbable that it was through the agency of Margaret. Relations between the older Yorkist aristocracy and the Woodvilles were strained. The reasons for this animosity are clear enough. Sir Richard Woodville had served in the household of the Duke of Bedford, Henry V's brother, and after the Duke's death had married his widow, Jacquetta of Luxembourg. As she was related to Margaret of Anjou, the wife of Henry VI, the Woodvilles had naturally supported the Lancastrian party in the Wars of the Roses. Sir Richard's family consisted of five sons and seven daughters, including Anthony, the future Earl Rivers, and Elizabeth. The latter became Edward IV's wife; both were patrons of the printer. Elizabeth was at first married to Sir John Grey, by whom she had two sons. Sir John, likewise a Lancastrian, was killed at the second Battle of St Albans in 1461. The male members of the Woodville family had continued to fight for the Lancastrian party until Edward established

---

[1] Calendar of Close Rolls, Henry VII, No 203.

himself on the throne in 1461, when they withdrew from public life. Their fortunes, however, underwent a sudden change in 1464, when in April Edward IV married Elizabeth. The marriage was at first kept secret because it was realized that it would not be popular. Edward had married below himself. In order to rectify this, he started to advance the Woodvilles by the grant of peerages and by arranging favourable marriages. Thus Elizabeth's father was made Treasurer of England and Earl Rivers in 1466. The rise of the Woodvilles naturally caused resentment and jealousy among the older Yorkist nobility, who remembered their former Lancastrian leanings. So when Warwick rebelled against Edward in 1469, he showed no mercy to those Woodvilles he captured. The Queen's father, Earl Rivers, and one of her brothers, Sir John Woodville, were beheaded on 12 August. Anthony, another brother, thus became Earl Rivers, by which title he will be styled in future in this book. The new Earl accompanied the King on his flight to the Low Countries in 1470. He was evidently a favourite of Edward's, for he had been made a Knight of the Garter in 1466 and later he was made a member of the Prince of Wales's Council and in 1473 the Prince's governor.[1]

It is probable that Caxton and Rivers met for the first time towards the end of Caxton's stay in Bruges. The first book that Rivers patronized was *Dicts or Sayings*, which Caxton issued in Westminster on 18 November 1477. In a prologue Rivers mentions that he had read and enjoyed the book in its French version in 1473 on a pilgrimage to Compostella. Later, realizing it would be suitable for the Prince of Wales, whose governor he was, he had translated it. It was this translation which Caxton printed. Rivers showed the translation to the printer to look over, just as Caxton had shown his own translation of the *History of Troy* to Margaret of Burgundy. It goes without saying that Caxton found no fault with the Earl's style. However, the Earl had omitted two passages from his translation, the letters sent by Alexander, Darius and Aristotle to one another and the sayings of Socrates about women. In his prologue Caxton made some playful remarks as to why Rivers might have failed to include the latter section, which he decided to reinsert. Nowhere else does Caxton joke publicly with one of his patrons; his tone is usually that of the utmost deference. One must assume that the relations between the two men were very cordial at this time for Caxton to have taken such liberties

[1]For a biography of Elizabeth see MacGibbon 1938. There is no adequate modern life of Earl Rivers, but see Hittmair, *Anglia*, lix (1935), 328-44.

with his patron. He would not have included the sayings if he had thought that their inclusion would anger Rivers; he did not reinsert the letters. Or if he felt that they had to be included, he need not have drawn attention to them so ostentatiously. The evidence in the prologue of this cordiality suggests that Caxton and Earl Rivers had been acquainted for some time before the book's publication in November 1477. If so, it is possible that Earl Rivers had had some hand in Caxton's return to England, perhaps by granting him financial assistance. Caxton had already received a 'good reward' [30] from him before he printed the *Dicts or Sayings*.

That Caxton and Rivers had been on friendly terms for some time is suggested also by *Jason*, the only translation Caxton made in the four years following his return to England. There is no date or place of printing in the work, which is, however, usually assigned to 1477. If this is correct, it would have appeared before the *Dicts or Sayings*, which would mean that Caxton started that translation shortly after his return to England or even that he had commenced it before he left Bruges. *Jason* is a continuation of the story in the *History of Troy*, and both works were made by Raoul Lefèvre for Duke Philip of Burgundy. The close connexion of the two books makes it remarkable that *Jason* was not also dedicated to Margaret of Burgundy or one of her kinsmen. There is a noteworthy break in patronage here. Caxton did not dedicate the volume to Edward IV because he assumed that Edward already had a copy in French. This was simply an excuse, since the existence of several French copies of the *History of Troy* in the Burgundian library did not prevent him from presenting his translation of that work to Margaret. With the licence and approval of the Queen, Elizabeth Woodville, Caxton presented his translation of *Jason* to the Prince of Wales so that he might learn English from it. The Prince, who was born on 2 November 1470, was not yet seven. The Queen's approval was evidently more important than the presentation to the Prince. Nevertheless, we may recall that Earl Rivers had been governor of the Prince since 1473. Quite probably he suggested that *Jason* should be presented to the Prince and he may have been responsible for introducing the printer to the Queen. Certainly Caxton's relations with the Queen were not at this stage very close, whereas he was on friendly terms with her brother, as we saw from his prologue to *Dicts or Sayings*. If this reasoning is correct, it would mean that Caxton and Earl Rivers would have known each other at least by the beginning of 1477. Rivers made frequent visits to the continent and was often at the court of Charles of Burgundy. Caxton could easily have met him in Bruges and the two could have formed some sort of association there.

Whatever the date of its inception, their relationship progressed happily. On 20 February 1478 Caxton printed another translation by Earl Rivers, the *Moral Proverbs* of Christine de Pisan. Little need be said about it, except that Caxton implies in his epilogue that Rivers had a secretary who attended the printing or who proof-read the text afterwards. In 1479 he printed the *Cordial*, a third translation by Earl Rivers. The French version of this work had been printed by Caxton in Bruges, and it was this text which Rivers used to make his translation.[1] In the epilogue to the English translation Caxton expatiates on the career of Earl Rivers. He mentions the various pilgrimages that Rivers had made as well as the indulgences he had acquired. In only one other instance, as we shall see, did Caxton enlarge upon the exploits of a translator—a fact which suggests that he took a special interest in the Earl's life. He certainly continued to receive many gifts from him. The impression created by these works is that in the period following Caxton's return to England, Rivers was the printer's major, or even sole, patron. He helped Caxton financially and provided him with texts to print. He may even have made suggestions about other texts.

Most of the other texts printed during these first years were poetical ones, as we saw in the last chapter, though there was also an occasional book in Latin. However, there is one text printed in these opening years which deserves further comment. In 1478 Caxton printed *Boethius*, Chaucer's translation of the *De consolatione philosophiae*, 'atte requeste of a singuler frende & gossib of myne' [37]. No indication is given as to the identity of this friend. It cannot have been Earl Rivers or any other member of the aristocracy, for Caxton did not address them in this way. The phrase 'a singuler frende & gossib' is echoed in two later prologues. The *Royal Book* was printed for 'a synguler frende of myn, a mercer of London' [101] and the *Book of Good Manners* for 'a specyal frende of myn, a mercer of London named Wylliam Praat' [99,. The similarity of these phrases suggests that the patron of the *Boethius* was a mercer, possibly the same William Pratt. If the patron had been Earl Rivers or a member of the nobility there would have been no reason for Caxton to conceal the name. If he

[1] Mulders, n.d. p. xxxiv.

was a mercer or merchant, Caxton might have decided not to mention it. At Westminster he was trying to build up a noble clientele for his books. The introduction of a mercer's name in the prologue would not have helped the sale of the book in such a market, and may even have hindered it. As it was, however, any noble customer would merely have seen that it was asked for by a friend of Caxton's. If this friend who recommended the *Boethius* was a merchant, as I suggest, it underlines what I have stressed earlier: Caxton remained a merchant and continued to have dealings with his colleagues, even though that side of his life finds little expression in the prologues and epilogues. His mercer friends recommended books to him and may have had some financial stake in the press. He no doubt printed the *Boethius* because it was by Chaucer and would have appealed to a courtly audience; the elegance of Chaucer's style is stressed in the epilogue. There would be no need for him to undermine this effect by stating that the book had been requested by a merchant, though he may have felt obliged to make some reference to his friend, who had perhaps made some financial contribution.

In 1480 Caxton issued the *Chronicles of England*, which he claimed had been printed at the request of various gentlemen, none of whom are named. Probably this claim is another way of saying that he hoped it would appeal to his gentlemen clients, for it echoes his phrase in the epilogue to the *History of Troy* to the effect that he had promised copies of that work to various gentlemen. In 1481 he issued the volume containing *Of Old Age*, *Of Friendship* and *Declamation of Noblesse*. It is not known who translated the first of these, though the translation was made for Sir John Fastolf, about whom Caxton gives us some information. This may well have come from a preface to the original translation, for there is no evidence that Caxton had had any connexion with Fastolf or his family. The other two works were translated by John Tiptoft, Earl of Worcester.[1] This Earl, executed in the temporary Lancastrian revival of 1470-1, is now remembered for his contribution to the growth of humanism in England.[2] It is natural, therefore, that many have seen in the publication of two of Worcester's translations a readiness on Caxton's part to support that revival of classical learning associated with Italian humanism. Before accepting this conclusion, it is necessary to consider why he printed these works and his attitude towards the Earl. Caxton made the following points about him:

[1] On Worcester see Mitchell 1938.
[2] Weiss 1957 pp. 109-22.

(i) he was recently killed; (ii) he excelled in 'vertue & cunnyng', and among the nobility none was his peer 'in science & moral vertue' [45]; (iii) he made other 'vertuous werkys, whiche I have herd of' [47]; (iv) he visited the holy places of Jerusalem; (v) he visited the Pope, who received him with honour; and (vi) 'I am enformed he ryght advysedly ordeyned alle his thynges as well for his last will of worldly goodes as for his sowle helthe, & pacyently and holyly without grudchyng, in charyte' [47]. Although Caxton thus expressed a high opinion of Worcester, there is nothing in what he wrote which specifically links Worcester with humanism. He valued his learning, but that was not necessarily the New Learning. Indeed the way in which *science* is coupled with *moral vertue* suggests it is not. Furthermore, Worcester is praised for such medieval virtues as going on pilgrimage and visiting the Pope; Caxton had praised Earl Rivers for the same things. Nothing is said of Worcester's studies in Italy or of his bequest of books to Oxford (though perhaps point (vi) could be interpreted to refer to this). More important than this question of Worcester and humanism is the indication from Caxton's prologue that he had an informant who was familiar with Worcester and presumably favourably disposed towards him, though he had been unpopular. It is not known who this informant was, but it may have been a Woodville, possibly Earl Rivers himself. Worcester had acted as the umpire in the famous tournament between Anthony, the future Earl Rivers, and the Bastard of Burgundy in 1467, and Rivers and Worcester doubtless met on numerous other occasions. It has also been suggested that Worcester was on friendly terms with the Queen. It may have been through Elizabeth's influence that he was made Treasurer and Constable in 1470. Then just as the first Earl Rivers and Sir John Woodville were beheaded in 1469, so was Worcester in 1470; and the deaths of all three were brought about through Warwick. This alone would have endeared his memory to the Woodvilles. There is no evidence that Caxton ever met Worcester, though he speaks of him warmly. Consequently, considering Caxton's relations with the Woodvilles, it is best to assume that his informant was a member of that family. We cannot doubt that Rivers would have approved of the publication of Worcester's translations both as a memorial of the man and for the content of the works.

Caxton followed this volume with his version of the crusade of Godfrey of Bouillon (1481). The book reflects an attempt to capitalize on the interest shown in crusading at this time. It follows on also from the praise Caxton had bestowed on Rivers and Worcester for their crusading ventures and pilgrimages. As an English crusade could be organized only by the monarch, the book is dedicated to Edward IV. Two other books, *Jason* and *Of Old Age*, had been produced under the nominal protection of the King, but this was the first one to be presented to him. Yet even in this volume the two young princes are included in the dedication. We do not know what the relations between the printer and the King were. It is doubtful whether Edward, despite his interest in manuscripts, took much interest in the press, even though Caxton is described in a contemporary note as being the 'royal printer'.[1] He owed his success as a printer at court more to the Woodvilles than to the King himself. In this same year he translated and printed the *Mirror of the World*. The edition was requested and paid for by Hugh Bryce, a mercer and alderman of the city of London, who intended to present the book to Lord Hastings. There was little love lost between the Woodvilles and Lord Hastings, and it may have been for this reason that Caxton made it quite plain that Bryce had asked for the edition. He would not have wanted to antagonize his own patron, Earl Rivers, even for the sake of a fellow mercer.

So far I have commented on the more important texts Caxton issued. The books mentioned were not the only titles to issue from the press, which was very active. I have merely used some representative texts to show how the press developed in its early years. In general, they were good years for the press and the printer, who, under the protection of the Woodvilles, was able to produce a constant stream of printed material—and, we may imagine, able to dispose of it fairly easily. In April 1483 Edward IV died, an event which was bound to have repercussions on Caxton because it had been the King who had raised the Woodvilles to their position of wealth and influence and without his help it would be difficult for them to retain it, for they had made many enemies. Edward's death was therefore followed immediately by a struggle for power between his brother, Richard Duke of Gloucester, and the Woodvilles. Richard won and became Richard III. Elizabeth Woodville lost her two sons and was forced to seek sanctuary in Westminster Abbey, where she became a close neighbour of Caxton's, though one who was in no position to offer any substantial assistance to the printer. Caxton also lost his principal patron, Earl

---

[1] Supra pp. 75–76.

Rivers, who was beheaded in June 1483. The situation created new problems for him.

The first intimation of the new conditions is found in his edition of the *Golden Legend*, which he finished translating in November 1483. In view of the length of the book and the variety of sources used, Caxton probably started work on it at least twelve months before it was printed. After he had started, his project was overtaken by the political changes in the country, just as had happened with the *History of Troy*. Caxton does not refer to these events; he claims instead that he intended to abandon the edition because of its length and of the expense involved. These reasons, like the faultiness of his English which, he said, caused the temporary abandonment of the *History of Troy*, were mere excuses. As he had translated and printed long works before, it is difficult to accept that either the translation or its financing was an insuperable problem. Indeed, the speedy completion of the project after a few words of encouragement from the Earl of Arundel confirms that his reasons were not the real ones. Naturally he was anxious about the distribution of the text now that he had lost his patrons and political conditions had turned men's attention away from such things as the purchase of books. The problem facing him in April 1483 was whether the conditions then prevailing justified the investment of a considerable sum of money in one book. However, his position was somewhat different from what it had been in 1469. Then he had only just started his translation and had no press; he could earn his living by trading in other goods. In 1483, on the other hand, he had a well-established printing business with many employees. The postponement of a project could cost him money. All he needed to keep going was a guarantee of support from some nobleman.

This he obtained from the Earl of Arundel; and it is doubtful whether the work suffered any serious interruption. Caxton probably made the first move, as he had done earlier with Margaret of Burgundy, for not only did he need the patronage desperately, but also the Earl took little personal interest in the press, the negotiations being conducted on his behalf by John Stanney. The Earl did not patronize any further volumes. In both 1471 and 1483 the patrons helped Caxton only for the one volume; neither played any further part in the history of the press. Arundel's help consisted of a promise to take a 'resonable quantyte' [70] of the finished books and of the gift of a buck in summer and a doe in winter. This help, welcome as it must have been, was not so important as the mere fact of having a patron who looked as though he would have an important role to play in the government of Richard III; he had recently been appointed Master of the Game of all the King's forests, chaces and parks south of the Trent. Through Arundel's protection Caxton may have hoped to sell his books to a different section of the nobility. It may be for this reason that he inserted in his prologue a list of some of the works he had previously translated. The list served as both a testimonial for him to new clients and an advertisement for works still in stock.

As Arundel patronized only one book, Caxton was forced once more to turn elsewhere for support. With his next book, *Caton*, finished in December of the same year, he attempted to develop a different approach to patronage. Up till now books had been produced without a dedication or under the patronage of a nobleman. The *Boethius*, it is true, had been produced for a friend, but this fact was glossed over. *Caton* marks a break with the past, for it is dedicated to the City of London. Not only did he dedicate it to London, but he stated his own allegiance to that city in no uncertain way; the prologue opens: 'I, William Caxton, cytezeyn & coniurye of the same [i.e. liveryman of London], & of the fraternyte & felauship of the Mercerye,' [77]. Such a statement is completely unexpected: nothing like it is found in any of his other books. The work itself may have inclined him to make it, for in his prologue he compares the customs of Rome with those of London. The book was designed to improve the morals of merchants rather than to amuse the nobility. Even so, Caxton had previously printed books for the merchant market without stating his allegiance to the merchant community. So political conditions may have prompted his actions now. He may have felt that his own safety would be guaranteed by withdrawing publicly from the Woodville camp and by announcing his connexion with the merchants. Since the former were in no position to buy his books at the moment, it was commercially more sensible to concentrate on a market largely unaffected by the recent disturbances. As we have seen, Caxton had retained close links with the mercers of London, though generally in his prologues and epilogues he tended to ignore that association because he was aiming to sell his works to the nobility. In *Caton* he merely stressed that side of his support which he normally chose to ignore.

Conditions, however, did not remain so desperate that Caxton was unable to offer books again to his noble clientele. On 31 January 1484 he printed the *Knight of the Tower*. The appearance of this work had been delayed, for the translation, which had been requested by a

'noble lady' [86], was finished by 1 June 1483. From hints in the prologue this lady has been identified as the Queen, Elizabeth Woodville,[1]
who in 1484 was in sanctuary at Westminster Abbey. Since Caxton
had finished his translation by the previous June, it is likely that she
had commissioned it before Edward's death in April. The change in
political conditions had created a problem for Caxton and he had
delayed its printing. He could hardly expect the now impoverished
Queen to grant him any reward, and her patronage would not assist
the sale of the book. He decided, therefore, to print the book while
withholding her name, which is more or less what he had done earlier
with the *Boethius*, though for different reasons. In this way he could
satisfy his patron without offending those in power. If they had bought
copies of the *Golden Legend*, they might also be persuaded to buy the
Knight of the Tower. The publication of this book introduces a period of
what we may call anonymous patronage. The reasons for the anony-
mity are the same in all cases, as our examination of the *Curial* will show.

This work, a copy of which had been delivered to Caxton by a
'noble and vertuous Erle' [89], at whose request he translated and
printed it, is also dated to 1484. The Earl has been identified as Earl
Rivers,[2] who had been beheaded in June 1483. So the manuscript was
doubtless delivered to Caxton prior to the late King's death. Once more
he had delayed the translation and printing. However, the omission of
the Earl's name in this volume should be considered alongside its
retention in the third edition of the *Dicts or Sayings* (c. 1489). Caxton
had shown how sensitive he was to political conditions when he
reissued the *Game of Chess*, for in the second edition (c. 1483) he was
careful enough to excise the name of the Duke of Clarence, the
original patron, who had been beheaded for treason between the
publication of the two editions. In view of this Caxton would hardly
have retained Earl Rivers's name in the third edition of the *Dicts or
Sayings* if this would have worked against the book's sale. The Earl's
name, omitted in the *Curial* in 1484, was deliberately retained in the
Dicts or Sayings (c. 1489). The reason is not difficult to find. The
Curial was published when the Woodvilles were in disgrace. But
in January 1486 Henry VII married Elizabeth, daughter of Elizabeth
Woodville and Edward IV, and this marriage paved the way for
the re-emergence of the Woodvilles. The patronage of Earl

---

[1] N. F. Blake, 'The "noble lady" in Caxton's *The Book of the Knyght of the
Towre*,' *Notes and Queries*, ccx (1965), 92–93.
[2] Blades 1882 p. 297.

Rivers was an asset in 1489, whereas it had been a liability in 1484.

Two other books of anonymous patronage are dated to 1484, the *Order of Chivalry* and the second edition of the *Canterbury Tales*. The first of these was translated at the request of 'a gentyl and noble Esquyer' [82], though he has yet to be identified. It is more than probable that he was of the Woodville faction since that would provide the best reason for the omission of his name. Possibly he had died or been killed recently, for though the translation had been commissioned by him, the finished work was dedicated to Richard III. This replacement of one patron by another is unique in Caxton's works, and it could indicate that the squire was either too unimportant or else no longer in a position to object. It would reflect better on the printer to think that the latter was the reason. Caxton, who had tried to find favour with the new regime through the Earl of Arundel, now took the next logical step which was to arouse the interest of the new King. This development had to come sooner or later, for Caxton wanted to make his position as secure as possible. It must be added, though, that this was the only book he did dedicate to the new King, a fact which may indicate that Richard showed little interest in the press. The works which followed continued to be issued without the patron's name, which would hardly have been necessary if the King had been willing to help the printer. The second edition of the *Canterbury Tales* was issued, according to Caxton, because 'one gentylman' [91] had told him that the first edition was textually unsatisfactory and that his father had a more reliable manuscript. The new edition was then set up from the first one after it had been corrected against this manuscript. Caxton wished to include this story because it would redound to his credit as editor and to the value of the edition, but he felt obliged to leave out the gentleman's name. Once again the reason can be only that it would have been politically, and hence commercially, inexpedient to include it. The gentleman has not been identified.

In 1485 Caxton printed *King Arthur*, his version of Malory's famous romance. In his prologue he does not specifically state that one man asked for the edition, though this can be inferred. To the enquiry from many noblemen why he had not printed a book about Arthur, Caxton replied that many considered Arthur a fiction; 'wher to they answerd and one in specyal sayd' [93] that there were many proofs of his existence. This *one* would appear to be the person with whom Caxton discussed Arthur and for whom he printed the edition. Certainly the manuscript he used was sent to him for this purpose, for, as he writes, the book was set up 'after a copye unto me delyverd' [94]. The whole prologue indicates that he is once more concealing the identity of a patron; again, we can surmise only that it was political conditions which caused this suppression of information; and once more we cannot identify the man. Whoever did recommend the work to him made a good choice, for the following year the son born to Henry VII was christened Arthur.

King Arthur is the last book of this group published for anonymous patrons. The evidence which the group provides is of great value in evaluating the history of the press. It shows that Caxton considered patronage important. He could have omitted all reference to his patrons instead of merely concealing their names. Yet in order to sell his books at court he felt it beneficial to have some form of recommendation from a member of the nobility; it guaranteed the courtliness of the contents. It was unfortunate for him that when he had gained a suitable patron in Earl Rivers, the Earl's death should upset all his own plans. This led him to seek for new patrons among the supporters of Richard III, though he can have met with only limited success since he continued to produce the works commissioned earlier by the Woodvilles. Nevertheless, the flow of books from the press in the period 1483–5 shows that he was not working on a hand-to-mouth basis; he had a full order book at the death of Edward in 1483. The press was evidently well-established and able to survive the upheaval of the two usurpations of 1483 and 1485. We saw in an earlier chapter how the political unrest of 1469–71 had resulted in the postponement of the project to have an English press. In 1483 the press went on working, though Caxton had naturally to tread somewhat warily. Even so, the troubles did not leave the press entirely unscathed.

The translation of the historical romance, *Charles the Great*, concluded on 18 June 1485, was printed on 1 December; in the meantime Richard III had been killed on 22 August. The edition had been asked for by 'a good and synguler frende' [99] of Caxton's called William Daubeney. Caxton does not refer to any offices that Daubeney held under Richard III, but calls him a Treasurer of the Jewels of Edward IV. We know little about the man except that he was a Treasurer of the Jewels and a Searcher of the Port of London under both Edward IV and Richard III. Since Caxton was a large importer of books and since his name occurs frequently in the customs accounts of the Port of London, he may have become acquainted with Daubeney through the latter's office as Searcher of the Port. As Daubeney was his good friend, Caxton must have known that he had been confirmed in his offices by Richard III. No doubt he omitted this information on account of the political conditions which prevailed when the book was printed. What Daubeney's position was under Henry VII we do not know, but there are hints that he was not in sympathy with the new regime.[1] However, for us the importance of Daubeney is that with this volume Caxton has reverted to a named patron. Perhaps the supply of books commissioned by the Woodvilles before April 1483 had become exhausted by now. Even so, the patronage of the book by a man like Daubeney is unusual. Caxton normally chose sponsors from among the ranks of the higher nobility. Daubeney did not belong to that class. His patronage is a sign that Caxton was finding it difficult to recruit further aristocratic patrons. Daubeney is on a par with the merchants, and his patronage thus carried on the tradition introduced by *Caton* and continued in later volumes. For the next few years in the history of the press were lean ones. Books were printed which had been commissioned by mercers, but at first Caxton made little headway with the members of the new government. There were few books printed in these years and such as did appear were of a technical nature. Many of these were printed without a date and it is difficult to be certain when they were issued. In 1486 there was only the first edition of *Speculum Vitae Christi*. The year 1487 witnessed the *Book of Good Manners*, the *Donatus*, the *Commemoratio*, the *Directorium Sacerdotum*, the first edition of the *Image of Pity*, the second edition of the *Golden Legend*, and perhaps the *Royal Book*. No edition is assigned to 1488.

Both the *Royal Book* and the *Book of Good Manners* were ordered by mercers during the period 1483–5. Pratt, who requested the latter, died in 1486; the former was commissioned in 1484, according to Caxton's epilogue, though it was apparently not printed for another three or four years.[2] It is possible that Pratt instigated the printing of

[1] Herrtage 1880–1 pp. vii–xii.

[2] This view (see Blades 1863 ii. 187–9) has recently been questioned by J. E. Gallagher, 'The Sources of Caxton's *Ryal Book* and *Doctrinal of Sapience*', *Studies in Philology*, lxii (1965), 40–62. Blades argued that the type in which the book was printed suggested a later date for its printing; but Gallagher argues that Caxton's words mean that he both translated and printed the book in 1484. However, in both prologue and epilogue Caxton says only that the translation was finished in 1484. Since he did delay printing some of his translations at this time, there is no reason why he might not also have done so with the *Royal Book*. The decision of the date of its printing must be based on the book's typography, and until a new investigation of this is made, I have accepted Blades's theory.

3   Margaret of Burgundy

That made hir body to kevde •
wonder cleer on the ryght syde •
But as I aspyen koude •
hir lyffe was shadewed with a clowde •

And whanne that I byhelde the guyse •
Off alle hir queynte marchaundyse •
Madame quod I in certeyn •
wonder faygne I wolde veyn •
Somwhat off youre thynges heere •
yeue so were ye wolde lere •
To me by short conclusioun •
youre name and youre condicioun •

¶ Gyographie •

Iam quod she cheeff nowyce •
To alle ffolkes that fleen vyce •
No cloyster is worthe wyo looke aboute •
On no syde whan I am oute •
I make cloystris fferme and stable •
worschype and honowrable •
And my name yeue thow lyste se •

4 A Medieval Bookshop

both books. They are exceptional in their reference to mercers. Apart from Hugh Bryce in the *Mirror of the World*, who was named for the special reasons already enumerated, William Pratt is the only mercer to be named in a Caxton prologue. This may have been done because the aristocratic book market was at a low ebb at this time and because Caxton thought the book suitable for merchants. He opens his prologue: 'Whan I consydere the condycions & maners of the comyn people' [99]. Under those conditions the patronage of a mercer could have been an asset. He may also have wished to honour the name of his dead friend. The name of the mercer who requested the *Royal Book* is not given. This book, however, differs in quality from the *Book of Good Manners*, for it was 'made in Frensshe atte requeste of Phelip le Bele, Kyng of Fraunce' [101], and was therefore suitable reading for all members of society, but particularly for noblemen. Caxton may have been trying with this book to regain the aristocratic market. The same reason for the omission of the friend's name in the *Boethius* may account for the omission of the mercer's name here: Caxton did not want to alienate his noble customers by introducing a merchant's name. On the other hand, loyalty to the person who made the request and who perhaps made some financial contribution to the book's printing would demand that some reference to the mercer be included. It may seem strange to us that Caxton should behave in this way, for in the latter case he does not even conceal the fact that his friend is a mercer. There is a parallel to this behaviour in many of the books published in 1483-5. He refers to some of the patrons of those books in such a way that they can confidently be identified; but he does not include their names.

By 1489 Caxton had gained new patrons who were important members of the new government. The most assiduous of these was John de Vere, Earl of Oxford. Though responsible for placing several orders with Caxton, he was not a liberal patron. In the prologue to the *Four Sons of Aymon*, printed under his patronage in 1489, Caxton complained that he had printed the book at his own expense and had so far received no reward from the Earl for it. Furthermore, he had also translated a version of the deeds of Robert de Vere, one of the Earl's ancestors. We may imagine that he had received little reward for that task either,[1] and introduced the information about it here in order to

[1] Caxton refers only to the translation of the work, not to its printing. He may not, therefore, have printed his finished translation. But as the actual translation would have cost Caxton little, his point is much stronger if we assume that he had sunk money in a printed edition.

D

jog the Earl's memory as to his obligations towards the printer. From this information we can deduce that even before 1489 Caxton had established himself with the new rulers. The translation of this work on Robert de Vere, and its printing if it was printed, should probably be dated to about 1488. Oxford was evidently also responsible for the next commission Caxton received. On 23 January 1489 he received from the King in the Palace of Westminster a copy of the French version of *Feats of Arms* by Christine de Pisan, an allegory on chivalry and a knight's equipment. The manuscript was handed to Caxton by the Earl of Oxford, through whose agency he was presumably presented at court. The translation 'was finysshed the viiij day of Iuyll the sayd yere [i.e. 1489], & enprynted the xiiij day of Iuyll next folowyng & ful fynyshyd' [103]. If the 'next following' refers to the year then the book was not printed till 1490, but if it refers to the day, it was printed less than a week after the completion of the translation. The latter interpretation would be possible if we could accept that the printing and translation proceeded simultaneously.[1] Also dated to 1489 is the romance, *Blanchardin and Eglantine*, which Caxton translated at the request of Margaret, Duchess of Somerset, the mother of Henry VII. How long Margaret had taken an interest in Caxton is not clear, but he had sold her the manuscript of the French text 'longe to fore' [105]. She was also to commission another work. Just as before 1483 it is not Edward IV but Earl Rivers and Elizabeth Woodville who take an interest in the press, so after 1485 it is the Earl of Oxford and the Duchess of Somerset who patronize the printer rather than Henry VII. If Henry did not patronize the press much, he was quite prepared to employ the printer on official business. Payments from the Exchequer were made to him 'for dyvers appoyntments to be made for the See and otherwise' about this time.[2] For Caxton 1489 must have been a satisfying year. He had regained the position as printer and royal factor which he had acquired before 1483 and which he had apparently lost in the political upheaval following Edward's death. For a man of his years to fight back in this way is in itself a considerable achievement.

Yet even towards the very end of his life Caxton was thinking about the future. His edition of *Eneydos*, the medieval adaptation of Virgil's

---

[1] Byles 1932 pp. xxix-xxx.

[2] Crotch 1928 pp. clviii. The exact nature of this business is not clear, though the entry may refer to the provision of ships for the king, since the Channel is probably meant by 'the See'.

poem, was presented to Prince Arthur, eldest son of Henry VII. We may recall that *Jason* had also been dedicated to the then Prince of Wales, and the same reason may have been operative in both cases. It is as well to ensure one's future position by gaining the favour of the heir to the throne, and parents tend naturally to be flattered by gifts made to their children. Furthermore, the governor of the Prince of Wales in 1477 had been Earl Rivers, and the tutor of Arthur in 1489 was John Skelton. Both were well known literary figures, whose help would be useful to the printer. Skelton was recognized as the leading rhetorician in England. Caxton, who was ever eager to persuade his clients of the courtliness of his style, probably felt that the introduction of Skelton's name in the prologue would serve as a guarantee for the quality of his prose. *Eneydos* was presented to the Prince of Wales, and in the following year the edition of fifteen prayers, known as the *Fifteen Oes* because each prayer begins with O, was commissioned by his mother, Elizabeth, and by his paternal grandmother, Margaret. Caxton may justifiably have felt by this time, when his death was near, that he had re-established his business on a sound footing with the patronage of royalty and nobility fairly certain.

It has been noted that Caxton issued only religious books in 1491, the probable year of his death, though it is doubtful whether we should attach any significance to this fact. He had, according to Wynkyn de Worde, just finished a translation of the *Lives of the Fathers* before he died.[1] This work was later printed by Wynkyn. The old man was active to the very end, a fitting conclusion to a life of industry and perseverance. The exact date of his death is not known. He was buried at St Margaret's, Westminster, for in the Parish Accounts for 1490-2 payments to cover the expenses of his burial are recorded. That his death occurred in late 1491 or early 1492 is confirmed by entries in the Sacrist's Roll in the Westminster Abbey Muniments. In the entry for 1491-2 the shop rented by Caxton is entered in his name and Wynkyn's, implying that the latter had taken over the tenancy during the course of the year. This would place his death between Michaelmas 1491 and Michaelmas 1492. Blades thought the position of his burial payments in the Parish Accounts of St Margaret's indicated that

---

[1]Wynkyn's colophon to his edition (1495) reads: '[this book] whiche hath be translated out of Frensshe in to Englysshe by Wyllyam Caxton of Westmynstre, late deed, and fynysshed it at the laste daye of hys lyff' (fol. 346vb).

Caxton had died in late 1491.[1] This is the major evidence for 1491, the date generally accepted; but there is no objection to a date in early 1492. No will of Caxton's has been found, though it appears he made one since some of his bequests to the parish of St Margaret's are recorded in the Parish Accounts. Records, however, have been found of an unhappy round of litigation which followed his death. The details of this dispute, which centred on Caxton's son-in-law, Gerard Crop, are of little concern to us here. They are of value in showing that Caxton was presumably married for he had a daughter, Elizabeth (we have no evidence of his marriage or of other children), and that his assets at his death were not inconsiderable. Caxton's intention, which was duly performed, was that Wynkyn should inherit the press and the business, and as we have seen, Wynkyn started paying for his old master's tenement immediately after his death. As few works issued from the press in the two years following Caxton's death, it has usually been thought that the legal difficulties surrounding the will may have caused some delay. This may be so, though the settlement was not finally made till 1496 by which time Wynkyn had printed many books.

Caxton's printing career in England may be divided into four periods. The first, from his return to the death of Edward IV in 1483, is characterized by the patronage of the Woodvilles and the publication of many smaller pieces during the establishment of the press. In the second, 1483–5, Caxton made many translations which had been ordered earlier and attempted to find some patron to take the place of the Woodvilles. From 1485 to approximately 1487, the third period, he issued many technical works, reprints and books for merchants. Political conditions forced him to develop a different market. But he had set his heart on selling books to a noble clientele and he won this market back about 1488, when he was taken up by the new regime. This last period extended to his death. Although he produced many courtly books, this period is also notable for a high proportion of religious texts.

[1] Blades 1861 i. 75. Blades also refers to a contemporary manuscript note quoted by J. Ames in his *Typographical Antiquities* from an edition of *Fructus Temporum*. The evidence of this note, which puts Caxton's death at 1491, is of doubtful value; it is not extant.

6

CAXTON AS EDITOR

In an earlier chapter I discussed what reasons dictated Caxton's choice of books to print. In the following chapters I shall consider how he prepared those books for the press. Since most people today think of Caxton primarily as the first printer of Chaucer and Malory and since those editions have contributed more than any others to that modern approval of his literary taste and scholarly method, it may be as well to consider first his activities as editor. Later chapters will be devoted to his work as translator and to his contribution to the English language. It will not be possible to scrutinize every edition he issued; I will select representative ones to illustrate how he approached his texts: whether he can be regarded as a scholar, to what extent he respected the text of the authors he published, why he made alterations in and additions to the texts, and what his general method of procedure was. The editions to be discussed are some of his editions of Chaucerian works, Malory's *Morte Darthur*, Trevisa's translation of Higden's *Polychronicon*, and the *Golden Legend*. The works of the first two authors are particularly important and have received considerable attention in the past, not always well-informed. The *Polychronicon* has been chosen because of Caxton's continuation, and the *Golden Legend* because he was here working from three versions of the book. Apart from the last work, for which he had Latin and French versions as well as an English translation, these works were all in English. I have deliberately chosen such works for this chapter, because the next one will be devoted to translations.

Of all his prologues, that to the second edition of the *Canterbury Tales* is the one which modern scholars have welcomed most warmly, for it has been used to show time and again not only that Caxton regarded Chaucer as the greatest English poet, but also that he did everything he could to publish his works accurately.[1] For most scholars

---

[1] 'But it is in the *prohemye* to the second edition of the *Canterbury Tales* that we get the fullest light both on the conscientious attitude of Caxton toward his work as a publisher and on his regard for the writings of Chaucer.' (Aurner 1926 p. 165).

there is thus a happy union of the talents of the greatest medieval English poet with those of the first English printer: the latter being a humble, though worthy, acolyte at the shrine of the master. Regrettably, I find it difficult to view their relationship in this way. I have already considered why Caxton chose to print the *Canterbury Tales* rather than *Piers Plowman*. The choice was determined more by current literary fashion than by the printer's own discrimination. Furthermore, as many manuscripts of Chaucerian works were being produced in the fifteenth century there were many copies of Chaucer's works in circulation. Blades's assertion that it would have been difficult for Caxton to find a good text of the *Canterbury Tales* is doubtful.[1] He printed the manuscript given to him; it probably never crossed his mind to look for another. In medieval times one manuscript was considered as good as another; scribes and printers freely altered individual words and phrases as long as they kept the general sense and plan of the original. Caxton was no different from his colleagues in this respect.

What exactly is it then that Caxton says in his prologue to the second edition?[2] After an enthusiastic appraisal of Chaucer's contribution to the English language, he states that he is now intending to issue a new edition of Chaucer's *Canterbury Tales*. This edition he has 'dylygently oversen and duly examyned' [90] to reproduce Chaucer's original poem accurately as many manuscript versions are abridged or have added verses. A manuscript with a faulty text was brought to him six years earlier, and, thinking it an accurate copy, he had printed it. Copies of the edition were sold to various gentlemen. One of these gentlemen came to him to complain of its corrupt text. Caxton assured him that he had followed the manuscript carefully. The gentleman replied that his father had a manuscript of the poem which he would borrow if the printer was willing to issue a new, corrected edition. Caxton agreed to this in order to 'satysfye th'auctour' Chaucer, whose work he had inadvertently damaged. The gentleman later brought him his father's manuscript, from which he corrected his first edition.

Caxton's first edition was printed from a copy 'delivered' to him. The most reasonable interpretation of this statement is that someone wealthy enough to own what was no doubt a luxury manuscript of the poem requested him to print it, just as many patrons suggested titles to him. Caxton did not choose of his own accord to print the

[1] Blades 1882 p. 89.
[2] Printed in full in Chapter Eight.

Canterbury Tales; he did it to please some wealthy, and probably noble, client. He does not tell us who this client was, for he criticizes the inferior text of his manuscript. The name of the gentleman who requested the second edition is withheld for different reasons. Both editions were apparently done by request. The manuscript from which the first edition was set up, which is not extant, belonged to what is known as group *b* of the *Canterbury Tales* manuscripts.[1] The manuscript was evidently printed faithfully for this edition is textually very similar to two other manuscripts in this group. This is to be expected: there would be no reason to alter the text. It was only when the second manuscript was brought to him that any problem would arise.

There is little to suggest that Caxton had any independent view about the quality of the manuscripts he used. He did not suspect that the first manuscript might not contain the best available text until someone else pointed it out. He agreed to print a second edition from another manuscript before he had seen it. He cannot have formed for himself any reasonable idea as to its quality; he merely accepted the word of his gentleman-client that it contained a better text. It is doubtful, therefore, whether his primary motive in printing the second edition was to produce a good text; his motive may have been a desire to oblige a noble customer, or simply a publisher's realization that a new, revised edition might sell well. Furthermore, Caxton never went out of his way to establish a good text. Many of the better publishers on the continent employed scholars to produce accurate texts. There is no evidence that Caxton did this for the works in English he printed.[2] As the *Canterbury Tales* was often copied in the fifteenth century, it should not have been difficult for him to acquire several manuscripts if he had wanted to collate the text. He was not enough of a scholar to do this himself or to get anyone to do it for him: he printed the manuscript he had available and accepted its authority. Then, in his prologue he gives no indication as to why the second manuscript was better than the first. He does say that some manuscripts contain additions or omissions—a general statement which is entirely unsupported. He does not give a single example of the first manuscript's inferiority. We can only guess what he thought of it by comparing the two editions.

[1] J. M. Manly and E. Rickert, *The Text of the Canterbury Tales* (Chicago, 1940), i. 80–81.

[2] Febvre and Martin 1958 pp. 217–22. But Carmeliano did apparently see *Sex Epistolae* through the press; see Chapter Ten.

It has been shown from collations of the two first printed editions of the *Canterbury Tales* that Caxton did not set up his second edition from his second manuscript.[1] Instead he wrote in corrections to the text in his first edition, which was then reprinted. This, we may well think, was an extraordinary way of going about a new edition. It meant that the first edition, which Caxton himself realized had a bad text, remained the basic text for the second edition. Why did he not print the second edition from the second manuscript? The answer to this is twofold. The first reason is technical. It was easier and much cheaper for compositors to set up a new edition from an older edition than from an expensive, and no doubt bulky, manuscript. It would be simpler to judge from a printed book how much type would fit on one page and thus to break down the book into parts which could be distributed among several compositors. Furthermore, any corrections made by the editor could be noted in the first edition, thus obviating the necessity for making any marks in a borrowed manuscript. The second reason lies in Caxton's attitude. Although he expressed concern for the text of his first edition, this may have been little more than publisher's talk. He was not sufficiently worried that he felt he had to produce a completely new text. He thought it sufficient to make one or two minor adjustments. This somewhat cavalier attitude has by no means disappeared from the publishing trade today, so we should not be surprised to find it in Caxton. Few people today take a publisher's 'blurb' at its face value, and there is no reason to do so with Caxton's prologues, which serve the same function.

The changes that Caxton made to the text of his second edition are of two kinds: changes in the order of the tales and changes in the actual words used. The order of the tales in his first edition is represented schematically as $AB^1F^1E^2DE^1F^2GCB^2HI$, which is the order of group *b* manuscripts. In the second edition F^1 and F^2 are united and put after E. Expressed more simply, this means that he found the link between the *Squire's Tale* and the *Franklin's Tale*, which he therefore joined together and put in a different position. As this link is found in the majority of the manuscripts which belong to group *a* and not in the manuscripts of other groups, it is probable that the second manuscript belonged to group *a*. But all known manuscripts of group *a* contain

---

[1] On the two editions of the *Canterbury Tales* see T. F. Dunn, *The Manuscript Source of Caxton's Second Edition of the Canterbury Tales* (Chicago, 1940), and Blake, *Leeds Studies in English*, New Series i (1967), 19–36.

other links between tales and other characteristic features of order *not* found in Caxton's second edition. If the second manuscript belonged to group *a* and contained these additional links, why did he not take all the links to be found in the manuscript he was using? The answer is that he worked too quickly. We shall see in the next chapter how many of his translations are marred by the speed at which he worked. It is only natural to assume that his editions of English authors suffered from the same fault. He probably made a hasty comparison of the two texts, merely taking over into his new edition anything that caught his attention. At the same time he omitted to include things in the second manuscript which would have improved the arrangement of his first edition.

This method of procedure can be seen even more clearly from the changes in the words and word-order made in the second edition. These changes show that the second edition was an edited text, and also that he did not spend sufficient time and trouble over the corrections. In the *Miller's Tale*, the line which in most manuscripts reads 'A clerk had litherly biset his whyle' [113] appeared in the first printed edition as 'A clerk had lowdly biset his whyle'. Caxton's second manuscript had the regular reading, for he crossed out *lowdly* and entered *litherly* in the margin in front of the line. When the compositor came to set up this line, he read it exactly as it stood in the corrected first edition with the result that he set up 'Lytherly a clerk had biset his whyle'. This, and other examples like it, prove that the second edition was printed from a corrected version of the first edition. Other changes show that Caxton failed to take sufficient care when correcting. Most manuscripts read at line 905 of the *Merchant's Tale* 'I chees thee for my wyf and my confort'. But the first four words had appeared in the first edition as 'I care for thee'. When he corrected the first edition he merely crossed out *care* and substituted *chees*. Consequently the second edition reads 'I chees for thee my wyf and my confort', which makes complete nonsense of the passage. He noted the difference between the two major words and corrected the line accordingly; but he cannot have read the line in its context or he would have realized what he had done. The fact that he was willing to edit Chaucer's work in this way shows that he did not have that tender regard for Chaucer's style and language which some scholars have claimed for him. The second edition was made hastily and without proper care. He borrowed some things from his second manuscript; but the changes were made haphazardly. For this reason it is difficult to discover which manuscript he used for his second edition, though there seems no reason to doubt that it belonged to group *a* of the *Canterbury Tales* manuscripts. There is nothing in the changes made for the second edition to suggest that he approached the text in a scholarly manner; in general he was inspired more by commercial than by academic considerations.

From his edition of the *Canterbury Tales*, we may pass on to a consideration of his edition of the *House of Fame*. The first thing to be noticed is that the poem is entitled 'The Book of Fame made by Gefferey Chaucer'. Caxton's edition is the first text which ascribes the authorship of the poem to Chaucer, an ascription which has never seriously been questioned. Whether he got the information from his manuscript is not known, but as Chaucer refers to his *bok of fame* in his *Retracciouns* which Caxton printed at the end of the *Canterbury Tales*, the second edition of which was printed about this time, Caxton could easily have made the deduction for himself. That he put Chaucer's name so prominently at the head of the poem is attributable to his desire to make the edition more attractive to any would-be purchaser. Chaucer was popular and his name would help the sale of the edition. Unfortunately the manuscript which Caxton used for his edition was defective. It is not extant, but it finished at line 2094, whereas the two major manuscripts of the poem continue to line 2158, though even in these manuscripts the poem is incomplete. It is generally agreed that Chaucer left the poem unfinished. Caxton's source lacked, therefore, about sixty lines, probably representing the final folio of a manuscript. Because his copy of the poem was incomplete, he was faced with the problem of what to do about it. He decided, rather surprisingly perhaps, to provide a metrical conclusion of his own composition consisting of twelve lines. That the composition is his own is proved by the word *Caxton* which is printed in the margin opposite the first line of his conclusion. The new conclusion is followed by a short prose epilogue.[1] To judge from those twelve lines of verse, Caxton's metrical abilities were not of a high order—several of the lines are little better than doggerel. Nevertheless he based them on Chaucer's conclusion to the *Parliament of Fowls*, which he had printed about 1479.

In his prose conclusion Caxton says that Chaucer has left the poem incomplete 'as fer as I can understonde'. This could mean either that he had inferred this from his own copy which he assumed contained all

---

[1] Blake, *Leeds Studies in English*, New Series i (1967), 25–26.

that Chaucer had written or that, although he was aware that his own manuscript was incomplete, he nevertheless knew that the poem had never been completed. The former is clearly the correct conclusion, as may be proved by his own words. His 'metyng of lesyng and sothsawe, where as yet they ben chekked' echoes two lines towards the end of his own text and shows that he did not expect anything else to follow. Line 2093 reads 'They were a chekked bothe two'; and line 2089 reads 'A lesynge and a soth sayd sawe'. The latter line is particularly interesting, for the manuscripts here read 'A lesyng and a sad soth sawe'. In view of the *sothsawe* in his epilogue it is difficult to escape the conclusion that his manuscript copy also read *sad soth sawe*. The reading in the printed edition must be a typographical error, by which *sad* has become *sayd* and has also been transposed in the line. Caxton cannot have checked his printed edition; he was not such a conscientious proofreader.

This epilogue reveals that he thought he had as much of the poem as Chaucer had written. If he thought it was complete, why should he have bothered to add a conclusion? It is impossible to reach any definite answer. The impression one gets is that his is an attempt to tidy up the text; he wished to print an entire poem. Yet he was not sufficiently moved by the poem to think how it might have finished; he had neither the talent nor the inspiration for that. His addition is in no sense a continuation; it is simply a way of drawing the poem to an end as quickly as possible. Although it might be thought presumptuous on his part to write a metrical conclusion to a Chaucerian poem, his ending shows not only a basic commonsense in using the conclusion of another Chaucerian poem as a model, but also his usual caution: he did not like to go too far on his own initiative.

Our investigation of the printed editions of these Chaucerian poems has shown that Caxton was not a scholar in any modern sense of the word. He may have wished to issue a good text of the poems, but he did not give as much care to his work as he might have done. His performance does not match his intentions. However, he was not a trained scribe, and may consequently have been unaware of the difficulties of reproducing a text accurately. It is also clear that he did not wish to introduce alterations into a Chaucerian poem. A poem, and this goes as much for the works of Gower and Lydgate as for those of Chaucer, had a fixed form which a printer should not alter. The changes made for the second edition of the *Canterbury Tales* were an attempt, albeit a very imperfect one, to restore the poem's original form. Where a poem was left incomplete by the poet, Caxton evidently felt there was no harm done in trying to round it off. Though we may be surprised at his presumption, there was no attempt at deception. The continuation to the *House of Fame* is labelled as Caxton's work, and this care reveals in itself a respect for the genuine writings of Chaucer.

The recognition of the permanent character of a poem's form was not extended to prose. This may be the result of a tendency to value poetry more highly than prose for, although prose had become more popular in the fifteenth century, it did not have the same cachet as poetry. It was functional, and therefore adaptable. Caxton's version of Malory's *Morte Darthur* reveals that he did not accord it the same respect he gave to Chaucerian poems; and he did not approach Malory's work with that appreciation given it by modern readers. He printed it because it was the text in the manuscript lent him by one of his clients. For Caxton, *Morte Darthur* was merely one version of the Arthur story, a version which was in English and therefore suitable for printing after it had been edited. He treated it in the same way he treated the English translation of the *Legenda Aurea*. Indeed since he altered Malory more than this latter work, he evidently felt Malory's prose style needed refining. However, the alterations in Malory's language will be discussed in a later chapter; here we are more concerned with the broader changes in Caxton's edition of *King Arthur*.

This edition was for long the only text of Malory available. In 1934, however, the unique manuscript was found at Winchester College. The find of this manuscript led to a controversy, not yet resolved, as to whether Malory had written the various component tales of his Arthur story as one work or as independent romances.[1] Since I am concerned with Caxton, I do not wish to contribute to this controversy. Caxton's editorial activities must be evaluated within the framework of the following details. He used one manuscript (he mentions only one manuscript in his prologue), which included all the tales; and those tales appeared in his manuscript in the order in which he printed them. Not only is the order of the tales the same in his text as in the Winchester manuscript, but also there is no reason to suppose that he would have made changes in their order. He did, on the other hand, frequently alter the language of his copy and add or delete episodes. As the

[1] Vinaver 1967 p. xxxv ff.

Winchester manuscript is not the one he used in setting up his text, it is not certain that the differences between the printed text and the manuscript should be attributed to Caxton rather than to the scribe of the manuscript he was using; but it seems most probable and will be assumed here.

Whatever Malory's concept of structure may have been, there can be no doubt that the modifications made by Caxton tended towards unity and order. He treated all the tales as part of a single work on Arthur, which he divided up into twenty-one books and 507 chapters. Consequently he omitted the explicits to all tales except the last, for their retention might have worked against the unity he was striving for. It is characteristic of the man that he failed to extend this policy to many of the episodes which make up the individual tales. Thus book two ends in the printed edition, following the manuscript, 'Thus endeth the tale of Balyn and of Balan', and book three 'Explicit the weddynge of kynge Arthur'. But usually Caxton carried out his policy of excision and adaptation with thoroughness. He followed hints in his manuscript when making his divisions into books, many of which correspond to tales or episodes in Malory. He tried also to make each book of about equal length and to be built round a single theme. Sometimes his material proved intractable; for example, he was content to let the break between books nine and ten occur in the middle of a conversation. Similarly, it is quite possible that many of the chapter divisions were suggested by paragraph marks in the text, for his divisions correspond with many such marks in the Winchester manuscript. Even if this were not so, there are plenty of expressions in the text like 'Now leave we', 'Now turn we to' to help an editor. The majority of his chapters are sensibly arranged, though some are too short because formulas like the ones quoted above occurred too close together.[1] Occasionally the chapter division has been made for dramatic reasons to increase the suspense; and often a chapter begins and ends with impassioned direct speech, because he felt that the opening and close of a chapter should be more rhetorical.[2] Some chapter divisions, however, appear to have little more justification than that the editor thought the chapter already long enough. Whereas generally the divisions followed hints in the manuscript and occurred

---

[1] For an account of these and other changes made by Caxton see Sally Shaw, 'Caxton and Malory', in *Essays on Malory*, edited by J. A. W. Bennett (Oxford, 1963), 114–45.

[2] Cf. Blake, *Bulletin of the John Rylands Library*, xlvi (1963–4), 321.

naturally, occasionally he was not prepared to look for a suitable break or to rewrite the passage to create one with the result that the division jars upon the reader. This is largely what we might have expected from what we already know of Caxton.

This division into books and chapters made Malory's work much more like the other books issuing from the press. The romances he translated from the French were all divided into episodes. This division was characteristic of the prose adaptations from poetry which were so common in the fourteenth and fifteenth centuries in Burgundy, and it is more than likely that Caxton became accustomed to the division of prose works into smaller units while abroad.[1] Such an arrangement makes a book easier to read and to handle, a factor which a publisher would also take into consideration. The way in which the work was edited was bound to throw more emphasis on the principal character, Arthur, and to give the book more unity. The Winchester manuscript of Malory consists of individual tales in reading which it is possible for a reader to confine his attention to one particular tale in which Arthur may not have been mentioned; but the division of the printed version into books makes each book part of a whole, and some connexion, however tenuous, is made between all books and King Arthur. This consideration may have had some weight, for Caxton printed the book to satisfy the demand for a work dealing with England's sole representative among the Nine Worthies. He was also to publish accounts of the exploits of Charlemagne and Godfrey of Bouillon, the two other Christian Worthies—and it is with these two volumes that his edition of Malory should be equated. Although these three volumes are all built round a main, central character, the unity of a tale, as we understand it, was not important to late medieval taste: it was concerned with the moral implications and lessons to be drawn from a holy war undertaken by a Christian king. Consequently, although Caxton's treatment of the text seems to give it greater unity by making the whole action revolve round Arthur, paradoxically it also makes the text more fragmentary: each small episode tends to become the illustration of a moral and can be read independently. The work has become something like a sermon on chivalry with innumerable, carefully indexed, exempla. As Caxton himself wrote in the prologue 'al is wryton for our doctryne, and for to beware that we falle not to

---

[1] G. Doutrepont, Les mises en prose des épopées et des romans chevaleresques du XIV⁰ au XVI⁰ siècle (Brussels, 1939).

vyce ne synne, but t'exersyse and folowe vertu' (cxlvi),[1] and the book as a whole 'treateth of the noble actes, feates of armes of chyvalrye, prowesse, hardynesse, humanyte, love, curtosye, and veray gentylnesse, wyth many wonderful hystoryes and adventures' (cxlvi). His reason for making the chapter and book divisions is the same in Malory as it was for including the table of contents in the *Polychronicon* or the *Golden Legend*: to enable a reader to select quickly a story or illustrative example of any particular virtue and vice. It was not for what we today would think of as literary reasons. He was more interested in the concept of chivalry than in any particular exponent of the chivalric code, though it was useful to relate the stories to a central personage as famous as Arthur.[2]

Although Caxton made changes in all books of *King Arthur*, he rewrote book five, the story of Arthur's conquest of the Emperor Lucius; the changes in that book reveal his motives and prejudices most clearly. The story is greatly reduced. Firstly, Caxton eliminated · detailed descriptions of battles. He was more interested in the results of battles and the attitude of the participants than in the battles themselves. Secondly, and closely related to the excision of the battle descriptions, he reduced the number of geographical references, with the result that the actions became more generalized. Thirdly, he cut out episodes dealing with minor personages, such as the wounding of Sir Kay. Finally, he omitted heroic speeches by minor characters, as in the deliberations of Arthur's knights about what answer they should send to Lucius. These excisions bring out the thread of the narrative more clearly and emphasize the deeds of the main protagonists. In particular the exploits of Arthur and Gawain are retained, though it was the virtues they stood for as Christian knights which he valued rather than their personalities or individual characters. This is shown by the retention of two digressions which might have been cut out without damage to the story, but which were not: Arthur's dream, followed by the fight against the giant, and Gawain's duel with Priamus. The former is retained because it contrasts a man who respects

[1] Page or page and line references in brackets after quotations from Caxton's edition of Malory are from Vinaver 1967 and not from Crotch, whose text is incomplete.

[2] It is interesting to note that Arthur's name does not appear in the table of contents as frequently as it might, a thing we might have expected if Caxton was particularly interested in Arthur. For example, book five 'treateth of the conqueste of Lucius th'emperour' (cxlvii) without mentioning Arthur.

women and children with a tyrant who respects nobody, and because it affirms that such a tyrant may be overcome only with God's help. It is fitting, therefore, that God should be thanked for his goodness by the foundation of a church. The tone of this digression is chivalric and religious; and this cannot be said of the wounding of Sir Kay. The latter digression contains a duel between a Christian and a pagan knight. Once more the tone of the episode is religious for, as Caxton's chapter heading states, it shows 'a bataylle doon by Gauwayn ayenst a Sarasyn whiche after was yelden and became Crysten' (183). In fact Priamus is not called a Saracen in the chapter, but the heading underlines what Caxton thought of the passage: it was a fight between Christian and Saracen in which the only result can be a Christian victory. The participants themselves are not as important as the doctrine that grace works through a good Christian for the overthrow of evil.

The emphasis of book five is upon two things, Christianity and chivalry. Both elements are of course to be found in the original, but they appear with greater force in Caxton's edition because so much else has been eliminated. The Christianity is expressed in terms of a holy war between good and evil. The nobility and virtues of Arthur are stressed. The enemies are referred to as Saracens, 'admyrales', sultans, giants born of devils and in other ways characteristic of books dealing with Christian crusades against the heathen. Caxton keeps all these references, as well as pointing incidentally to the luxury of the Emperor with his silk pavilions and to his pride in uttering vain words (192/2)—the 'vain' being a Caxton addition. Such moral and religious references as there were in the original are kept and often made more pointed. Arthur's war comes to resemble Charlemagne's crusade in Spain and the conquest of Jerusalem by Godfrey of Bouillon; and crusading, we should remember, was much in the public mind in England at the end of the fifteenth century. Much of the moral lesson of the story is presented through Arthur's character, for he behaves in a way that all should emulate. His foundation of the church after the battle with the giant has been noted. He attacked the giant to relieve the wretched people of the countryside; his concern for the poor people is often stressed (cf. 206/9). Arthur adopts a protective attitude towards women and children (241/8 ff.), a quality not found in his opponents. Caxton retains Arthur's prohibition against rape at the sack of Urbino and how he restrained his own men from attacking the Emperor's messengers. After one of the many battles Arthur sent back the bodies of the dead Romans to Rome so that they might be buried (225). In all things Arthur acts with that wisdom and mercy we expect of a Christian king.

Apart from the moral interest in the story, Caxton was clearly impressed by the trappings of chivalry. The ceremonial at court is elaborated. The messengers arrive carrying olive branches in token of peace and they do 'theyr obeyssaunce in makyng ... reverence' (185/19). The kings and emperors are addressed in a more elevated manner. The speeches made in Arthur's council are clothed in a more pompous and high-flown oratory. Caxton probably enjoyed and admired the hierarchical structure of court life and the pomp of office, a taste he may well have acquired at the Burgundian court. The inclusion of such details may also reflect the popularity which they enjoyed among his public. Typical of these are that Arthur buried his men according to their rank (224), and that Priamus was overjoyed that he has been conquered by a knight like Gawain and not by a simple yeoman as he had at first feared (232); both of which details are retained from the original. When the messengers leave Arthur's court, Caxton added that they were given gifts, and after Arthur has slain the giant the gold and money are left there to be distributed equitably among the people. The Christian ideal of abstinence is fused with the chivalric one of generosity. Even some of the incidental aspects of chivalry are retained, such as the description of Priamus's shield, though it has no bearing on the story.

To summarize: Caxton modified Malory's story to bring out the Christian morals and chivalry in it. Both are to be found in Malory's original, but by cutting out much other material he is able to throw them into greater prominence. At the same time he emphasizes the roles of Arthur and Gawain, not because he is particularly interested in them as persons, but because they represented for him the ideal of a Christian knight. Although one result of his alterations has been to give the work greater unity, this may not have been his intention. He was perhaps more concerned to break the story down into short episodes illustrative of various Christian morals.

Although Malory's book cannot be shown to have achieved much popularity before Caxton printed it, the next work that we shall consider had been popular for some considerable time. This is the world history, Higden's *Polychronicon*, which had been written in Latin in the first half of the fourteenth century and translated into English by John

Trevisa in 1387.[1] Historical works were popular with aristocracy and merchants alike, and the *Polychronicon* was no exception.[2] To understand how the *Polychronicon* fits into Caxton's output, it is necessary to give an outline of the historical works he published. In 1480 he printed a book which he called the *Chronicles of England*—a version of the popular chronicle known as the *Brut*. He printed it with one modification, and that a characteristic one, namely the introduction of a table of contents 'to th'ende that every mon may see and shortly fynde suche mater as it shall plese hym to see or rede'.[3] In this same year Caxton printed the section from Trevisa's translation of Higden's *Polychronicon* containing the description of the British Isles. This small book was probably intended to be issued as part of or at least in conjunction with the *Chronicles of England*. Certainly he mentions this work in his prologue, and the two books are often found bound together. He also added, as we would expect, a table of contents to this part of the *Polychronicon* published separately. In 1482 he issued two historical works: *Chronicles of England*, reprinted without change, and Trevisa's translation of the *Polychronicon*.

Caxton made several changes to Trevisa's translation. He added his own prologue, based ultimately on a prologue by Diodorus Siculus,[4] and he inserted a table of contents. This table is quasi-alphabetical; it does not follow the contents of each chapter chronologically. I say 'quasi-alphabetical' because although all the initial letters are grouped together, the arrangement of the entries within each letter is erratic. Trevisa's book is then printed much as it appeared in the manuscript Caxton was using, except that he modernized the language. Trevisa's prologue and colophon are given as well as Higden's own prologues. After Trevisa's colophon, Caxton added the epilogue which introduces the final book, often referred to as the *Liber Ultimus*, that he had decided to include with the *Polychronicon*. Trevisa's translation had ended in 1357; Caxton's continuation carried it down to 1461. However, in the epilogue which precedes the *Liber Ultimus* Caxton mentions that his own addition is not to be compared with Trevisa's work and that he

---

[1] See J. Taylor, *The Universal Chronicle of Ranulph Higden* (Oxford, 1966).

[2] C. L. Kingsford, *Prejudice and Promise in Fifteenth Century England* (repr. London, 1962), pp. 41–42. It was the mercer Roger Thorney who got Wynkyn de Worde to print his edition of the *Polychronicon*.

[3] Blades 1863 ii. 109.

[4] Workman, *Modern Language Notes*, lvi (1941), 252–8.

has therefore separated the two parts of the volume. He has gone so far, he writes, as to divide off the table of contents for the last book from that for the rest of the work. This is so, but in a rather curious way. All the entries under *a* to the last book are to be found in the table of contents at the end of the other entries of *a*, and so on with the other letters. Since the table is not fully alphabetical, a complete separation is hardly achieved. These entries appear to have been added to avoid a complete recasting of the table rather than to separate the last book from the others.

Two features of this book are noteworthy. The first, the alphabetical arrangement of the table of contents, represents a distinct advance. However faulty it may be by modern standards, it is the first index to an English printed book. It enables a reader to find a story about any particular person with ease. It continues that process of fragmentation which we noted in the edition of Malory. History has become a series of examples which a reader can select at will. The second, the addition of the last book, presents us with some interesting problems. Why did Caxton feel it necessary to bring the history down to contemporary times? Why did he choose to do it in the way he did, keeping the continuation separate from the rest of the book? And what sources did he use for his continuation, which was described by Blades as 'the only original work of any magnitude from our printer's pen'?[1]

It is natural to assume that he added the last book for the sake of completeness. However, the way in which the book is added suggests that Caxton may not originally have intended to include it. It is kept so much apart from the rest of the work; in this respect this addition is not typical either of Caxton's works or of contemporary history writing. Additions to the *Brut*, for example, were freely made; and Caxton thought nothing of rearranging Malory's text. On the other hand, in his edition of the *Polychronicon* he kept Trevisa's colophon as well as adding his own epilogue to book seven. The reasons he gave for not wanting to link this last book more closely with Trevisa's work were that he had few sources from which to compose it and that his own capabilities were so inferior to Trevisa's scholarly and literary attainments. Nevertheless, he did not hesitate to modernize the 'rude and old Englyssh' [68] of Trevisa's translation. There can be no doubt that Trevisa's translations were admired in the fifteenth century; and Caxton himself mentions two of the other translations executed by

[1] Blades 1882 p. 257.

Trevisa.[1] Consequently it is probable Caxton felt that his reputation
was such that he ought not to rearrange his work as he had done
Malory's, but that a modernization of the language did not constitute
tampering with the text. His modesty, which is so often a mere formula, may here be genuine, and the continuation may not, therefore,
be an afterthought. If so, this would support the results of our investigation of his editions of Chaucer. The works of authors with an established reputation were not changed, whereas other books could be
altered to suit the requirements of the publisher. The answers to our
first two questions are therefore related. Caxton wished for completeness in his historical work, but he also wanted the advantages which
the name of Trevisa would bring him in promoting the book. Hence
he kept his own continuation apart, just as he had done in the *House of
Fame*.

The impression one gets from Caxton's epilogue to book seven is
that he composed the *Liber Ultimus* himself, though this is perhaps not
an impression he wanted to create. He mentions two sources available
to him, Caspar Rolewinck's *Fasciculus Temporum* and an unidentified
book which he called *Aureus de Universo*. This latter book is similar to
Walsingham's *Historia Anglicana* and it may have been John Tinmouth's
Historia Aurea, which in one manuscript, Corpus Christi College,
Cambridge, B 1. 2, extends down to 1377.[2] Certainly down to 1377
Caxton made use of the two sources he mentions. From that date onwards he based his work on the *Brut*, though it is not mentioned in his
list of sources. From 1377 to 1419 he had two versions of the *Brut*, for
in his description of the death of Richard II, for example, he mentions
two accounts of how he died. Although one of these is described as
'the comyn oppynyon of Englysshmen', both are taken from the *Brut*
and no attempt is made to distinguish which one has the greater
probability. Caxton does not approach history in a critical way. Up
to 1419 Caxton's version is somewhat abbreviated though based on
two versions of the *Brut*; after 1419 Caxton's edition is a straight
reprint of his own *Chronicles of England* with only one or two corrections and additions. The *Liber Ultimus* is thus a compilation of other

---

[1] See also D. C. Fowler, 'John Trevisa and the English Bible', *Modern Philology*,
lviii (1960–1), 81–98, and 'New Light on John Trevisa', *Traditio*, xviii (1962),
289–317.

[2] F. W. D. Brie, *Geschichte und Quellen der mittelenglischen Prosachronik—The
Brute of England oder The Chronicles of England* (Marburg, 1905), pp. 122–3; and see
C. L. Kingsford, *English Historical Literature in the Fifteenth Century* (Oxford, 1913).

texts to which he contributed little. Though it may have been difficult to get other books about this period, he was evidently unwilling to add something from his own experiences or even to make comments about what had happened. It looks as though he started out trying to make a compilation, and then because of a lack of material or just as a result of a general impatience he tended to rely more and more upon one book. Even though this meant he had to repeat what he had printed already, he no doubt felt that the completeness achieved in this way was important.

The final work I shall consider is the *Golden Legend*, a collection of saints' lives. In content it has much in common with the *Polychronicon*, as Caxton himself recognized in his prologue to that work which was under preparation about the same time. The *Polychronicon* embraced the history of the world and naturally included accounts of many biblical figures and saints. Although these two works were similar in content, they differed in their structural organization, for whereas the *Golden Legend* contains stories to be read on a certain day in the Church's calendar, in the *Polychronicon* the stories are part of a continuous narrative organized on a chronological basis. Hence his additions to the latter work took the form of an extension of the chronological narrative to his own times. This method could clearly not be adopted with the *Golden Legend*, since the Church's calendar forms a complete unit in itself. Any additions had to be entered in their appropriate place in that calendar or they had to form a separate section.[1]

To appreciate the difficulties involved it is necessary to review the development of the *Legenda Aurea*, the original Latin version of the *Golden Legend*. The original work, written in Latin between 1250 and 1280 by a certain Jacobus de Varagine, Archbishop of Genoa (1292-8), contained about 180 sections, each designed to be read on a particular feast-day in the Church's calendar. The sections were arranged in accordance with the ecclesiastical calendar starting with Advent and the Feast of St Andrew. The range of subject matter included lives of martyrs, virgins and apostles, apocryphal stories, and episodes from the life of Christ. The work became so popular that additions were made to it in the author's own lifetime. In the fourteenth century at least two independent translations into French were made, a relatively free one by Jean Belet and a more literal one by Jehan de Vignai; both these translations exist in various versions. A feature of some texts of the

---

[1] Hence it is the one which 'seems to be the most independent and original' of all his works as editor; Aurner 1926 p. 116.

latter version is that the episodes from the life of Christ are grouped in a section which is separated from the rest of the lives. About 1438 an English translation of the *Legenda Aurea* was made. This earlier English translation is known as the *Gilte Legende*, a title it has in one of the manuscripts, to distinguish it from Caxton's own *Golden Legend*. The author of the *Gilte Legende* introduced into his work the lives of many English saints.[1] Each of these three versions of the *Legenda Aurea* existed in many copies, for it was one of the most popular works of the late Middle Ages.[2]

Then in 1483 Caxton published his own translation of the text, now known as the *Golden Legend*. As he informs us himself, his translation is based on three versions of the book, a Latin, a French and an early English one. His Latin text remains unidentified. His French text was a fifteenth-century redaction of Vignai's translation, which is represented by British Museum MS Stowe 50-51, and his text of the *Gilte Legende* is most closely represented by British Museum MS Additional 35,298. Apart from these three texts which he tells us he used, he had access to other sources. He inserted a whole new section containing lives of biblical and apocryphal people. These were Adam, Noah, Abraham, Isaac, Jacob, Esau, Joseph, Moses, Joshua, Samuel, Saul, David, Solomon, Rehoboam, Job, Tobit, and Judith; and the section also includes a small commentary on the Ten Commandments linked with the life of Moses.[3] He also translated a Latin life of St Roch not found in the *Legenda Aurea*, and he included many personal comments and reminiscences.[4] The sources of his edition are therefore many and they pose two problems for the modern scholar: how Caxton combined three texts of *Legenda Aurea* into a coherent narrative, and how the additional sources were woven into the framework of the book already provided by the three texts of the *Legenda Aurea*.

With respect to the first of these problems it is interesting that Caxton felt it necessary to justify himself in making a new version when an English translation was already available. His justification is simple: his Latin and French texts contained stories not in his English one, and in his edition he intended to include as much as possible from each

[1] For a general discussion of English Saints' Lives see T. Wolpers, *Die englische Heiligenlegende des Mittelalters* (Tübingen, 1964).

[2] R. F. Seybolt, 'Fifteenth Century Editions of the *Legenda Aurea*', *Speculum*, xxi (1946), 327-38.

[3] Printed in Ellis 1892 pp. 105-244.

[4] Jeremy, *Modern Language Notes*, lxiv (1949), 259-61, and lxvii (1952), 313-17.

version. Although he may have introduced this apologia simply to draw attention to his editorial activities and hence to enhance the value of his edition, comprehensiveness was a principle which often guided his actions and was certainly a factor here. The method he adopted was to use the French text as his basic one, for reasons discussed later, and to incorporate into this framework additional stories from the English and Latin versions. But even his translation itself is in any passage usually an amalgam of two or three of his texts. This is shown by the following example, in which he has apparently borrowed words from all three sources:[1]

Latin:	Tunc illa constans effecta tortores hortabatur ...
French:	Et fu celle ferme et amonnoistoit les martyreurs ...
Early English:	And than þis blessid queen was made fulle of sad feithe and commaundid the turmentours ...
Caxton:	And she was constaunte and ferme in the feythe, and bad the tormentours ...

His procedure here is no different from the one he followed in the *Canterbury Tales* or the *Polychronicon*. Evidently when he had more than one source available, he felt he had to make use of them all; he did not attempt to choose between them.

Nevertheless, if he had used all the material found in the three texts, his edition would have reached gargantuan proportions. It was necessary to do some pruning. But many of the omissions may not reflect a desire to prevent the edition from growing too large; they were made because in some places, Caxton felt out of sympathy with his sources. One of the characteristics of the Latin *Legenda Aurea* is a certain reserve on the part of the author towards the veracity of the stories. It is this expression of a critical spirit which modern readers of Varagine's work most admire. Although these expressions of doubt are generally kept by Vignai, they are frequently omitted by Caxton who obviously felt that they were unsuitable. Thus Varagine's comment that many of the bones said to be of the Holy Innocents are too big to belong to children under two is omitted. The exclusion of this type of passage 'not only impairs the quality of his version and misrepresents its original but also detracts from his editorial stature'.[2] Probably Caxton was an uncritical admirer of the Church who would tolerate no doubt

---

[1] Kurvinen, *Neuphilologische Mitteilungen*, lx (1959), 353–75; the example is taken from this article.

[2] Jeremy, *Speculum*, xxi (1946), 215.

or backsliding, for whom accuracy was less important than truth, though he may have omitted such passages because he assumed that his clientele would not approve of them. He also omitted other passages, which have been described as '(a) narrative episodes, most of which are variants of incidents already narrated; (b) panegyric passages; (c) citation of authorities; (d) scriptural quotations, especially when grouped; (e) controversial or doctrinal dialogues'.[1] The result of these excisions is that his work is based more firmly on narrative and moral than that of any of his predecessors; it is simpler and less questioning.

His handling of the three texts of the *Legenda Aurea* follows the pattern we have come to expect. How did he manage to amalgamate his other sources into his translation? An answer to this question must first consider the nature of his major addition and what his source or sources for it were. The legends in the additional section are of two types. One group consists of stories which, though based on the biblical account, are considerably expanded by the inclusion of apocryphal elements and of facts and comments culled from the works of early scholars and commentators. Thus the story of Adam and Eve follows the outline found in Genesis, but it includes apocryphal tales like the quest for the oil of life by Seth and individual details from the works of Bede, Methodius, Josephus and Strabo. The earlier stories up to and including the life of Moses with its excursus on the Ten Commandments belong to this type. The second group, beginning with the life of Joshua and extending to the end of the additional material, consists of stories which appear to be direct translations of the Vulgate. But the Vulgate account is often considerably shortened, and this group is notable for a host of personal reminiscences by Caxton. The story of Job is a good example. The narrative section of the Vulgate account has been translated, but the middle section of the biblical book in which Job discusses his misfortunes with his three friends is dismissed in a couple of sentences. The interest of the translator lay in narrative rather than in speculation. The stories in this second group differ in another important characteristic from those in the first one. Whereas the earlier stories are complete, independent narratives, the later ones cannot be read in isolation. The accounts of Saul and David must be read together to make them meaningful; and the tale of Rehoboam lacks any cohesive structural framework. It opens by following the Bible literally, then goes over to paraphrase and finally the translator

[1] *Ibid.*

breaks it off with 'And here I leve alle th'ystorye and make an ende of *Booke of Kynges* for this tyme &c. For ye that lyste to knowe how every kyng regned after other, ye may fynde it in the fyrst chapytre of Saynt Mathew, whyche is redde on Crystemas day in the mornyng to fore Te Deum, whyche is the genelagye of Our Lady' (Ellis, p. 218). No attempt has been made to round the tale off, and it could not be read aloud to any effect. It was therefore different not only from the earlier biblical stories, but also from the other legends in the *Golden Legend*. These differences between the two groups of stories in this additional section suggest that each was taken from a different source.

As for the earlier biblical stories, it is possible to think that either Caxton composed the lives himself by making use of all the authorities mentioned or he took over all stories in that group from one source. The latter is the only acceptable hypothesis. Not only is it improbable that he had access to so many different sources, but also if they had been available to him, he would have made greater use of them since he aimed at comprehensiveness in his editions. Generally he preferred to adapt an existing source than to compose a new account. This source could conceivably have been attached to one of the three versions of *Legenda Aurea* he used. Thus at the end of MS Additional 35, 298 of *Gilte Legende* there are several quasi-biblical stories which did not come from its French source. However, these stories differ considerably from those in the *Golden Legend* so that it is impossible that Caxton based his own stories on them. In other words Caxton had access to certain apocryphal stories of biblical material which he chose to ignore in favour of another version. This detail confirms that he used only one source for these earlier biblical stories, since from what we know of him he would not have disregarded a version which was available in order to compose a similar one himself. He disregarded the version in *Gilte Legende* because he had access to a more complete one; and it was its greater comprehensiveness that appealed to him.

It is likely therefore that his source for the earlier biblical stories was an independent English work,[1] possibly an English Temporale, that part of the breviary and missal containing the daily offices as distinct from those proper to saints' days found in the Sanctorale. This hypothesis is quite possible even though no suitable manuscript which he might have used has been found. If his source was of this type, it is

[1] My article 'The Biblical Additions in Caxton's *Golden Legend*', which is to appear in *Traditio* (1969), discusses this point in more detail.

easier to understand how he approached some of the editorial problems involved in preparing the edition of the *Golden Legend*. With a Temporale and three versions of the *Legenda Aurea*, he would naturally choose that version which allowed him to include the Temporale with least trouble. That was the French one, in which the episodes from the life of Christ and the lives of the saints were arranged in independent sections. This arrangement obviated the necessity of putting each new tale in its appropriate position in the ecclesiastical calendar. It also made for a contrast between the episodes from the life of Christ (New Testament) and the early history of the Jews (Old Testament), and between the material of the Temporale and the lives of the saints (Sanctorale). The central section thus provided a link between the other two sections. Unfortunately the Temporale was arranged to follow the chronological sequence of the Bible. It started with Adam and Eve; but that part of the Bible was read at Septuagesima. Hence the central section of his *Golden Legend* started at Septuagesima, whereas the other two commenced at Advent and the Feast of St Andrew. Caxton was not prepared to adapt his source to make it harmonize with the rest of the book; that would have involved too much trouble.

When he had decided to adopt this plan, he was faced by a further problem: the source he was using for the early biblical stories finished with Moses. He had to decide whether to continue the narrative or not and, if he continued it, what source to use. He did carry on and he chose the source most immediately available—the Bible. It is of course possible that he used an English translation of the Bible already available. The available evidence, however, suggests that Caxton made his own translation of the Vulgate, which would in any case have been more easily accessible to him than any English translation. The manner in which the continuation was made certainly suggests that he was the translator. It is incomplete, even though Caxton recognized that a Temporale would include more material than his translation did. Possibly he got tired of his self-imposed task, a view which is confirmed by the brevity of some of the stories. The life of Joshua is little more than the bald statement of a few details from his biography; it is certainly very far from being a true *vita*. Yet if he had used an English translation, there would not have been the same necessity for such drastic abbreviation; the earlier lives are very full.

The growth of Caxton's edition was as follows. He had three texts of the *Legenda Aurea* and another source, possibly an English Temporale.

As both works contained readings for the Church's year he thought they could be satisfactorily united in one volume. In order to accommodate the Temporale in the text most easily, he chose to follow the French version of the *Legenda Aurea* rather than the English one. While he worked basically from that text, he included additional stories from the other versions and often adapted his translation by borrowing words from them as well. In his new section he followed his Temporale source as far as it went, and then set out to complete the readings for the Temporale by translating the Vulgate. His decision to translate parts of the Bible was thus prompted by the particular conditions of one volume, and it cannot be assumed that he ever intended or even wished to produce a translation of the complete Bible. No doubt because the translation of the Vulgate was his own, he introduced many personal reminiscences into it. He evidently tired of the task he had set himself and left the translation unfinished, though he did not draw attention to this defect. Perhaps its incompleteness is the reason why Caxton did not refer to this new section in his prologue. As he followed the arrangement of the Temporale, his central section follows a different plan from that of the other sections. He was prepared to stitch the two sources together, but not to weld them into a unified work. And the haste which led to careless mistakes in so many of his books is to be found in the *Golden Legend* as well. The task he had undertaken was perhaps too large for him and he left it incomplete; yet one cannot but be amazed at the scope of the plan. The final result may not be an entirely satisfactory amalgam; but we must perforce admire the energy and dedication of the man who attempted such a compilation. Even in its modern edition (1892), his book runs to more than a thousand quarto pages.

I must now summarize the conclusions that have emerged in this chapter. Some texts were altered more than others by Caxton. When he felt obliged to alter a book because of its style, he took the opportunity of bringing the story more into line with his own prejudices. This meant in effect that speculation and controversy were cut down so that the narrative with its moral of the triumph of Christianity stood out more clearly. Poetry texts were not altered because they were thought to have a fixed form and because of their prestige. A problem arose only when differing manuscripts of a poetic text were available. Caxton cannot be said to have faced up to this problem. His practice was to print the manuscript he had without concerning himself about the quality of the text. But when a client complained of his text of the

Canterbury Tales, he was forced to take some action. He did not print the new manuscript as one might have supposed; instead he produced a conflated text, as though both manuscripts had equal authority. Indeed when he had more than one source, it was his habit to draw on them all. There was no question of trying to decide whether one was better than another. Similarly there is no evidence that he ever tried to find out the best text or the most authoritative account of anything. He tended to take what he had to hand and print it. If he had one text, all well and good; if he had more than one, he conflated them. When he made these conflated texts, he worked in haste without paying sufficient attention to the meaning or textual accuracy of what he was printing. We cannot justifiably think of Caxton as a scholar.

His attitude towards his texts depended on the reputation of the author and whether he had written in the fashionable, courtly style. Texts by such writers as Chaucer, Rivers and Worcester were not altered. Trevisa's text was modified because though a well-known translator he was a little outdated, and Malory's text was changed considerably because he had no reputation as a translator and because his book, though in prose, was in the alliterative tradition. When a text fell into his hands, if it was a poetic one he printed it without much alteration. If it was a prose text, he would normally divide the work up into books and chapters, and add a table of contents. In some books an index was also included. He even added a table of contents in his edition of Gower's poem, *Confessio Amantis*. He treated this poem differently because the manuscripts of it are conveniently divided into small sections each of which has a short chapter heading in Latin. He merely translated the Latin headings to form his own table of contents.[1] This example shows his opportunism: he made use of what was available. It also shows that he was not prepared to go out of his way to introduce this innovation into other poetic editions, even though he seems to have thought a table of contents desirable. Caxton often added a prologue as well. In his handling of texts Caxton exhibits a blend of the medieval and the modern. His cavalier attitude to textual authority is typical of the medieval period; but his presentation of the texts with table of contents, chapters and index gives many of them a modern appearance.

[1] Blake, *Anglia*, lxxxv (1967), 282–93.

7

CAXTON AS TRANSLATOR

Although Dr Johnson may be correct that 'the great pest of language is frequency of translation', no serious study of Caxton can neglect to make an evaluation of Caxton's translations for they form the major part of his total printed output. Evaluations of his merit as a translator have varied from the enthusiastic to the despairing. As an example of the varied results so obtained, let me quote from two editors. Sommer wrote of the *History of Troy*:

> The language of the first English printed book is, to say the least of it, very peculiar, owing to the facts, that Caxton's 'rude englissh' had probably become somewhat rusty during his long absence abroad, and, that his knowledge of French must have been rather superficial. It is therefore not wonderful when William Fiston, who corrected the text for Th. Creede's edition (1607), doubted Caxton's being an Englishman.[1]

Kellner, however, in his introduction to *Blanchardin and Eglantine* claimed:

> I contend that he was as good and free a translator as any of the 15th century, and in his style certainly not inferior to Peacock, the greatest prosaist of his time. What makes Caxton's style appear so awkward in the eyes of a modern reader, is his repetitions, tautologies, and anacolutha. But these irregularities are, for the most part, conscious sins, committed not only by him, but also by all the writers of his time.[2]

Only Byles in his edition of the *Order of Chivalry* has attempted to unite conflicting assessments by different editors into a comprehensive view of Caxton as translator by suggesting that there was a development in his translations. The differences arose, in his opinion, because Caxton improved as a translator as he went along.[3] However, if there is an improvement in Caxton's later translations, this is a

[1] Sommer 1894 p. 801.
[2] Kellner 1890 p. cxi.
[3] Byles 1926 p. xliv.

change in degree, not of kind: his approach to translation does not seem to have undergone any significant alteration throughout his printing career. All editors of Caxton texts, whether they are early or late texts, note how closely he follows his original; his unashamed transference of French words and idioms into English; and his frequent misunderstanding of the French. The type of mistake Caxton made in his first translation, such as the confusion of pronominal forms, he can still make in his later translations. There is a striking example of this in book eleven of his *Ovid's Metamorphoses* where Iris is referred to as 'he' or 'she' quite indifferently. Although Caxton doubtless became a little more aware of the pitfalls of translation, he is just as likely to get into difficulties over a difficult French passage in a late translation as he is in an early one. The difference between the views of Sommer and Kellner quoted above is the result not so much of the different quality of the two translations, as the different expectations and outlooks of the two modern editors. The mistakes in the two works are comparable, but Kellner viewed them in relation to other fifteenth-century translations, whereas Sommer looked at them with a modern eye. Admittedly there are more mistakes in the *History of Troy* than in *Blanchardin and Eglantine*, but the mistakes and infelicities are of the same kind.

How then did Caxton approach a text for translation? He often claims that he has kept as close as he can to his original; but statements of this sort are found in all fifteenth-century translations. Caxton doubtless included such statements because he felt obliged to, rather than that they accurately reflect his own views on translation. His method was to finish the translation as soon as possible in order to set it up in type. Since he was translating to keep his own presses in work, it is only natural to assume that there were many occasions when financial gain took precedence over literary responsibility. To keep the presses working may have appeared more important than a finely wrought phrase. After all, this state of affairs is not unknown today; and we do not necessarily have to blame Caxton for this attitude.

Modern literary expectations in Caxton will be disappointed: but he was not primarily a literary man. When he translated a text, Caxton never recast the story. In some cases this is only to be expected: the romances he published naturally take place in exotic lands, and there would be little need to adapt plot or localization for English readers. The story of Charlemagne had to retain its French and

Spanish localization. However, with some romances Caxton might have made the hero English, if he had wanted to; he never does. The exploits of such heroes as Paris and Blanchardin remain firmly continental. A story like *Reynard the Fox*, which does not depend upon a particular locality for its effect, could easily have been retold with an English, possibly Kentish, setting. Caxton did not change it, though in this respect he shows less originality than the earlier English adaptors of French romances. Such a reorganization would have involved too much time and trouble; hence only minor adjustments are made. And if Caxton chose to publish texts which were fashionable in Burgundy, he might have wanted to keep them in a form identical with the copies being read there.

This does not imply that Caxton made absolutely no concessions to his English audience. There are in most of his translations a few details which are omitted or added for what are called by most editors 'patriotic' reasons. Patriotism is perhaps too lofty an ideal to invoke; often the change reflects an attempt simply to make the story more suitable for an English audience. The *Mirror of the World* contains several of these additions and omissions. As we saw in Chapter One, he leaves out the story of tailed Englishmen. Whenever Paris as a seat of learning is mentioned, he adds Oxford and Cambridge. The King of France becomes the King of England and France. Bath is included among the great health-giving centres of Europe. In the *Feats of Arms* he omits two uncomplimentary references to the English, one to the effect that they kept some castles from the French illegally and the other that they had broken a truce with the French. In the same translation Caxton substitutes Cambridge for London in a context where the author is speaking of the rights of scholars. Occasionally in *Reynard the Fox* he alters a Dutch placename: Zyricxzee, for example, is altered to London. In *Paris and Vienne* small additions are made for the 'glorification' of England.[1] In the *Knight of the Tower* he omits a sentence in the French which implies that there are many immoral women in England.[2] These are small alterations carried out in the process of translation. Although they were made haphazardly, for some uncomplimentary remarks about England are not excluded, they

[1] Leach 1957 p. xxx.

[2] Mrs M. Y. Offord, who is preparing an edition of the *Knight of the Tower* for the Early English Text Society, very kindly placed all her material for this edition at my disposal. My examples from this text are taken from her forthcoming edition.

do show that Caxton did not want to repeat disparaging remarks about England or the English.

Caxton did sometimes make longer additions—and these usually reflect his own experience. These additions are mostly either religious or chivalric. Typical of the religious interpolations is the famous passage he added about David in the *Golden Legend*.[1] One day as he was riding from Ghent to Brussels with Sir John Capons, a councillor to the Duke of Burgundy, the latter told him an account of David's penance. In some ways the interpolation illustrates both types of addition, for, though basically a religious exemplum, it contains considerable information about the aristocratic narrator. His titles and some of his biography are related. It also underlines Caxton's caution: he gives his source for the story. He rarely passes on information of this sort without giving some indication of how he learned it. In relating a miracle of St Augustine he introduces it with 'I wylle sette here in one myracle whiche I have sene paynted on an aulter of Saynt Austyn at the Blacke Freres at Andwerpe' [75]. In the *Golden Legend* in the section on the Nativity of Our Lord, he says he will omit all the miracles about it 'sauf one thynge that I have herde ones prechyd of a worshipful doctour', and in that on the Nativity of Our Lady he writes 'It is so that I was at Coleyn and herd reherced there by a noble doctour . . .'[2] What he heard was a story about St Jerome. In writing about St Ursula he states that while in Cologne he learned that as well as the virgins there were fifteen thousand men who suffered martyrdom. From these interpolations we get the impression of a regular worshipper who visited different churches and relics assiduously.

Nevertheless, his acceptance of miracles or holy places was not uncritical. St Patrick's Purgatory in Ireland, about which many legends were current in the Middle Ages, is introduced into the *Mirror of the World*. Caxton had spoken with many people about it. Two of these, a High Canon of Waterford and Sir John de Banste of Bruges, told him they had slept in the Purgatory and had not suffered in any way— as legends current about it intimated they should. However, in true medieval fashion, Caxton does not reject these legends out of hand; he placated both sides by suggesting that the experiences related in the legends happened in the past, even if they do not appear to do so now. He was not prepared to flout tradition completely.

[1] Crotch 1928 p. 74.
[2] For Caxton's additions to the *Golden Legend* see Jeremy, *Modern Language Notes*, lxiv (1949), 259–61.

An interesting example of religious interpolation is a passage from the *Game of Chess* which is not well known because it was not included by Crotch.[1] In it Caxton mentions that he had had dealings with the 'White Freris' at Ghent, who lived a life of abstinence and had all things in common. These 'White Freris' may have been the Brothers of the Common Life, but more probably they were Benedictines, since this was the name they had in Ghent at that time. Possibly Caxton supplied them with English cloth, for we know that he was often in Ghent. His relationship with them may have been primarily a mercantile one, yet he evidently reflected upon their way of life.

The other additions are those I have termed chivalric. From these Caxton appears to have been convinced of the necessity of maintaining the existing social structure, in which each man had a definite place according to his birth. In the upper ranks of this hierarchy were the king with his knights, and they were expected to model their behaviour on the code of chivalry. His epilogue to the *Order of Chivalry*, in which it is regretted that knights do not always live up to the code, expresses this concept forcefully, and that lament is paralleled by the picture of England's general decline in an interpolation in the *Game of Chess*.[2] She was once glorious and feared; but now she has lost her former position. Although not specifically concerned with chivalry, the passage does criticize the leaders of the country who are failing in their duties. The health of a nation is determined by the quality of its leaders; and their worth Caxton measured in chivalric terms. More typical of his chivalric additions is his inclusion in the *Golden Legend* of details about St George's Chapel, Windsor, the home of the Order of the Garter—an interpolation paralleled by the description of the castle of Hesdin found in his prologue to *Jason*. Caxton was clearly interested in all the appurtenances of chivalry and the aristocracy. This interest comes out particularly in such a work as the *Order of Chivalry*. The modern editor of this work has commented on his interest in this way:

Caxton stresses the aristocratic conception even more than Lull. An ardent lover of chivalry, he insists that it is the preserve of a privileged class ... At one point in this connection he makes a most significant departure from his original. He enforces the argument that noble birth, not good looks, is essential to chivalry by adding that if this were not so women might be dubbed knights; then at the end

[1] Axon 1883 p. 88.
[2] Axon 1883 pp. 161–2.

E

of the same passage he ... substitutes the statement that chivalry is 'moche more syttynge to a gentyl herte replenysshed wyth al vertues than in a man vyle and of euyl lyf'.[1]

Similarly the editor of *Paris and Vienne* has noted that he sometimes adds a phrase in glorification of chivalry or of the aristocracy. He includes the dubbing of Paris as knight and the establishing of the *lystes* at a tournament.[2]

Some of these additions are extensive, but the majority of them involve perhaps a clause or only two or three words. The smaller ones are inserted into the text without comment; only a comparison of Caxton's text with his source enables us to detect them. The larger additions are more easily recognized, for they have a more personal tone even if the opinion expressed is not Caxton's own. Only occasionally does he make a comment of his own, as when he questions the geographical accuracy of the author of the *Mirror of the World*: 'And how be it that the auctour of this book saye that thise contrees ben in Affryke, yet, as I understonde, alle thise ben within the lymytes and boundes of Europe'.[3] A more ambiguous example of his opinion occurs in the *Game of Chess*, in which the legal profession is attacked though it is too long to quote here.[4] It is ambiguous, for although it could, as some scholars think, reflect Caxton's own views about the legal profession, the attack may have been a literary, rather than a personal, one; the legal profession was regularly accused of avarice by medieval writers, as readers of *Piers Plowman* will recall. Caxton may be following the fashion in this onslaught. On the other hand, he had dealings with the legal profession throughout his business life and he may have acquired a distaste for its members. However, the interest of this interpolation lies in the knowledge exhibited of the legal profession in England and of the composition of the various courts at Westminster. Yet he finished translating the *Game of Chess* on 31 March 1475, over one year before his return to England. In spite of his residence abroad he knew of the Hell, a small room where some of the Exchequer clerks worked which was so dark that it had received this name. It was not, as far as we can tell, a word in wide usage—yet it was known to Caxton. This detail emphasizes the point made in an earlier chapter: Caxton did not cut himself off from England by becoming a merchant

[1] Byles 1926 p. xxxix.
[2] Leach 1957 p. xxxi.
[3] Prior 1913 pp. 93–94.
[4] Crotch 1928 p. 14.

adventurer. He was well informed of affairs in England, no doubt because he was frequently there.

To what extent he altered his sources on the basis of his own reading is an interesting problem, though it is impossible to present a comprehensive survey for, as so few of his texts have been satisfactorily edited, it is difficult to be certain how much Caxton added. He did on occasion make use of his reading to adorn or correct his translations. In *Reynard the Fox* among the animals who complain to the King about Reynard are 'Chantecler the cock, Pertelot wyth alle theyr children', though none of the Dutch texts has any reference to Pertelot either here or elsewhere. Caxton has presumably introduced her from Chaucer's *Nun's Priest's Tale*. Similarly, towards the end of *Reynard the Fox* there is a clear echo of a line in the tale: one sentence, for which there is no equivalent in the Dutch, finishes 'blame not me but the foxe, for they be his wordes and not myne'. These words are an adaptation of Chaucer's 'Thise been the cokkes wordes and nat myne'.[1] Another example of the fusion of two sources is to be found in his translation, *Ovid's Metamorphoses*. In a description in book eleven of the God of Sleep's abode, there are many striking phrases which have no parallel in Caxton's French original. Thus Caxton's account of Iris's preparations reads 'And the messagier made hyme redy thyder as hys lady sente hym, and *dyde on his rayny cope*'. Later when Iris arrived at the God of Sleep's house, Caxton describes the god's bed as 'softe, rychely aourned of an olde coverlet; the cowche was made of Hebenus, *that sleepy tree*'. The italicized phrases which were added by Caxton are taken from book four of the *Confessio Amantis* in which Gower tells the same story from Ovid.[2] The two corresponding passages read:

> This Yris, fro the hihe stage
> Which undertake hath the Message,
> Hire reyny Cope dede upon (ll. 2977–79);

> and of his couche
> Withinne his chambre if I schal touche,
> Of hebenus that slepi Tree
> The bordes al about be (ll. 3015–18).

We cannot tell whether Caxton relied on his memory or not here, but

[1] Blake, *Bulletin of the John Rylands Library*, xlvi (1963–4), 309–10.

[2] Bennett, *Modern Language Review*, xlv (1950), 215–16. Caxton uses the phrase 'his rayny cope' also in the recently discovered part of *Ovid's Metamorphoses*, bk. I ch. 14.

he printed the *Confessio Amantis* only in 1483—three years after the completion of *Ovid's Metamorphoses* (1480). Caxton evidently did read his English authors. He certainly plundered the English poets when he wrote his prologues and epilogues, as we shall see.

So far in this chapter I have been concerned with the larger and more personal changes made by Caxton in the texts he was translating. It is time now to turn to a more detailed consideration of how Caxton made a translation. It may seem from what I have said that he made fairly extensive changes. This is not so. In view of the great bulk of his translations the number of examples quoted is very small. In general Caxton sticks to his original very faithfully, or, as Axon puts it, 'he is content to follow his author with almost plodding fidelity'.[1] Such changes as are found, apart from the bigger interpolations already mentioned, are usually of a minor nature. Consequently there are two difficulties an investigator faces when making a detailed study of the translations. As the compositors made changes and mistakes, the printed book may not accurately reflect Caxton's written translation. This difficulty is too complicated to be discussed here; but I shall use examples in which there is no reason to suspect compositorial bungling. Secondly, if Caxton's changes are minor ones, it is essential to have the manuscript he used, for otherwise the changes might have been made in his source. Thus where the French manuscript of the *Knight of the Tower* which is closest to, but not identical with, the one Caxton used has *et personne ne leur osoit dire riens*, his translation reads *and the parson durst not withsaye hym*. As *personne* means 'no-one' in this passage, it would be tempting to think that Caxton had either misunderstood or wished to improve his source. However, as other French manuscripts of the same work read *la personne* 'the parson', Caxton's source may also have had this reading; *parson* would then be an accurate translation. As Caxton's original has not been identified, we cannot be certain in this instance whether this is so or not. Nevertheless there are cases where, no matter what the reading in the source might have been, he cannot have paid attention to what he was translating. The result is usually nonsense. In one episode in Peter the Hermit's march to Constantinople in the *Siege of Jerusalem*, a hundred Germans remained behind at Nish in Jugoslavia after the departure of Peter and the main host to revenge themselves on the townspeople. Having set fire to some outlying districts, the Germans hurried after the main body.

[1] Axon 1883 p. xxxiv.

The townspeople gave chase, and, according to Caxton, when they *fonde thise thre malefactours*, they killed them. Where Caxton's text reads *thre*, such French manuscripts of this work as I have consulted read *tyois* 'German'. Either Caxton misread *tyois* as *trois* 'three' or he had a manuscript which actually read *trois*. In either case he cannot have paid any attention to the meaning of the passage, for the reading 'these three malefactors' makes little sense: he evidently translated each clause separately without considering what relation it bore to what preceded or followed. Although this example could be paralleled from all his translations, a proper estimate of his abilities as a translator is to be had from a consideration of those translations for which the original has been identified. As Caxton also made translations from printed books, it is in practice most sensible to confine an investigation to them, for all copies of a printed edition may for our purposes be regarded as identical. The French text he used for his translation of *Charles the Great* was *Fierabras* printed by Garbin at Geneva in 1483; the Dutch version for his translation of *Reynard the Fox* was that printed by Leeu at Gouda in 1479.[1] In the following detailed examination of Caxton as translator I shall base my remarks upon *Charles the Great*. Where necessary, I shall also support these observations either from other translations of French texts or from *Reynard the Fox*. As the latter is a translation from Dutch, it will enable us to decide whether he adopted a different principle of translation for different languages.

To begin with I should perhaps substantiate my opening remark that Caxton's cardinal principle in making a translation was speed. The following characteristics of his texts bear this out. Firstly, he keeps very close to the French original and often seems to take each clause as an independent unit without worrying about the sense of the passage in general, as the example in the preceding paragraph showed. This occurs in many fifteenth-century translations. Secondly, he often omits passages unintentionally. Usually this happens because his eye has slipped down from one word to a similar word two or three lines further down. As these mistakes could have been made by the compositor, their value is equivocal. Yet there are the corresponding places where Caxton translates a line or two twice, which is the same mistake in reverse. As the passage appears in a slightly different form the second time, it seems very probable that Caxton rather than the compositor was responsible. Thirdly, in his translations he sometimes takes over a

[1] S. J. Herrtage, *Sir Ferumbras* (London, 1879), pp. vi-viii, and Blake, *Bulletin of the John Rylands Library*, xlvi (1963-4), 298-311.

French word, whereas at other times he translates the same word into its English equivalent. Finally, he often misreads what is in front of him or makes an elementary mistake in translation. These elementary mistakes cannot be attributed to his faulty command of French, because he translates a similar word or idiom accurately on many other occasions.

As the last category is perhaps the most convincing, I shall start with that. In *Charles the Great* Caxton translates *fille*, which in the context means 'girl', as 'daughter' so that the resulting phrase reads somewhat curiously as *Agabondus, uncle of thys doughter* [13/17].[1] As he translates *fille* accurately as *mayde* a few lines later [13/21], it cannot be ignorance which caused the mistake. In his haste he did not stop to think which of the two meanings was appropriate. Occasionally he misreads. Thus in the sentence: 'I praye to God that he be in thy comfort and that he have pyte of thy soule' [154/1-2], the *he be in thy comfort* is awkward as it implies that God will receive solace from Richard of Normandy. The corresponding passage in the French reads *qu'il te soy en bon confort*, and the mistake arose from a simple misreading of *bon* as *ton*. The important point is that Caxton translated the clause as he read it without worrying about the sense of the sentence as a whole. It is reasonable to assume that this type of mistake is the result of haste in translation. Similar examples are found in *Reynard the Fox*. In his translation of *Segt ons bellijn* 'Tell us, Bellin' as *saye on, Bellyn*, he misread *ons* 'us' as *on*. On another occasion he misread *hoep* 'crowd' as *loep* 'running' without apparently worrying about the sense of the sentence. Similar examples occur in all his translations. In the *Knight of the Tower* he read *lange*, i.e. *l'ange* 'the angel' as *lange* 'language, tongue'. In the *Feats of Arms* he misread *espies* 'spies' as *espees* 'sword' and translated the passage as 'thoos that fought ayenst a folke that men called Heryteos toke the swerde of theyre enemyes and made hem to confesse & telle there couvyne'.[2] This example from the *Feats of Arms*, printed in 1489, two years before Caxton's death, shows that he could make an elementary misreading right at the end of his life. All these mistakes, whether from an early or late text, show the same hastiness and lack of care in translation. It is unlikely that he revised or corrected what he had once written.

[1] Page and line references are to Herrtage 1880-1. The corresponding French passages are from Garbin's edition of *Fierabras* (1483). The language of the French text has been slightly normalized.

[2] Byles 1932 p. 112.

The same conclusion is suggested by those cases in which Caxton omits a passage or twice translates a passage. As it is not usually possible to tell whether omissions were made by Caxton or the compositor, I shall go straight on to a consideration of passages which are translated twice. An interesting example of the repetition of a passage in *Charles the Great* concerns the baptism of King Clovis by St Remigius. The French text reads:

Tout cecy condicionné, le roy fut tout prest de recepvoir le saint sacrement de baptesme, auquel le bon amy de dieu Saint Remy commenca dire par faconde maniere: 'Sire roy, il est heure que vous debuez de pure intencion relinquir les dieux ausquelz aultres fois vous avez donné creance'.

The English translation of which is this:

Whan al this was done the Kyng was al redy to receyve the holy sacrament of baptesme, to whome the frende of God Saynt Remyge began to say by faconde manere. 'Syr Kyng, it is tyme that ye ought wyth pure entencyon to forsake the false goddes to whome tofore this tyme ye have gyven fayth'. And thenne the Kyng was al redy to receyve the holy sacrament of baptesme. To whom Saynt Remyge began by fayr manere: 'Syr Kyng, it is tyme that ye ought of pure intencion to forsake the goddes to whome here afore tyme ye have byleved on'. [19/32–20/5]

A part of the French is translated twice, though the two translations are not identical. The variations between them make it certain that the two versions were made by Caxton rather than by the compositor; they can be paralleled from other parts of his translation. Thus in the second version he omits 'the frende of God' in the description of St Remigius. Similarly in the baptismal ceremony following the passage quoted a dove appears with an ampulla containing the holy oil for the anointing of the king. Here after the words *douve shynyng* [20/30] he omitted the French phrase *et estoit tout envolée en l'air*. Likewise a few lines later the French author mentions that his sisters and three thousand men of his army were baptized with Clovis. Caxton's text reads only *In that tyme were baptysed . . .* [21/4–5], where after *tyme* the French adds *que le roy jadis fut baptisé*. Most of these omissions are descriptive, and their absence does not usually affect the sense. Yet in view of the general faithfulness of the translation, their omission was probably accidental. This is confirmed by examples where an omission does cause a break in the sense. During the battle around the tower of Floripes, Gerard says: 'My brethern & lordes, who wyl here-after have playsyr & be honoured, it is tyme that he shewe hym, for often by one unhappy man a valyaunt man is in daunger' [128/23–26]. The last clause is awkward, because immediately before it Caxton has omitted this passage from the French: 'et n'est pas mestier que entre nous en soit congneu ung seul desloyal'. Not every omission in *Charles the Great* was accidental for, as we saw earlier, Caxton can make deliberate omissions; however, it seems certain that the majority of minor omissions are purely fortuitous.

Another interesting point of comparison between the two Caxton versions of the French passage is that he twice uses different words to translate a word in the French. This variation forms my third category mentioned above to show that he made hasty translations, so it will be convenient to tackle it here. The French *par faconde maniere* is translated first as *by faconde manere*, and then as *by fayr manere*. Similarly the French *avez donné creance* is translated at first by *have gyven fayth*, and then by *have byleved on*. It should not be assumed from these two examples that Caxton normally takes over a French word into his own translation when he meets it for the first time, and then uses an English word for it when it occurs a second time. Consider for example the case of the French verb *vituperer* in *Charles the Great*. At 91/21 this is translated as *repreve;* at 116/30 Caxton used *vytupered;* at 160/17 it is translated as *shamed;* and at 182/19 as *vytupered* again. Other words show the same variation. *Force* is translated as either *force* [93/33, 102/8] or *strength* [27/8, 132/1]; *puissant* as either *puyssaunt* [101/12, 140/7, 8] or *mighty* [96/3, 150/19]; and *createur* as either *creator* [149/30] or *maker* [101/22, 107/15]. In some cases Caxton shows a preference for one of the two words. *Createur* is generally translated *maker*, and only rarely *creator*. He normally uses *force* only when translating the phrase *a grant force;* otherwise he uses *strength*. He invariably uses *(al)mighty* as a translation for *(trez)puissant* used to describe the deity, but either *puyssaunt* or *mighty* when *puissant* is applied to human power. Other examples, such as *lette/empessche, staffe/baston*, are manifold. A similar variation is to be noticed in translations of French idioms, though the common ones are given an English equivalent. Caxton only exceptionally fails to use the English passive to translate the French construction with *on* plus an active verb. The French reflexive is normally omitted in English so that *cité qui se disoit Aigremoire* becomes *cytee named Agrymore* [85/34]. Occasionally he slips up and writes, for example, *this paynym nameth hym self Fyerabras* [42/24–5]. Similarly although at 84/5–6 the French *force luy fut de retourner* is rendered *it was force to hym to retorne*, this construction is normally translated as 'it behoves' or 'it is necessary'.

It is time now to summarize what the comparison of Caxton's two versions of a single French passage has revealed. The repetition of a passage and the variation in the translation of individual words show that Caxton often worked in haste. He did not go over what he had written, or he would have eliminated one of his two versions. Similarly he did not usually give himself enough time to find the right word in English for a French word whose meaning was known to him. Examples in which this happens are found in all his translations; it is not necessary to labour the point by giving further examples.

Many characteristics of a Caxton translation have now been mentioned. But when one picks out infelicities in a translation to illustrate certain points, one often unwittingly creates an impression that the translation as a whole is poor. This is not fair to Caxton; and in order to show him in his full powers as a translator, it is necessary to quote a longer passage. It will also provide a convenient starting-point for a discussion of other features of his translations.

Fierabras	*Charles the Great*
J'ay parlé devant ou premier livre superficiallement du premier roy de France baptisé en descendant selon mon propos jusques au roy Charles, duquel on ne scauroit pas bonnement racompter la vaillance de luy et ses barons que se dient pers de France, desquelz a leur endroit je feray mencion selon que j'en pourray concepvoir en verité. Mais ce que j'ay dessus escript, je l'ay prins en ung auctentique livre nommé *Mirouer Historial* et es croniques anciennes, et l'ay tant seullement transporté de latin en francoys. Et la matiere suyvant que sera le	I have spoken tofore in the fyrst book superfycyally of the first kyng of Fraunce baptysed in descendyng after my purpoos unto Kynge Charles, of whome may not wel be recounted the valyaunce of hym and of hys barons, whych were named & called pyeres of Fraunce. Of whome & of their behavyng I shal make mencion after that I shal mowe conceyve by trouthe. But thys that I have tofore wryton I have taken it oute of an autentyke book named *Myrrour Hystoryal* and in auncyent cronycles, and have onelye translated them oute of Latyn in to

second livre est d'ung rommant
fait a l'ancienne facon sans grant
ordonance, dont j'ay esté insité
a la reduire en prose par chapitres ordonnez. Et se dit celluy
livre selon les aulcuns et le plus
communement *Fierabras* a cause
que celluy Fierabras estoit si
merveilleulx, come j'en feray
mencion, que fut vaincu par
Olivier et a la fin se baptisa et
fut apres saint en paradis.

Frensshe. And the mater folowyng whyche shal be the second
book is of a romaunce maad
of th'auncyent facyon wythoute
grete ordynaunce in Frensshe,
wherof I have been encyted for
to reduce in prose by chapytres
ordeyned. Which book after
somme and moost comunely is
called *Fyerabras* by cause that
thys Fyerabras was so mervayl-
lous a geaunte, as I shal make
mencyon, whyche was van-
quysshed by Olyver and at the
laste baptysed & was after a
saynt in heven. [38/17–39/2]

The English passage has a generally French flavour about it, but for
the most part it reads easily and is readily intelligible. This is the virtue
of the French text rather than of the English translation, for the read-
ability of Caxton's texts is determined by the sources he used. If his
source is muddled, the translation is likely to be clumsy; if the source
is fluent, the translation will be equally so. I do not mean by this that
all difficulties in his translations are attributable to the source he was
using, for he creates some of his own; but the stylistic characteristics
and peculiarities in vocabulary and syntax of a French text will be
reflected in his translations. There are of course many places where he
has kept too close to the French so that a modern reader is puzzled at
first. His 'the first kyng of Fraunce baptysed in descendyng after my
purpoos unto Kynge Charles' brings a reader up with a jerk. This is
the result partly of the retention of the past participial adjective after the
noun it qualifies, for we would have expected 'the first baptized (or
Christian) King of France', and partly of the retention of the French
words and word-order in the rest of the sentence. Caxton has not
attempted to recast the latter part of the sentence into an English form
to express the author's meaning, namely that it was his plan to follow
all the Christian kings of France from the first, Clovis, to Charles.
These failures reduce the fluency of the translation. However, there are
times when Caxton has superseded a French construction or French
word-order by its English equivalent. He changes *es croniques anciennes*

into *in auncyent cronycles*. Likewise where the French has inversion of verb and subject as in *Et se dit celluy livre*, he alters it to give the English pattern with the subject first: *Which book . . . is called*. In this same example the French reflexive is also transformed into the English passive. Regrettably his attempts to put a French construction into English are too often half-hearted. Thus where the French has 'je l'ay prins *en* ung auctentique livre . . . et *es* croniques anciennes', he translates the first part as 'I have taken it *oute of* an autentyke book'. When, however, he got to the second part of the parallel construction, he had forgotten how he translated the first part and was reduced to translating literally 'and *in* auncyent cronycles'. This failure may be attributed to his taking each sense-unit independently. A comparable, if less clear-cut, instance is to be found in this same sentence. He translates *ce que j'ay dessus escript, je l'ay prins* quite acceptably as *thys that I have tofore wryton I have taken it*, with the *it* referring back to *thys that I have tofore wryton*. When he comes to the parallel phrase *et (je) l'ay tant seullement transporté*, he translates *And have onelye translated them*. He has been confused by the intervening reference to ancient chronicles to put *them* instead of *it*, even though the reference is to *thys that I have tofore wryton*. The instance is less clear-cut because it might be claimed that Caxton made the change deliberately. However, since he frequently confused pronominal forms and since the change is no improvement, it is probable that he had merely forgotten the earlier part of the sentence and consequently misunderstood the French. In some cases it is the second part of a parallel construction which is changed. In a description of Charles, the French text introduces a series of parallel clauses composed of three elements. The clause is introduced by the part of the body being discussed; this is followed by *avoit* 'he had'; and the clause is completed by the descriptive characteristic of that part of the body. Caxton commences by imitating the French: 'The armes and thyes he had ample and large'. He soon realized that the clauses could be rendered in a more English fashion by putting 'he had' first. So he goes on 'he had the face deduyte in lengthe . . . he had hys nose reysed upon a roundnes' [26/24–29]. He made no attempt, however, to bring his earlier clauses into line with this new pattern.

It is doubtless the French element in Caxton's vocabulary which strikes a modern reader most forcefully in the comparative passages above. The great proportion of the nouns, adjectives, adverbs and verbs are taken over directly from the French source. The only English words in this category are common ones such as *book, speak, first* and *king*. It is the French words which give the passage its weightiness and its exotic qualities: *valiance, peers, conceive, authentic, romance,* etc. We today can distinguish among the French words those which are introduced for the first time, those which have been in the language for some time, and those which extend the meanings of words already in the language. It is not to be thought that Caxton distinguished them in the same way. He merely copied the French word in front of him, unless there was a common English word which came into his mind first. It does not seem to have made any difference to him whether the word was known in England by then or not. In the passage words such as *authentic, ancient, conceive* and *vanquish* are recorded from earlier English works, but *superficially* and *incite* are not. This cannot have been known to him or made any difference to his method of translation. As it happens both *superficially* and *incite* are still current in English, but many of the words which he used in his translations are found only there. Such words from *Charles the Great* include *atediacion, confirmator* and *descircle*. Of the other words he introduced some have since become obsolete, though others are still used. The following list will give some idea of their variety: *autentykly, compose* (build), *deduyte, esbatements, exaltation* (elevation), *exercite* (practice), *exercite* (army), *frequented, illumynatour, passion* (to torment). Whether he used a word or not depends entirely on whether it was in one of his sources. The words in his sources he took over wholesale and almost certainly without any plan to enrich the English vocabulary.[1]

Apart from introducing new words Caxton also extended the meaning of French loanwords already in the language. The verb *reduce* which he used in the above passage is a good example. On the basis of the meanings of the French *reduire*, he uses *reduce* in English in the new senses 'to translate', 'to record in writing', and 'to transfer from verse to prose'. It is interesting, however, to note that in the passage quoted he employs *translate* to render *transporter*, although he uses *reduce* to render *reduire*. This difference introduces another aspect of his vocabulary, namely that he often uses an English word (in which category I include loanwords already established in English) which is suggested to him by the spelling or the sound of the French word in the text he is translating. Clearly he used *translate* to render *transporter* because they both commence with *trans-*. Similarly when he came to *reduire* it suggested *reduce* to his mind, which he then used even though

---

[1] For a contrary view see Leach 1957 p. xxvii.

reduce had not been used in this sense before in English. A very interesting instance of this suggestiveness of words is provided by his translation of the French verbs *cheoir* and *tomber*, both meaning 'to fall'. The former occurs most frequently in the French text and he regularly translates it as *fall*, as at 81/33 where *he fyl to the erthe* translates *il cheust a terre*. Occasionally the French text uses *tomber*, and he always renders this by the English verb *tumble*, spelt *tomble* in Caxton, which was doubtless suggested to him by the similarity of the two words. Thus in *they tombled doun to the grounde* [181/16] the *tombled* translates French *tomberent*. Only in one instance does he use part of the verb 'to fall' to translate *tomber*, and then he makes use of the doublet *fyl and tombled* [142/27] to translate *tombeoient*. He never uses the verb *tomble* unless the French text has *tomber*: it is never used to translate *cheoir*. Clearly the verb 'to tumble' was less commonly used than 'to fall' then, as now. It was probably not part of Caxton's everyday speech. It was only when the verb *tomber* suggested, on account of its similar spelling, the verb *tomble* to his mind that he used 'tumble' in his translation. There are many other examples like this. The French verb employed in *Fierabras* for 'to blindfold' is *bender*. Sometimes he translates this with a part of the verb 'to blindfold', as at 82/1 where they *blynfelde hys eyen*. At other times the French verb suggested 'to bind' to him, as at 129/27 where they *bounde hys eyen*. The meaning 'to blindfold' is not recorded in the *Oxford English Dictionary* for the verb *bind*, and it seems likely that Caxton has merely extended the meaning of this common English verb to include this sense on account of the similarity in form between *bind* and *bender*. Among other examples we may note that French *robustement* is always translated *boystously*, and *remply* as *replenish*. French *roidement* is translated *rudely* at 171/7, but more correctly as *myghtely* at 172/16. The vocabulary of a Caxton translation was influenced by its original more than one might at first expect.

There are two further points about Caxton's vocabulary which must be discussed. In the two parallel passages where the French text has *se dient*, the English version has *were named & called*. This use of doublets, in which two words are used instead of one, has aroused some controversy among Caxton scholars as to whether he used too many of them. It is easy to exaggerate his use of doublets, for the unfamiliarity of this rhetorical device to a modern reader makes it conspicuous, even though in this passage it is used only once. The doublet was a form of stylistic embellishment used widely by English and

French authors. It occurs frequently in the works he translated, though there do tend to be more doublets in his translations than in their sources. But their use in Caxton as in most other authors is generally reserved for passages in the high style or for statements which call for particular emphasis. Consequently in his works we find it particularly in his prologues and epilogues, and also at the beginning and end of paragraphs and chapters.[1] It is used elsewhere, as this passage shows; but it is less commonly found in passages of narration. He no doubt used doublets partly because they would lend distinction to his translation, and partly because there were many doublets which had become stereotyped by his time. Such pairs as *laude and honour*, *fere and drede*, *synne and vice* and even *named and called* were so common as to be traditional. Often his use of doublets may have been largely involuntary. Consider for example his renderings of *louenge*. Sometimes this is taken over as *loange* [25/32]; sometimes a doublet is used such as *thankynges and laude* [25/14], *laude and honour* [26/1] or *lawde & praysyng* [181/19]. There does not seem to be any pattern in his usage except that *loange* is not used in a doublet. The common words come together more easily, though whether 'the epithets are sweetly varied' is a matter we are not at this moment concerned with. It does of course happen that a less common French loanword is glossed by an English word in a doublet, such as *strengthe & corobere* [24/9]; but generally where a doublet occurs it is made up of two words which had been in the language for some time, or were indeed both words of Anglo-Saxon origin. The more difficult words in the French sources are rarely made part of a doublet if they are taken over into his English. Possibly this was because Caxton was not sure of their exact meaning. It is doubtful whether his use of doublets was inspired by a desire to enrich the English word stock. It is a stylistic device which he sometimes used unconsciously, and at other times merely to give his English a more dignified and fashionable appearance.

The other point about his vocabulary is suggested by his translation of the French *paradis* as *heven*. To us today this rendering may appear as an improvement rather than a translation, but in Middle English, as in Old French, *paradise* meant 'heaven'. Caxton, however, almost regularly translates *paradis*, which occurs frequently in the French, as *heaven*; only occasionally does he use the expected translation *paradise*, as in *Lord God of paradys* [106/12]. The importance of this substitution

---

[1] Blake, *Bulletin of the John Rylands Library*, xlvi (1963–4), 319–23; see also Lenaghan 1967 p. 21.

of heaven for paradise is that, although he normally keeps very close to the French, and although *paradise* would in the fifteenth century have been a sufficient and quite intelligible translation of French *paradis*, he nevertheless felt obliged to use *heven*. Indeed he uses it to translate not only *paradis*, but also *ciel*, no matter whether that word in the French means 'sky' or 'heaven'. Similarly, as we have seen, whenever the French uses *(trez)puissant* of the deity, Caxton translates it *(al)mighty*, though he employs *puyssaunt* of Roland or Charles. He uses *maker* to translate *createur*, except in those instances where he has slipped up and used *creator*. These examples suggest that he found such expressions as 'saints of paradise', 'God all puyssaunt' or 'Creator of sky and earth' uncomfortable. They did not sound right to him, even though there was nothing incorrect about them. This was presumably because religious expressions were already becoming ossified, and an Englishman in the fifteenth, as in the twentieth, century would expect 'saints of heaven', 'God almighty' and 'Maker of heaven and earth'. The expressions had become or were becoming so stereotyped that even Caxton, who normally takes over the French word, felt obliged to use them rather than to translate literally. It is only because he is such a literal translator that we today can appreciate what expressions had become so hackneyed that they forced themselves upon him. Expressions of this sort are not confined to religious terms. Caxton invariably translates *oeuvre* as 'work' and *publique* as 'public' or 'open'; but when he comes across *l'euvre publique* he renders it *comyn wele* (at 22/8 and elsewhere). From this translation we may assume that *common weal* had become a stock phrase by the fifteenth century, even though dictionaries record few examples of it before 1500. Another interesting example is that involving French *putain*. Caxton always translates this literally as *putain* when it occurs by itself; but when *filz de putain* is used as a term of abuse, that is translated as *whoreson*. From which it might be suggested that although *whoreson* was in common use as a term of abuse, *whore* itself was less frequently used. The author of *Fierabras* used *face* and *visaige* indiscriminately. Although a modern translator would render both of these by *face*, for *visage* is now somewhat archaic, Caxton uses only *visage*. Although both *face* and *visage* had been in the language some time by the fifteenth century, it is possible to assume from Caxton's usage that *visage* was more commonly heard in the fifteenth century.

There are many similar examples in *Charles the Great*. Together they form a feature of Caxton's translations which has not yet received attention from modern investigators, though a study of his translations might reveal interesting facts about fifteenth-century usage and vogue words. It could be one of the more positive results to be gained from an intensive study of his translations. Admittedly one cannot always be sure that an invariable departure from the original represents a common fifteenth-century usage rather than an idiosyncrasy on his part. Nevertheless the results gained from a study of his translations could always be tested against other authors, and if it could be discovered that these usages were confined to Caxton it would not be without interest to find out why this was so. At the moment we only know roughly when words like *face* or *visage* were introduced into written English; we do not know the relative popularity of the two words in different centuries. A study of Caxton's translations might help to clarify the position for the fifteenth century.

In the French and English passages given earlier, there are statements in Caxton's version which are quite inappropriate for an English translation, particularly the author's claim that he translated the book from Latin to French. As we saw earlier, Caxton does sometimes make concessions to his English audience either by omitting uncomplimentary remarks about England or by adding small details about English affairs. It is surprising, therefore, to find that he has not altered any details about the French translation. Likewise at the beginning and end of the work he includes all that the French author had to say about the genesis of his work and for whom it was made. This information is often very valuable for the modern scholar, but it must have been confusing for the contemporary reader. It is not clear whether he left this sort of information in purposely, because he felt it would increase respect for his book or would lend it authenticity, or whether he was too lazy or too busy to omit it. At the very least he could have re-organized the passage so that the reader would know who the 'I' was, for the inclusion of *in Frensshe* after the mention of *a romaunce maad of th'auncyent facyon wythoute grete ordynaunce* only confuses us in our attempt to identify this 'I'. The absence of any significant modification suggests that it was laziness or haste which prevented any alterations from being made. This view is supported by the consideration that it is not unusual to find a modification only half-completed in a Caxton translation. In the chapter of *Charles the Great* which tells of Charles's visit to Constantinople, he fails to carry through an adaptation. Whereas in the French source Archbishop Ebroin was present on that occasion, Caxton evidently intended to replace him in his translation by Turpin, who plays a much larger role in the Charlemagne stories. At the beginning of the chapter all references are to Turpin (e.g. 35/23). Then in the middle of the chapter Ebroin appears from nowhere and Turpin vanishes. This failure to complete changes or even to initiate them can only be attributed to the speed at which Caxton worked. It is parallel to the slovenliness by which many French words are sometimes taken over literally into the translation, and sometimes replaced by an English equivalent. He was unwilling to make any substantial changes in the books he was translating, though his source demanded modification; and even the minor alterations he attempted are often botched.

It is unfortunate that Caxton did not take more trouble over his translation, for some of his small changes indicate that he did on occasion follow the story closely. After Oliver's battle with Fierabras, several Frenchmen including Oliver are captured by the Saracens and thrown into prison. Among them is Gerard of Mondidier. In prison they are visited by Floripes, who in the French text has a conversation with a Richard. This Richard is changed by Caxton into Gerard. Clearly he thought that the Richard in his source was Richard of Normandy, who could not have been in prison then for he was one of the peers of France sent by Charles to Ballant to request the release of the prisoners. This change, admittedly a minor one, was probably made by Caxton as he translated; there are other examples like this one.

In one of the many battles between Christian and pagan, the pagan Duke Basin is killed. His son then threw himself on his body 'and there he *was slayn and* abode' [129/19–20]. The italicized words were added by Caxton and they do enable the reader to understand the meaning of the passage more quickly. Similarly when the French barons are in prison, the water rises in it with the tide. Oliver had been wounded and when 'he felte hym bayned *in the salte water* he fyl doun a swoune' [89/20–21]. This addition is not essential to the sense of the passage, but it makes us appreciate that it was the salt in the water which caused Oliver's wounds to smart so much that he fainted. The inclusion of the italicized words adds considerably to the overall effect of the sentence.

Other small changes might have been made from his own knowledge and experience. Where *Fierabras* records that the relics Charles had brought from Constantinople were on view in Aachen every June, he alters this to July. As this alteration is made twice, it was doubtless intentional. Since Caxton might have visited Aachen, possibly on his way to Cologne in 1471, and since he was interested in relics, he probably made this alteration as a correction. Several of the inclusions mentioned in this paragraph aid the flow of the narrative: if Caxton had given himself sufficient time, he might have produced a much better translation.

The conclusions put forward so far in this chapter may appear somewhat conflicting. Some examples show Caxton making additions and changes, others show him following his text faithfully. This conflict is more apparent than real. He generally follows his source closely, though he also occasionally makes minor changes—changes which involve no recasting of the text. This method of translation was probably dictated more by the speed at which he worked than by any theory of translation, though like many medieval translators he claimed to follow his text accurately. The speed of his translations also accounts for the mistakes and infelicities, for his knowledge of the languages from which he translates appears to be competent. There is no evidence to suggest that Caxton improved as a translator to any considerable extent. There may be fewer mistakes numerically in the later translations, but the same kind of mistake is found in all his translations—both late and early ones.

The larger additions in Caxton's translations tend to be centred on a few texts. There is no major addition in *Charles the Great*, for example, but several are found in each of the *Golden Legend*, the *Game of Chess* and the *Mirror of the World*. The reason for this is that *Charles the Great* belongs to a different genre: it is a historical romance. Although the purpose of the story might be to show the victory of Christianity over paganism, the book is presented in a narrative form in which there is little scope for personal additions by the translator. Likewise there are few major additions in similar works such as *Paris and Vienne*, *Blanchardin and Eglantine*, the *Siege of Jerusalem*, the *History of Troy* and *Eneydos*. Books like the *Golden Legend* and the *Game of Chess*, however, are collections of saints' lives, miracles, or exempla. These works are episodic, and often one section has little organic connexion with the next. It is much easier and more tempting to introduce additions here. There is more scope for a divergence of views, or for an additional story about a moral problem. People might disagree about the story of St Patrick's Purgatory, but the account of Charles's expedition to Spain was accepted as a narrative of historical fact. Of the episodic works, the *Golden Legend* contains the greatest number of important additions, not only, perhaps, because the book was episodic, but also on account of the special circumstances in which it was composed. Since Caxton was drawing on now one, now another source, it would have been easier and more natural for him occasionally to include his own observations and experiences.

This does not mean that Caxton translated his French source for the *Golden Legend* more accurately than any other French source he used. On the contrary, there are proportionately more mistakes in the parts of the *Golden Legend* taken from the French *Légende dorée* than there are in *Charles the Great*. There are more mistakes for the same reason that there are more additions. *Charles the Great* is a narrative work, and like most narratives the style is simple and fluent. The *Golden Legend*, besides being episodic, is more contemplative, discursive and philosophic, though it also includes many short stories. Consequently the style is often more involved and complicated, because the book is concerned with more profound matters than are found in *Charles the Great*. Caxton, like the rest of us, found it more taxing to translate a contemplative work than a narrative one. There is neither space nor, I think, need to include an investigation into a translation belonging to a different genre from *Charles the Great*, for the results gained would not be materially different. The reader must accept that though my general conclusions are based on an examination of only one text, they are representative of Caxton's work as a whole. An investigation of another text would only reveal the same characteristics with different examples; and I hope that the merits and failings of his translations have now been sufficiently revealed.

To conclude this chapter it is desirable to assess how Caxton's translations compare with others made in the fifteenth century. We have so far viewed his work in isolation in an attempt to elucidate its major characteristics. When his work is approached in this way, we judge it by modern standards; with the result that he is condemned as an inferior translator. It is fairer, as Kellner has shown, to judge him by the standards of his own time. Did other fifteenth-century writers keep as close to their source as Caxton? Did they import foreign words and constructions into their translations as readily as he did? Did they adorn their work with doublets and similar rhetorical devices? It is not possible to answer these questions finally, for many of the numerous translations made in the fifteenth century are not available in modern scholarly editions. By and large, however, it may be said that Caxton's translations are in no way exceptional. Naturally, because of the great number of fifteenth-century translations, all approaches to translation from the very free to the absolutely literal are found. Nevertheless, the greater proportion of them are to be located towards the more literal end of the scale; and it is there that Caxton's translations must also be placed. Yet the extent to which his translations reflect contemporary practice varies in respect of each of the aspects enumerated, viz. the general approach to translation, vocabulary and style.

The majority of fifteenth-century translators appear to have approached their sources in the same way.[1] It is rare to find a translation which renders the sense rather than the words of the original. On the contrary, each translator translated each sense-unit in his original in turn. Although the clause is often given a more English style, as for example by putting the verb after the subject or the adjective before the noun, the sentences in the original can be traced in the translation without any difficulty, for the sequence of clauses remains unchanged. There are omissions and additions, as there are in Caxton's works, but they are generally of a minor nature. As an example of a contemporary translation, I shall quote the opening lines of the *Cordial*, a translation by Earl Rivers, together with the corresponding French. The translation, printed by Caxton in 1479, was made from the French text printed by Caxton about 1475-6.

Eclesiaste dist en son septieme chapitre les parolles qui s'en suivent: 'Ayes memoire de tes dernieres choses et tu ne pecher-as jamais'. Saint Augustin dist aussi ou livre de ses meditations que plus fort fait a eschever seulement la souillure de pechié que quelconques craultez de tourmens infernaulx.	Ecclesiasticus saith in his seuenth chapiter thise wordes folowyng. Bere wel in thy mynde the last thingis. and thou shalt neuer fal in synne. Also. Seynt Austyn. saith in his book of meditacions. That man ought rather haue in fere and eschewe thabhominacion and filthe of synne than ony other crueltees of thinfernal turmentis.[2]

Here is an exact parallel of Caxton's method of translation. There is no departure from the general framework of the original, though some constructions are given an English equivalent and some expressions in the source are expanded. This close following of the sources is the common feature of fifteenth-century writings and it is found in the greatest works of the period. Even Malory, as C. S. Lewis has reminded

---

[1] See particularly Workman 1940.
[2] The text of the *Cordial* is available in Mulders n.d.

us, was 'at the mercy of his originals'.[1] In his translation technique
Caxton was the child of his age.

In the *Cordial* Earl Rivers did make some attempt to produce
English expressions for French ones: French *Ayes memoire* was translated *Bere wel in thy mynde*. Similarly he found a different word (or
words) to render the French *souillure:* he used *abhominacion and filthe*.
He did not transfer *souillure* into his English translation. It is doubtful
whether Caxton would have done the same, for he keeps closer to the
vocabulary of his French sources than many fifteenth-century translators did. Although all translations from this time use a vocabulary
which is strongly influenced by that of their originals, it is only in his
texts that there is such a concentration of nonce words borrowed from
the sources which occur nowhere else in English. Reference to the
Oxford English Dictionary will reveal how many words fall into this
category. His reliance upon his sources can be illustrated by comparing
one of his translations with another English translation of the same
French text. The following list contains a selection from the nonce
words in his version of the *Knight of the Tower*; none of these words
was used by the earlier translator (*c.* 1450) of the same work, who
either omitted them or found an English equivalent: *Attoured* (made
hem redy);[2] *attouchementis* (touchinge and handelinge); *affleblysshed;
bestourned; enchartered; eslargysshe* (the more largely saye); *queynteryes*
(gay arraye); *tresperce* (perisshe thorugh); *ventillous* (and euer beting her
eyelyddes togedre); and *yssue* (ende).

When the style of Caxton's translations is compared with that of
his contemporaries, it occupies a middle position: some authors used a
more ornate, others a less ornate style. All, however, made use of
rhetorical devices, such as the doublet, though many employed them
more frequently than Caxton. Though he claimed to be interested in
rhetorical colours and expressed an admiration for the poet John
Skelton, who was one of the abler exponents of the aureate style,
Caxton himself used few rhetorical devices other than the doublet.
An appreciation of how his translations compare with those by his
contemporaries may be obtained by comparing his prologue to the

[1] C. S. Lewis, *Studies in Medieval and Renaissance Literature* (Cambridge, 1966),
p. 107.

[2] The words in brackets are from the 1450 English translation, available in
T. Wright, *The Book of the Knight of La Tour-Landry*, rev. ed. by J. Munro (London,
1906). Where no form is given in brackets, the author of the 1450 translation
either omitted the word or rewrote the passage.

Polychronicon with the equivalent passages in the translations by Lord Berners and Skelton.[1] The passages are all based on Poggio's Latin version of a prologue by Diodorus Siculus, though Caxton translated from a French version of Poggio's text. Caxton cannot equal the 'stuffed and swelling bombast'[2] of the laureate Skelton's style. For example, his 'experyment of grete jeopardyes' pales before Skelton's 'experymentis of many maters with many-folde laborious trauaylles & ieopardies'. Skelton's style, however, is noted for its circumlocutions and aureate language. Likewise Caxton's version does not contain the rows of synonyms which characterize Lord Berners's style. Yet apart from the synonyms, Berners has a style which is terse and straight-forward; the meaning is immediately apparent. Although Caxton used the doublet less extensively than Berners, his style is otherwise more prolix and certainly less well organized. 'The comparison of these three men's treatment of the same text shows Caxton, indeed, less expansive and aureate than Skelton, but Berners far least so of all.'[3]

The faults and virtues of Caxton's translations noted in this chapter are typical of most fifteenth-century translations. In vocabulary he is more tied to his sources than most translators of his time, and in style he cannot equal the more famous exponents of the aureate diction. In general he can hardly be distinguished from the host of translators who crowd the fifteenth-century scene, except perhaps in the sheer quantity of his output. Of the 106 works printed by or attributed to Caxton, he translated at least twenty-eight; many of these books were large volumes. It is hardly surprising that he did not always have time to polish his version for the press.

---

[1] S. K. Workman discovered that the translations were from the same source, see *Modern Language Notes*, lvi (1941), 252–8.

[2] H. B. Lathrop, *Translations from the Classics into English from Caxton to Chapman 1477–1620* (Madison, 1933), p. 26.

[3] Workman, *Modern Language Notes*, lvi (1941), 253–4.

8

PROLOGUES AND EPILOGUES

In many of the previous chapters I have drawn extensively upon the prologues and epilogues. In them Caxton gives details not only of his own life, but also of contemporary fashions and prejudices. Up till now, however, I have plundered these prologues and epilogues for individual details in support of a particular hypothesis without considering them in their entirety. It may put some of those details in perspective if a chapter is now devoted to these pieces of Caxton's own writing. This chapter may also serve as a link between the last two chapters and the following one, for in his prologues and epilogues Caxton the editor and translator becomes a writer who has something to tell us of his contemporaries' attitudes to language and style. In these pieces he is most independent, though he never entirely abandons the supports of tradition and translation.

The question why Caxton wrote the prologues and epilogues may be answered by looking at the conditions of writing and book publishing prevailing in the fifteenth century. Dedications are of course known from classical times onwards. They became very common in the later medieval and renaissance periods, when men who did not enjoy the security of the cloister tried to live by their writings. They had to find a patron who would both support them and encourage the wider dissemination of their work. The dedication became the means by which a writer could thank or beg his patron for support. Caxton sought patrons for the same reasons as the writers and scribes of the fifteenth century: financial gain and the recommendation for a particular work which a patron's name gave. In his books he frequently mentions the receipt or the expected receipt of financial assistance from his patrons. However, it was the recommendation a patron's name gave a book which was of special importance to him when he was establishing himself as the court printer. Since the dedication would be the first thing a prospective buyer would see, the choice of patron may often have been crucial for a book's reception, especially with such a fickle commodity as fashionable literature. It may have encouraged 'impulse buying'. The patron's name rather than the contents may have been of more influence with many buyers, just as today we may be swayed by the name of a well-known reviewer.

Although self-interest may have been a motive for the composition of the prologues and epilogues, Caxton was also influenced by the well-established tradition of dedications, for his echo other fifteenth-century dedications. The two branches of that tradition which influenced him most were the dedications found in French prose texts and in English poetic ones, particularly those of Lydgate. Naturally he met with French dedications in many of the works he translated, though he also drew on French dedications in texts not translated from French as, for example, in his prologue to the *Polychronicon*. It had become customary for Burgundian writers, many of whom were employed as secretaries by the Dukes, to include a dedication. We have already seen that Caxton was influenced in many ways by the customs of the Burgundian court, and this applies to his prologues and epilogues.

His use of English poetic works has been almost entirely neglected by previous commentators, though I have shown the importance of the English courtly poets for someone who wanted to write in the courtly style. Caxton could not afford to neglect them, and in fact he pillaged them. Thus when he opens his epilogue to his edition of Earl Rivers's translation of *Moral Proverbs*:

Go thou litil quayer and recommaund me,

we may be sure that he based it on Lydgate's words in the *Churl and Bird*:

Go litell quayer and recomande me.

As a formula it was common enough,[1] and Caxton was to use a different version of it in the *Life of Our Lady*, but it is only in Lydgate's *Churl and Bird* that we find the identical words used. Furthermore, Caxton had printed Lydgate's poem in the year before he published *Moral Proverbs*, so that we may be pretty sure that he borrowed the expression from this source. These borrowings which are a feature of his prologues and epilogues are invaluable as an aid to dating his various publications, though they have as yet been disregarded by bibliographers.

There are three themes around which Caxton built his dedications: the value of the book itself, whether on account of its novelty, its

[1] Holzknecht 1923 pp. 116–23.

edifying stories or its courtly style; the nobility of the patron; and the humility of the printer-translator. These three themes, which are traditional, were filled out by details concerning the book's publication, by moral precepts, and by injunctions to behave virtuously and to read other books of the same type. The language in which these details are expressed follows a set pattern, often the same words being used again and again. When a reader is asked to rectify any mistakes he may find, he will be urged 'to correct and amend' the book. Such correction may be necessary even though Caxton has kept 'as nigh as is possible to my copy'. In some cases he does exhibit some development in his wording, for he may come across a phrase which will then stick in his mind and become part of his vocabulary from then onwards. Thus the way in which he describes the courtly style is modified throughout the prologues.[1] Usually, however, he went on employing the same formulas, and often he may have turned back to what he had written in a previous book for help with a later prologue. In addition to these more traditional elements he also gives us considerable information about when a book was printed and how long it took him to translate it. This information was hardly necessary for the sale of his books: possibly he included it because it was the habit of scribes to add details of this type.

Not all the books which issued from the Westminster press were furnished with prologue or epilogue. In general they were added to those books which were designed for the courtly market. The contents of texts intended for a specialized market would be a sufficient inducement for any prospective buyer; these books would not need a particular recommendation from the publisher. However, not even all the books which he printed for his aristocratic clientele were provided with prologue or epilogue. It was only those books which needed some form of introduction to a purchaser that would merit a dedication. Works by poets such as Lydgate and Chaucer would be well enough known already—at least by their titles. They would not need a preface. It was only when special circumstances were involved that a few words from the printer became desirable: the incompleteness of the *House of Fame*, the corrections in the second edition of the *Canterbury Tales*, and the rarity of manuscripts of Chaucer's prose translation *Boethius*. Otherwise, it was when he published a translation, his own or someone else's, of a French work that a dedication was essential, for the book would not be familiar to an English audience. It was neces-

[1] Blake, *Essays and Studies*, New Series xxi (1968), 29–45.

sary to point out what sort of book it was, how fashionable it was and under whose auspices it was printed. It is because so many of Caxton's printed works fall into this category that we have so many prologues and epilogues from his pen.

Before considering two of Caxton's prologues in detail, I shall briefly discuss how he approached the problem of providing a prologue. When he was going to print a work, he could be faced with two possibilities: the work already had a prologue, or it had none at all. In the latter case he had to compose his own dedication by the combination of set formulas with borrowings from other writers. In his edition of the *Polychronicon* he took a complete prologue from another work. We shall see later, by examining his prologue to the second edition of the *Canterbury Tales*, how he went about the composition of his own prologues. When the book he was publishing already had a prologue, he never omitted it, but either modified it and made it his own, or left it substantially intact, but added something to it. In the latter case he could keep the original prologue (perhaps in a modified form) quite separate, as he did in the *Golden Legend* and the *Polychronicon*, or he could tack on his own comments at the beginning or end, as he did in *Charles the Great*. When there is only one undivided preface it is difficult to disentangle what is Caxton's own and what is from the original, unless (as rarely happens) the exact source has survived. Scholars trying to put together Caxton's biography have often been misled by this mixture of original and borrowed material; just as they have failed to make allowances for the traditional elements in them. Without knowledge of the source, it would be easy to assume in *Charles the Great* that Caxton wrote the work for both William Daubeney and Henry Bolomyer; the latter is the patron of the French edition. Caxton translated the French *je* as 'I' without making any distinction between himself and the French author.

As in *Charles the Great* he added his own continuation to the original prologue, the Caxton contribution is not too difficult to identify. Often, however, he adapted the original dedication to suit his immediate purpose, and then his own contribution and the original prologue are woven together inextricably. To illustrate this, I shall compare his prologue to the *Mirror of the World* with the French prologue in British Museum MS Royal 19 A IX, the manuscript Caxton used.[1]

[1] Prior 1913 pp. vii-viii.

Consideryng that wordes ben perisshyng, vayne & forgeteful, and writynges duelle & abide permanent, as I rede *Vox audita perit, littera scripta manet*; thise thinges have caused that the faites and dedes of auncyent menn ben sette by declaracion in fair and aourned volumes to th'ende that science and artes, lerned and founden of thinges passed, myght be had in perpetuel memorye and remembraunce. For the hertes of nobles, in eschewyng of ydlenes at suche tyme as they have none other vertuouse ocupacion on hande, ought t'excersise them in redyng, studyng & visytyng the noble faytes and dedes of the sage and wysemen, somtyme travaillyng in prouffytable vertues. Of whom it happeth ofte that som men ben enclyned to visyte the bookes treatyng of sciences particuler, and other to rede & visyte bookes spekyng of faytes of armes, of love, or of other mervaillous histories. And emonge alle other this present booke whiche is called the *Ymage* or *Myrrour of the World* ought to be visyted, redde & knowen by cause it treateth of the world and of the wondreful dyvision therof. In whiche book a man resonable may see and understande more clerer by the visytyng and seeyng of it and

Considerant que parolles sont & demeurent vaines et escriptures permanentes,

ont les fais des anciens esté mis par declaracion en beaulx & aournés volumes, affin que des sciences acquises et choses passées fust perpetuelle memoire

pour les coeurs des nobles excerser en lisant & estudiant les fais des sages jadiz traveillans en vertus prouffitables.

Dont il advient que les ungs sont enclins a visiter les livres traitans de sciences particulieres, et les aultres a visiter les livres parlans de fais d'armes & d'amours ou aultrement. Et est ce present volume appellé *l'Ymage du Monde*;

the figures therin the situacion
and moevyng of the firmament
and how the unyversal erthe
hangeth in the myddle of the
same, as þe chapitres here
folowyng shal more clerly
shewe and declare to you.
Whiche said book was translated out of Latyn in to Frensshe
by the ordynaunce of the noble
duc, Johan of Berry and Auvergne, the yere of Our Lord
M.CC.xlv. And now at this
tyme rudely translated out of
Frensshe in to Englissh by me,
symple persone, William Caxton, at the request, desire, coste
and dispense of the honourable
& worshipful man Hugh Bryce,
alderman & cytezeyn of London, entendyng to present the
same unto the vertuous, noble
and puissaunt lord, Wylliam
Lord Hastynges, Lord Chamber-
layn unto the most crysten
kynge, Kynge Edward the
fourthe, Kynge of England & of
Fraunce &c., and Lieutenaunt
for the same of the toun of
Calais and Marches there; whom
he humbly besecheth to resseyve in gree & thanke. Whiche
booke conteyneth in alle lxxvij
chapitres & xxvij figures without whiche it may not lightly
be understande. And for to
declare more openly, it is
ordeyned in thre parties: of
whiche the firste conteyneth xx
chapitres and viij figures; the

et fu translaté de latin en
franchois par le commandement
et ordonnance du noble duc,
Jehan de Berry et d'Auvergne,
l'an .M. deux cens quarante
cincq.

Si contient cinquante cincq
chapitles et vingt sept figures
sans lesquelles il ne porroit estre
de legier entendu. Et pour le
mieulx declarier a esté ordonné en trois parties: dont la
premiere partie contient xiiij
chapitles et huyt figures; la

seconde partie xxxiij chapitres and ix figures; and the therde conteyneth xxiiij chapitres and x figures. Whiche was engrossed and in alle poyntes ordeyned by chapitres and figures in Frenshe in the toun of Bruggis the yere of th'yncarnacion of Our Lord M.CCCC.lxiiij. in the moneth of Juyn. And emprised by me, ryght unable and of lytil connyng, to translate & brynge it in to our maternal tongue þe second day of the moneth of Janyver, the yer of Our said Lord M.CCCClxxx in th'abbay of Westmestre by London. Humbly requyryng alle them that shal fynde faulte to correcte and amende where as they shal ony fynde. And of suche so founden that they repute not the blame on me, but on my copie whiche I am charged to folowe as nyghe as God wil gyve me grace. Whom I most humbly beseche to gyve me scyence, connyng and lyf t'accomplysshe and wel to fynysshe it.

seconde partie contient xix figures; et la tierce partie est de xxij chapitles et ix figures. Si fu grossé & de tous poins ordonné, comme dit est, en la ville de Bruges l'an de l'incarnation Nostre Seigneur Jhesu Crist mil quatre cens soixante & quatre par le commandement de Jehan le clerc, librarier & bourgois dicelle ville de Bruges.

Priant Dieu que tous ceulx qui le lirront ou orront lire y puissent tellement prouffiter que ce soit au prouffit et salut de leurs ames & a l'onneur et santé de leurs corps.

The comparison of these two versions shows how Caxton's text is modelled on his source. Whereas when he translated a whole text he was content for the most part to translate literally, as we saw in the last chapter, the prologue is modified considerably. He has expanded the original by the use of doublets or triplets and by the use of parallels. In the opening sentence, French *vaines* becomes 'perisshyng, vayne & forgeteful' and the French verbal doublet, *sont & demeurent*, appears as 'ben ... duelle & abide', two verbs being expanded into three. Similarly the sentiment of the opening sentence in the French is repeated in Caxton's version by the addition of the Latin proverbial expression. The exact source of this addition is not known; presumably he took it from some book when he writes 'as I rede' rather than he quoted it from memory, though similar expressions are attested from this period.[1] He included it not only because it formed a suitable parallel, but also because he, like other writers, was fond of quoting suitable aphorisms and proverbs. Several may be found in his prologues and epilogues. Thus by the simple expedient of various forms of parallelism, he is able to make the opening sentence more impressive and weighty. Examples of the creation of further doublets may be found throughout the prologue. The reason that he created more doublets in his prologues rather than in the body of his texts is the same as that which led him to have a patron. It is the prologue which is a book's advertisement. Its style must be fashionable and striking, just as its patron must indicate that it is suitable for members of the court. The reader must be convinced of the book's merits at the outset, and the prologue was designed to do just that.

The principal method Caxton employed to give weight to his prologues was the use of these parallels. Another method was the introduction of additional moralizing comments. Thus his noble readers are imagined to attend to this book 'in eschewyng of ydlenes at suche tyme as they have none other vertuouse ocupacion on hande'. Normally it is Caxton himself who seeks to eschew idleness. He translated the History of Troy 'in eschewyng of ydlenes' [7], and the formula occurs in many of his other prologues and epilogues. In the prologue to the Golden Legend he wrote, following his French source, that St Bernard had reproved idleness and that St Jerome had said that the devil should never find one idle—examples which show how typical of prologues a reproof of idleness was at the time, and which reveal that his predilection for a moral precept was shared by his contemporaries. Similarly the necessity for virtuous occupation is a theme which runs through his prologues from the History of Troy onwards, usually in close association with the need to avoid idleness.[2] The

---

[1] H. Walther, Lateinische Sprichwörter und Sentenzen des Mittelalters, II/2 (Göttingen, 1964), p. 750.

[2] For example, 'to eschewe slouthe and ydlenes whyche is moder and nourysshar of vyces and ought to put my self unto vertuous ocupacion and besynesse' (History of Troy); 'every man eschewe synne and encrece in vertuous occupacions' (Game of Chess). The sentiment and wording are traditional, being found in Lydgate's prologues, cf. Troy-Book, prol. 82–84.

introduction of these two formulas here brings this prologue into line with most of his others.

A little later Caxton alters *aultrement* to 'other mervaillous histories', a translation which continues the process of amplification and inflation already noted. This expression is another favourite with Caxton, who used it to recommend his books: although the moral precepts were familiar, the exempla used to illustrate them could be strange and novel. The *History of Troy*, the *Siege of Jerusalem* and the *Polychronicon*, to name only a few, were recommended in the same words. This example adds further evidence for my suggestion that certain stock ideas and expressions which filled his mind emerged whenever he composed a prologue or epilogue. His books are recommended for the same reasons: they were uplifting, but also unusual.

At this point the French scribe named the book for which this was the prologue. The book is, however, referred to in the manuscript as both the *Image of the World* and the *Mirror of the World*, so naturally Caxton includes both titles. The title leads him to think of the book's contents, so his prologue continues with an outline of the 'marvellous stories' that can be found within the book. He did this by the simple method of building up a sentence from one or two of the chapter headings which follow the prologue. At the same time he did not forget to refer to the illustrations which form one of the features of the book. It is in fact the first Caxton book with woodcuts. In this way he ensures that a reader would have some idea of the book's contents—and those who would know more are referred to the table of contents. Having made this addition Caxton returns to his source for the statement that the book was made for the Duke of Berry in 1245. Caxton never omits information of this sort, even though the Duke's name is erroneously associated with the volume through the Bruges adaptor's misunderstanding of his copy. If he ordered it, then the book must be worthy of every courtier's attention. The Duke's name was a good advertisement.

From here Caxton passes naturally to the circumstances of the English translation. Inevitably he describes his translation as 'rude', for this is an adjective that all writers of the time apply to their work; Caxton is no exception. We learn also it was made at the request and cost of Hugh Bryce, a mercer, who intended to present it to Lord Hastings. Bryce is a relatively unimportant link in the chain of events which brought the book about insofar as its public appeal is concerned, and he is given little attention in the prologue. But Hastings, who had not yet, as far as we know, seen or heard anything of this book, is described in the terms Caxton used for members of the aristocracy. He is *virtuous*, *noble* and *puissant*, terms which Caxton also used of such people as Earl Rivers and Margaret Duchess of Somerset. Hastings is also given many of his titles. This is not only a mark of respect to the man, but also a sign that the patron of the book is noble and out-standing. The reader need have no fears of the book's credentials since it was sponsored by the Duke of Berry and Lord Hastings.

After this insertion Caxton returns to his source. The chapters of the book are numbered, though he has gone to the trouble of correcting the figures, which are inaccurate in the French. The next section of the French prologue is the only part Caxton abbreviates. He includes only that the French book was made in Bruges in 1464, but he omits the name of the bookseller and the concluding remarks about the value of the book for the reader's soul. The Flemish bookseller would not be known in England and his name would add nothing to the esteem of the book. Caxton retained the information about the manufacture of the French book in Bruges, because Bruges was the centre of the book trade and, one might say, the home of good books. It was a further recommendation for a book that it had come from Bruges, for many of the most sumptuous books came from there to England and it was one of the residences of the Dukes of Burgundy. Edward IV had him-self spent some time there during his exile. Caxton omitted the final remarks in the French prologue because he wanted to include his own traditional ending. This involved the humility formula, which we have already commented on. The words used here are the same as those he employs elsewhere. The whole is then completed by the date of his translation and a prayer for the completion of the project.

As this brief comparison has shown, Caxton carried out his task of adaptation with considerable tact and ability. The prologue reads as a unit, and it would be difficult, if the French source had not survived, to realize that Caxton's prologue was such a mixture of his own and his original. By the use of his stock phrases he has made the prologue very much his own, even though it is solidly based on the French. Where he had something to work on, he usually managed to employ it to good effect.

He did not always have the benefit of a model. As an example of a prologue of this type, I have chosen that to the second edition of the *Canterbury Tales*.[1] As we have seen, this book was produced in the

[1] For a general discussion of Caxton and Chaucer see Blake, *Leeds Studies in English*, New Series i (1967), 19–36.

5 Death and the Printers

6 Earl Rivers presents his Book to Edward IV

troubled times of Richard III, and therefore Caxton could not use the patron's name to advertize his book. He was thus thrown back on generalities and abstract statements. It is necessary to quote the prologue in full:

Grete thankes, laude and honour ought to be gyven unto the clerkes, poetes and historiographs that have wreton many noble bokes of wysedom, of the lyves, passions & myracles of holy sayntes, of hystoryes of noble and famous actes and faittes, and of the cronycles sith the begynnyng of the creacion of the world unto thys present tyme, by whyche we ben dayly enformed and have knowleche of many thynges of whom we shold not have knowen yf they had not left to us theyr monumentis wreton. Emong whom and in especial to fore alle other we ought to gyve a synguler laude unto that noble & grete philosopher Gefferey Chaucer, the whiche for his ornate wrytyng in our tongue may wel have the name of a laureate poete. For to fore that he by hys labour enbelysshyd, ornated and made faire our Englisshe, in thys royame was had rude speche & incongrue, as yet it appiereth by olde bookes whyche at thys day ought not to have place ne be compared emong ne to hys beauteuous volumes and aournate writynges. Of whom he made many bokes and treatyces of many a noble historye as wel in metre as in ryme and prose. And them so craftyly made that he comprehended hys maters in short, quyck and hye sentences, eschewyng prolyxyte, castyng away the chaf of superfluyte and shewyng the pyked grayn of sentence, utteryd by crafty and sugred eloquence. Of whom emonge all other of hys bokes I purpose t'emprynte by the grace of God the book of the *Tales of Cauntyrburye*, in whiche I fynde many a noble hystorye of every astate and degre: fyrst rehercyng the condicions and th'arraye of eche of them as properly as possyble is to be sayd; and after theyr tales whyche ben of noblesse, wysedom, gentylesse, myrthe and also of veray holynesse and vertue, wherin he fynysshyth thys sayd booke. Whyche book I have dylygently oversen and duly examyned to th'ende that it be made acordyng unto his owen makyng. For I fynde many of the sayd bookes, whyche wryters have abrydgyd it and many thynges left out; and in somme place have sette certayn versys that he never made ne sette in hys booke. Of whyche bookes so incorrecte was one brought to me vj yere passyd, whyche I supposed had ben veray true & correcte. And accordyng to the same I dyde do enprynte a certayn nombre of

F

them, whyche anon were sold to many and dyverse gentyl men. Of whome one gentylman cam to me and said that this book was not accordyng in many places unto the book that Gefferey Chaucer had made. To whom I answerd that I had made it accordyng to my copye, and by me was nothyng added ne mynusshyd. Thenne he sayd he knewe a book whyche hys fader had and moche lovyd, that was very trewe and accordyng unto hys owen first book by hym made. And sayd more yf I wold enprynte it agayn he wold gete me the same book for a copye, how be it he wyst wel that hys fader wold not gladly departe fro it. To whom I said in caas that he coude gete me suche a book, trewe and correcte, yet I wold ones endevoyre me to enprynte it agayn for to satysfye th'auctour, where as to fore by ygnouraunce I erryd in hurtyng and dyffamyng his book in dyverce places in settyng in somme thynges that he never sayd ne made and levyng out many thynges that he made whyche ben requysite to be sette in it. And thus we fyll at accord. And he ful gentylly gate of hys fader the said book and delyverd it to me, by whiche I have corrected my book as here after alle alonge by th'ayde of almyghty God shal folowe. Whom I humbly beseche to gyve me grace and ayde to achyeve and accomplysshe to hys laude, honour and glorye, and that alle ye that shal in thys book rede or heere wyll of your charyte emong your dedes of mercy remembre the sowle of the sayd Gefferey Chaucer, first auctour and maker of thys book. And also that alle we that shal see and rede therin may so take and understonde the good and vertuous tales, that it may so prouffyte unto the helthe of our sowles that after thys short and transitorye lyf we may come to everlastyng lyf in heven.

This prologue, like that to the *Mirror of the World*, has a grand opening. In this case Caxton has used triplets which are balanced against one another: *thankes, laude, honour; clerkes, poetes, historiographs;* and *lyves, passions, myracles*. And triplets are a common feature of the whole prologue. The opening sentence is not, however, original, since he based it upon the prologue to his edition of the *Polychronicon*, which opens:

> Grete thankynges, lawde & honoure we merytoryously ben bounde to yelde and offre unto wryters of hystoryes, which gretely have prouffyted oure mortal lyf . . .

There are other verbal similarities between the two texts. Thus *monumentis wreton* echoes 'lyteral monumentis' [65], and the phrase *lyves, passions & myracles* appears in the *Polychronicon's* prologue in a different order, as well as in several other Caxtonian prologues. Even the way the whole course of history is expressed has a parallel in the *Polychronicon*, though in this case the verbal similarity is not pronounced. The correspondence between the two prologues reveals that in his wish for a grand dedication he modelled the opening sentence of this prologue on that in his prologue to the *Polychronicon*, though other of his historical works may also have been called on, for the word *historiograph* had been used by him earlier in his prologue to the *Siege of Jerusalem*. He was thus building his prologue on a well-established model, since the prologue to the *Polychronicon* was itself a translation of the French version of the prologue to the *Historical Library* by Diodorus Siculus. Yet if the sentence is read in its context, it is not really an appropriate opening for a prologue to the *Canterbury Tales*. Admittedly poets often did write historical works, but Chaucer's poem is not such a work. Indeed after the opening sentence about history, that subject is not raised again. On the contrary, after the introduction about historians Caxton goes on to praise Chaucer for his style; and later when he lists the topics to be found in the *Canterbury Tales*, history is not among them. So in this particular instance at least Caxton has borrowed material which was not entirely suitable thematically for his prologue, but which provided a grand opening sentence in the high style. It was this latter qualification which he doubtless considered the most important, for Chaucer was the father of English poetic style, as Caxton was about to point out. It was essential that his works should be introduced by the printer in a fitting manner. He was determined that his clients should feel that the greatest English poet was being produced by a printer who was worthy of him and them.

The central part of the prologue is devoted to Chaucer's style. In his praise of Chaucer, Caxton followed a trend which was already well established. As a publisher it was necessary for him to keep abreast of this fashion, but he went so far as to borrow the words which other writers had used for their own appreciations of Chaucer. Generally it is Lydgate who provided him with his critical vocabulary, though the printer also made use of other poetic texts which he had printed. He opens his eulogy by calling Chaucer a 'noble & grete philosopher'. The two adjectives were constantly employed by Caxton, for they are commendatory without being specific. *Noble* occurs several other times in this prologue. The description of Chaucer as a philosopher is less often found, though Caxton may have taken the hint from Surigone's epitaph.[1] He continues by praising Chaucer for his ornate writing in English for which he deserves the title of poet laureate. The attribution of *ornate* language to Chaucer was well established and Caxton had already used the word to describe Chaucer's writings in his prologue to the *Boethius*, into which he had introduced it from a line in the *Book of Courtesy*. It had become part of his stock ideas about Chaucer and may well have been repeated here almost spontaneously. To my knowledge the words *poet laureate* had not been used of Chaucer by earlier writers, though Chaucer's pre-eminence is often referred to in more general terms. Thus Lydgate in his *Life of Our Lady*, printed by Caxton in the same year as the second edition of the *Canterbury Tales*, described him as:

> The noble rethor poete of Breteine
> That worthy was the laurer to have
> Of poetrie. (II. 1629–31)

Chaucer had, however, used the phrase himself to describe Petrarch as 'the lauriat poete' (*Clerk's Tale* 31) and Caxton may have borrowed it from there. Otherwise, it is possible that Caxton took the phrase direct from another work which he had recently published, the *Court of Sapience*, formerly attributed to Lydgate. In that poem there is a passage in praise of Chaucer terminating with the poet's plea that those who think his writing dull should consult 'Galfryde the poete laureate'. The anonymous poet was referring to Geoffrey de Vinsauf, a thirteenth-century rhetorician who is cited as an authority by Chaucer himself. Caxton may have understood the reference to be to Geoffrey Chaucer and so taken over the phrase to use it in his honour. Furthermore, the phrase *poet laureate* was becoming more popular at the end of the fifteenth century and it was used both by Stefano Surigone, on his tablet to Chaucer in Westminster Abbey, and by Skelton to describe themselves. Its use here by Caxton may reflect the growing popularity of the expression at that time.

Having praised Chaucer the man, Caxton proceeds to Chaucer's contribution to the English language. This largely repeats what he has just written about him. Chaucer 'enbelysshyd, ornated and made faire' the English language. Not only is this an amplification of what he

---

[1] This is printed in C. F. E. Spurgeon, *Five Hundred Years of Chaucer Criticism and Allusion*, I. 1357–1800 (London, 1914), pp. 59–60. In the epitaph Surigone refers to the *fontes philosophie*, which may have given Caxton his hint.

has just written, it also repeats what he had written of Chaucer in his prologue to Chaucer's *Boethius*, in which he was described as an 'enbelissher in making the sayd langage ornate & fayr' [37]. The words are again largely borrowed by Caxton from other writers.[1] If Chaucer enriched the language, it must have been rude beforehand. So Caxton spends a few words on the barbarity of the English tongue. Once again this is a common theme in fifteenth-century writings, though in this case it is difficult to find exact parallels to all the words he used. He wrote: 'in thys royame was had rude speche & incongrue, as yet it appiereth by olde bookes, whyche at thys day ought not to have place ne be compared emong ne to hys beauteuous volumes and aournate writynges'. With this may be compared, as an illustration of the traditional nature of his remarks, the following passage from Lydgate's *Troy-Book*, a work known to the printer:

> Rude and boistous firste be olde dawes,
> Pat was ful fer from al perfeccioun,
> And but of litel reputacioun
> Til pat he (*i.e.* Chaucer) cam, & poruӡ his poetrie,
> Gan oure tonge firste to magnifie,
> And adourne it with his elloquence (III, 4238–43).

The use of *rude* to describe the earlier English language was regular, as this passage shows, though Caxton has himself added the word *incongrue*, for it is a word not used elsewhere in this type of context. He had used it in his translations and may have incorporated it from there. Similarly the expression 'beauteuous volumes and aournate writynges' was modelled on phrases he had used in his earlier prologues. In the prologue to the *Mirror of the World*, for example, he translated the French *beaulx & aournés volumes* as 'fair and aourned volumes'. It was a phrase he had taken over from his various French prologues and made his own. After the benefits that Chaucer had conferred upon the English language, Caxton mentions that the poet had written many works, in both prose and verse. We may note again the use of the colourless *noble* to describe Chaucerian works. The phrase 'in metre as in ryme and prose' is one which the printer used in many other prologues and which merely signifies all types of literary composition. It is used as early as the *History of Troy* and recurs in later works, though Caxton had by this time printed many Chaucerian works, including

---

[1] I have not thought it necessary to include examples; see either Blake in *Leeds Studies in English* (1967) or Spurgeon, *op. cit.*

the prose *Boethius*, and this statement may reflect that activity.

In his handling of the Chaucerian theme Caxton thus paid a compliment to Chaucer the man, commented on his enriching of the English language, and stated that he had written many works. It would be a natural progression to proceed to the one text for which this prologue was written; and if one momentarily leaves out the next section of the prologue, it will be seen how easily the prologue would have developed: 'Of whom he made many bokes and treatyces of many a noble historye as wel in metre as in ryme and prose. Of whom emonge all other of hys bokes I purpose t'emprynte by the grace of God the book of the *Tales of Cauntyrburye*'. The development of this prologue would then have been identical with that in the prologue to the *Mirror of the World*. But this is not how the prologue reads in the printed book, for Caxton has inserted an additional sentence. This sentence may well have been an afterthought on his part—an afterthought perhaps suggested by Lydgate's appreciations of Chaucer. Whether an addition or not, the sentence stands out from the rest of the eulogy of Chaucer, firstly on account of its inflated vocabulary: *superfluyte, pyked, sugred*; and secondly because a rhymed poetic work can be seen to form its basis: *prolyxyte: superfluyte; sentence: eloquence*. Instead of taking a word or a phrase from a source, Caxton has stolen several lines; the result being that the passage fits somewhat awkwardly into the prologue. Both the prologue's tone and its development are interrupted.

The work from which Caxton borrowed these lines appears to be Lydgate's *Siege of Thebes*, though there is no single passage in that poem which could have provided him with all that he includes here. He has conflated several different passages. The 'craftyly made' which he applies to Chaucer's works may be an echo of Lydgate's 'crafty writinge' (*Siege of Thebes 57*) used of Chaucer. However, Caxton had also used the expression before in his prologue to Chaucer's *Boethius*, in which Boethius is described as 'an excellente auctour of dyverce bookes craftely and curiously maad in prose and metre' [36]. Here the association of 'craftely' with the various books in 'prose and metre' may be significant, particularly since Caxton wrote in his epilogue to Chaucer's *House of Fame* that it also was 'craftyly made' [69]. The sentence continues to the effect that Chaucer 'comprehended hys maters in short, quyck and hye sentences', an expression which cannot be traced to Lydgate's *Siege of Thebes*, though Lydgate used expressions which may reflect this one.[1] Again it was a phrase Caxton

---

[1] Cf. *Troy-Book* III. 4248 'ful hiȝe sentence'.

associated with Chaucer, for in the epilogue to the *House of Fame* he had written that Chaucer's 'mater is ful of hye and quycke sentence' [69]. There is a close parallel from Chaucer's own Prologue to the *Canterbury Tales*, from where Caxton may have borrowed the expression. In the description of the Clerk of Oxenford occurs the line:

> *And short and quyk and ful of hy sentence* (l. 306).

It is of course possible that Caxton quoted the line from memory and that sometimes he remembered it more accurately than at other times. It is intriguing to speculate whether Caxton equated Chaucer with the Clerk of Oxenford. He had described Chaucer as a philosopher earlier, and the prologue links poets with clerks and historians. This idea is perhaps a little fanciful; it may merely have been a phrase which stuck in his mind.

The rest of the sentence in praise of Chaucer is taken direct from two passages in the *Siege of Thebes*:

> Be rehersaile of his sugrid mouth,
> Of eche thyng keping in substaunce
> The sentence hool withoute variance,
> Voyding the chaf, sothly for to seyn,
> Enlumynyng þe trewe piked greyn
> Be crafty writing of his sawes swete (52–57);

and

> In eschewyng of prolixite,
> And voyde away al superfluyte (1907–8).

The first of these two passages by Lydgate is in praise of Chaucer, though the second is not. Possibly Caxton had conflated the two unconsciously rather than deliberately.

After this digression on Chaucer's elegant style, he returns to the particular edition he is printing, the *Canterbury Tales*. As might be expected, it contains many 'noble' stories; and these stories are of 'every astate and degre'. The latter phrase is another favourite with Caxton, found as early as his first edition of the *Game of Chess*. He used it particularly frequently at this time, for it also occurs in *King Arthur* and *Charles the Great*. The contents of the book are then noted, as they had been in his prologue to the *Mirror of the World*. He refers first to the contents of Chaucer's Prologue, in which the pilgrims are described, and then to their stories. Although the contents of the *Canterbury Tales* were described by Lydgate in his *Siege of Thebes* and the *Fall of Princes*, the list in Caxton's prologue is independent of them, even though they naturally overlap in places. This is surprising as he had just borrowed two passages from the *Siege of Thebes*, unless the previous sentence in his prologue was an addition as I have suggested above. Caxton's list is longer than either of Lydgate's, and from his other prologues we know that he was partial to such lengthy lists; the best known one being his list of the different aspects of human behaviour to be found in *King Arthur*. The list in his prologue to the *Canterbury Tales* should be equated with that one in *King Arthur*. More importantly the list of contents shows that Caxton had read his Chaucer.

Caxton concludes this section of his prologue by saying that he has looked over the edition carefully to prepare it for the press because of the confused state of the manuscripts of the *Canterbury Tales*. I have shown in an earlier chapter that his attitude to Chaucer's text fell far short of what we might have expected from his own words. Some of those words form part of his general stock of critical vocabulary so that they may reflect what he considered ought to be in a prologue rather than what he had actually done. Thus the expression 'dylygently oversen and duly examyned' occurs in one form or another in many of his other prologues, particularly those to his later books. Yet we rarely have evidence of any careful textual scrutiny on his part. The phrase is more a literary embellishment than a statement of what has been done. The information that some manuscripts of the *Canterbury Tales* are faulty may have been given to Caxton by his gentleman-client, or he may have deduced it from what the client had said about the first edition; it is unlikely that Caxton had ever collated manuscripts.

The concluding part of the prologue describes the events leading up to the publication of the second edition. It is totally different in style from what has preceded. In the first part he made an effort to adorn his prose-style by borrowing from the works of other authors. He was able to do this because he was writing on a traditional theme: it was easy to adapt the words of others to one's own needs. The result is a fairly competent, elevated style, though the matter is somewhat lifeless. In the description of his relations with his gentleman-client Caxton had no previous tradition to fall back on. So he composed in a simple repetitive style, based on the pattern of 'he said ... I said'. The contrast is profound, not only in style, but also in content. The former part is abstract statement, the latter part is simple, quick-moving narrative. Although the earlier section is stylistically more proficient, the simplicity of the narrative section makes it more personal and lifelike. A similar type of difference between the two halves of a prologue is found in that to the *Polychronicon*, in which the first part, based on a French source, is an abstract discussion of the benefits of history, and the second is a straightforward account of the publication of the *Polychronicon*. Though the arrangement of this part of the prologue to the *Canterbury Tales* is simple and the language unadorned, many of Caxton's stock phrases reappear. His defence of his first edition is that he had copied his manuscript as closely as possible and that he had not 'added ne mynusshyd' anything. Even his claim that he had printed this edition to 'satysfye th'auctour' is found in other prologues. The habit was too strong to break. Nevertheless, when he finished his account of the dealings with the gentleman, he did try to round off the prologue in a slightly grander style. The sentence '. . . to gyve me grace and ayde to achyeve and accomplysshe to hys laude, honour and glorye' contains two doublets and a triplet. The triplet clearly looks back to the opening phrase 'thankes, laude and honour'; and the doublet *achieve and accomplish* is one of Caxton's favourites. It occurs from about this time in the *Golden Legend*, *King Arthur* and the *Royal Book*. He is attempting to bring his style up to its former level again. The final sentence continues this trend; it is modelled on many other prayers which conclude prologues in Caxtonian editions.

The investigation into these two prologues has shown how Caxton set about writing his original compositions. He wanted to compose them in a high style and consequently he was forced to borrow widely from the works of previous writers. He used his French sources, the poems of Lydgate and other poems he had printed to quarry his material. It is possible that he may also have used other works, for there are certain correspondences between his prologues and those by John Shirley.[1] As it cannot be proved that Caxton knew these, I have concentrated on those texts with which he was certainly acquainted. These provided him with a suitable terminology for only some well-defined themes. When he wished to comment on non-traditional topics, he had to rely on his own resources. This resulted in some of his favourite grand phrases being mixed into an otherwise very simple vocabulary and style. Unfortunately he was not able to weld the differing styles of his prologues and epilogues into a unity; and even when a prologue is based mainly on a foreign source there is a tendency towards patchiness.

The two prologues examined in detail are typical in their method of

[1] Cf. Spurgeon, *op. cit.* pp. 53–54.

composition of all his prologues and epilogues. Although new information is included in individual prologues, in general the tone and content of one are very much like those of any other. The prologues and epilogues are valuable in that they show how the stock contemporary phrases could be welded together in a literary composition. They reveal who were the popular authors and also illuminate Caxton's own tastes and prejudices.

9

CAXTON AND THE
ENGLISH LANGUAGE

Today we distinguish between linguistics and stylistics. In the fifteenth century such a distinction would not have been made, for style played a dominant part in any discussion about language. So a chapter on Caxton and the English language will have to consider his attitude towards style since most of his comments about English are stylistic. This situation prevented him, despite his residence abroad and his acquaintance with foreign languages, from examining the contemporary language objectively. This is unfortunate, as it was a period of rapid change. English sounds were being modified by the Great Vowel Shift; the vocabulary was being enriched with many foreign words; a standard based on court usage and the London dialect was beginning to emerge with the result that people were becoming more conscious of dialect and social differences in speech habits; and literacy was becoming more widespread. The purpose of this chapter is to see how changes like this affected Caxton, whether he made any attempt to contribute towards them, or whether he was even aware of them. The investigation will be limited to a consideration of syntax, vocabulary and orthography. Since the last subject is the one which involves stylistic considerations least, it will be simplest to begin with Caxton's attitude towards a standardized orthography.

Book production had become big business in the fifteenth century and Caxton had himself been associated with this expanding trade, as earlier chapters have shown. Although Caxton had links with professional scribes and booksellers, the connexion amounted to no more than a business association: the scribes cannot have helped him with his literary productions or with his writings in English. He was a man of some education, but no professional experience of writing. He had moved into the book business as a merchant to make money from books as items of trade. The scribe, on the other hand, had been trained to write, and spent most of his time doing just that. Consequently he would have accepted certain standards of spelling, vocabulary and usage. The standard he followed would depend to a large extent upon where he had been trained and where he worked. In comparison with such a man, Caxton appears in linguistic matters to be only semi-literate; or perhaps we may simply say he was not a professional.

It is wrong to imagine that monastic scriptoria were the only producers of manuscripts in England. During the fifteenth century many manuscripts were produced in shops staffed with professional scribes. These may have been smaller ones run by such men as John Shirley,[1] or what were no doubt larger establishments, producing de luxe editions of English works for the aristocratic market; the writings of Chaucer, Lydgate and Gower were frequently produced in these shops.[2] For our present purpose the important feature of these establishments was that they followed a local standard or even used a house style, so that today it is often possible to attribute a manuscript either to a locality or to an individual establishment not only on palaeographical grounds but also by reason of its spellings and vocabulary. Such a house style was not inflexible, but most of the scribes within a particular establishment would tend to conform. The result was that within the various localities there was a growing standardization in the language— a standard which tolerated more variation than ours today does, but which is nevertheless recognizable as such.[3] It is in London that the development towards a standard can be best seen. Let me quote a simple example of the growth of standardization in spelling. Among the many French words introduced into English in the Middle Ages is the group of words, of ultimate Greek origin, which today end in -ic, such as *music* and *rhetoric*. By the fifteenth century it was customary to spell this group of words with the ending -ik, or less often -ike. Gower, however, on account of some personal idiosyncrasy, which he was able to gratify because of his connexion with the scriptorium at St Mary Overy, preferred to spell these words in a French way. Thus early manuscripts of *Confessio Amantis* use -ique in these words. During the course of the fifteenth century these spellings in manuscripts of his poem were gradually replaced by -ik and -ike. As the French spelling was not part of the scribes' normal usage, they changed individual examples of -ique to -ik(e); but being human, they also overlooked

---

[1] Doyle, *Medium Ævum*, xxx (1961), 93–101.

[2] For information about these shops see J. M. Manly and E. Rickert, *The Text of the Canterbury Tales* (Chicago, 1940), i. 561–605 and *passim*.

[3] We shall learn more of this process of standardization when the results of the investigation into late Middle English by Professors McIntosh and Samuels are published. See also Manly and Rickert, *op. cit.* i. 545–60.

many examples which could have been corrected.[1] This small example illustrates that the scribes did have a standard in some matters and that they tended to bring the texts they were copying into line with it.

The preceding paragraphs have underlined two things: firstly, professional scribes were developing a standard in English; and secondly, Caxton had business connexions with some of the shops and scriptoria. It ought, therefore, to have been possible for him either to learn from the scribes what the acceptable standards of orthography were, or to employ a scribe to standardize the language of the books coming off the press. It should have been possible, if he had wanted to spell his books in accordance with the incipient standard. The evidence, however, suggests that he had no interest in this particular aspect of English.[2] Just as his vocabulary reflects that of the particular work he is translating, so his spelling takes on the colour of the language he is working from. Dutch, French and English spelling habits find their way into his books. This diversity may be accounted for both by a lack of interest in this matter on the part of Caxton and his clients and by the speed at which he worked. He knew that some spellings were more acceptable than others, but he did not give himself enough time to correct his mistakes. Consider his translation of *Reynard the Fox*, the only book he translated from Dutch. In this text we find the sporadic retention of Dutch spellings. The digraphs *oe* and *ae* are sometimes found as in *goed* (good), *roek* (rook), *lupaerd* (leopard) and *waer* (ware), though in his text these words are more often spelt in an English way. We find both *ruymen* and *rome* as variant spellings of the verb 'to make room', of which the first retains the Dutch diphthong and the second has been given an anglicized spelling. Consonants also are taken over from the Dutch source, as in the words *valdore* (falldoor, i.e. trapdoor) and *vlycche* (flitch), though forms with initial *f-* are also found. The numerous occasions on which he spells a particular word in the English fashion shows that he had spelling preferences which were largely in line with the development of orthography in the London area. But the instances in which he was influenced by his source are so many that he cannot have paid particular attention to how he spelt. The irregular

[1] I have taken this example from the M.A. thesis, *A Study in English Orthography*, presented by Miss E. J. Clarke to the University of Liverpool in May 1967.

[2] Wiencke 1930 has attempted to show from four of Caxton's translations that there was a development in Caxton's orthography and language. His conclusion has not been generally accepted, and Sandved 1968 has shown that Wiencke's results cannot be applied to Caxton's publications which were not translations.

spellings reflect carelessness arising from haste and lack of correction. Similarly his translations from French have a large proportion of words influenced by French spelling. Thus, to take the example discussed earlier, in his translations from French such as the *History of Troy* words in *-ic* are generally spelt *-ique* or *-icque* in imitation of the French source. On the other hand, when he issued the *Canterbury Tales* and other English poems, he spelt the identical words with *-ik* or *-ike* because these were the spellings in the manuscripts he was using. Thus in the *History of Troy* occur such spellings as *magique, musycque* and *practicqued*, whereas in his edition of the *Canterbury Tales* they appear in the forms *magik, musik* and *practik*. In all cases the predominant influence is that of the manuscript which he was working from, and the impression that these examples create is that he had no particular policy towards the spellings he used in his books.

This conclusion is of interest because, as today we are used to all printed books appearing in a uniform spelling, we naturally assume that the printing press was an agent of uniformity from its beginnings. On the contrary, there is much to suggest that at first the printing press led to variety rather than to uniformity. The printer may have been able to produce four or five hundred identical copies of a book, but this means that the confusion of one book will be multiplied by the number of copies printed. It is only when a printing house develops its own style that the multiplication of identical copies helps uniformity; until that time, it is a hindrance. The first result of the introduction of the press, therefore, was the flooding of the market with books in an irregular orthography. Whereas the scribes had been slowly working towards standardization in certain areas, printed books tended to undermine these efforts at first. This did not mean that professional scribes gave up their own spelling habits. They continued to provide certain types of book in their standardized language; and many booklovers preferred a manuscript to a printed book. It was more individual and could be executed to a patron's own wishes. But since one scribe can produce only a few books in comparison with a printing press, the output of the scribes would seem insignificant when compared with that of the press. Gradually, however, printing houses adopted the professional scribes' spellings so that printed books became more and more uniform in their orthography. As soon as that happened the printing press became an important influence in the spread of uniformity and the growth of a standard. But this development took place after Caxton.

When one realizes the opportunity to reorganize English spelling that was available to Caxton, an opportunity which he completely neglected, it is easy to blame him. A bold printer interested in language could perhaps have rid English spelling of some of its inconsistencies. Caxton, however, reflected the attitudes of his age too much to pursue an independent policy towards language: and since there was little interest in spelling at that time, he naturally gave it no attention. We may indeed criticize him for not conforming to one of the standards of orthography of the fifteenth century; but it is unjust to blame him because his century took no interest in spelling reform. Possibly he may have regarded spelling as little more than a mechanical exercise suitable only for scribes. Furthermore, the standardization of a text was the responsibility as much of the compositor as of the master-printer; and Caxton was impelled at first to seek his compositors from among foreigners, since Englishmen were not acquainted with the technicalities of printing. Thus although he must be held responsible for the introduction of the French and Dutch spellings in his translations from those languages, a competent English compositor might have eliminated them. Thus the language in Wynkyn de Worde's books has often undergone a process of standardization and modernization which may be attributed to the compositor. It is ironical that the books issuing later from the press of de Worde, a foreigner, had a more standardized English spelling than those printed by the Englishman Caxton. This may have arisen because de Worde employed English compositors whereas Caxton employed de Worde as his principal assistant. This difference in the output of the two printers can be seen in their editions of *Reynard the Fox*. Caxton issued two editions, in both of which the language and spelling are strongly influenced by the Dutch original; there is no indication that the second edition had been revised. However, de Worde's edition of *Reynard the Fox*, which used Caxton's second edition as its copytext, shows extensive revision and modernization; its spelling has undergone considerable standardization.[1]

If Caxton was insensitive to spelling, this does not mean that he took no interest in linguistic matters; his interest, however, was confined to vocabulary. In earlier chapters it has been shown how in his translations he took over many foreign words and, in his original writings, borrowed from other English authors. At the same time in his prologues and epilogues the style of those passages which he composed himself without the aid of borrowed phrases is simple. This contrast suggests

[1] A full investigation is found in Blake, *Studies in Philology*, lxii (1965), 63–77.

he was responsive to style, even if he was not always able to master it. It might be considered unusual for a merchant, who had engaged in business most of his career and who had turned to literature late in life, to have either a feeling for style or a large English vocabulary suitable for literary composition.

Studies into Caxton's personal vocabulary have revealed how small it was and how few in number were the words he introduced into English without the suggestion of some source.[1] Without this prompting he prefers simple, unspecific words such as *noble* and *great*, and his wordstock tends to be Germanic rather than Latinate. But when he elevates his style through borrowing from English authors or by basing his language on a foreign model, the number of words of Latin origin rises sharply. It is only in these cases that he uses such words as *laudable* and *incredible*. Like most Latinate borrowings, these words are polysyllabic and often of an abstract, generalizing quality. Thus on the basis of his French source Caxton used the expression '*lyteral* monumentis' in his prologue to the *Polychronicon*; when he reused the phrase in the prologue to the second edition of the *Canterbury Tales* it appeared as '*monumentis wreton*'. His English reasserted itself when the stimulus of the French source was removed. This example also underlines the lack of growth in Caxton's vocabulary; he may introduce a new word suggested by some source, but it rarely becomes part of his permanent vocabulary. He was an opportunist in linguistic matters, but he failed to educate himself. Occasionally he can remember a word from the text he is translating long enough to include it in the prologue or epilogue to that text. A good example is *contemplare* in the epilogue to book two of the *History of Troy*. This word occurs in the text towards the end of book two[2] and he remembered it long enough to use it in the epilogue; but he does not use it anywhere else in his original writings. Similarly he used *enseygnement* in the prologue and in the colophon to the *Knight of the Tower*. This word occurs frequently in his translation of that text, from which he took it to use on these two occasions. It is not used elsewhere in his prologues or epilogues; he reverted to *learning* and *teaching*, two much commoner words. His vocabulary was not enriched in any permanent way by his translating activities. Likewise, he did not import or coin new words in his own writings, unless some unusual circumstance was present. In his pro-

[1] See Blake, *Neuphilologische Mitteilungen*, lxvii (1966), 122–32, and Donner, *English Language Notes*, iv (1966–7), 86–89.

[2] Sommer 1894 i. 374.

logue to the *Life of Our Lady* the exigencies of the rhyme scheme forced him to invent the word *rudehede*, whereas normally he used either *rude* or *rudeness*. Whatever one may think of this new creation, Caxton himself invented it to overcome a particular difficulty; he did not use it again. He did, however, show more consistent originality in the use of the prefix *en-*. This was a favourite with him, and it enabled him to coin new words by the simple expedient of adding this prefix to a word borrowed from French. We saw how in the prologue to the *Mirror of the World* he translated *grossé* as *engrossed;* similarly in *Charles the Great* he translated *orné* as *enorned*; and in the *Knight of the Tower* he may have rendered *levé* as *enlewed*.[1] There are further examples of this use of *en-* in his works. But his predilection for this prefix was shared by many at the time, and it can hardly be said to reflect great verbal originality on his part. Not only was Caxton's vocabulary limited, but he also failed to develop it at all. Words were borrowed for a particular need and not to extend his own vocabulary.

Although Caxton had a small English vocabulary, he did, as I have shown, try to write in an elevated style when occasion demanded. He learned to appreciate what the high style consisted of through two principal influences: the conversations he had with members of the court and the critical comments which already surrounded the works of Geoffrey Chaucer. In the prologue and epilogues of the *History of Troy* Caxton dismissed his translation as a rude work containing rude English, even though he had followed the French original as closely as possible. Yet the French book was written in the 'fayr langage of Frenshe' [4] in a style 'well and compendiously [i.e. pithily] sette and wreton' [4]. We may note several points: the praise of French style, the slavish copying of the source, the barbarous English of the resultant translation, and, most importantly, the simple terms, *fair, well, rude*, of the critical vocabulary—apart from the word *compendiously*. This word, however, is one which he borrowed from Lydgate, in whose works it appears regularly. For example, in the *Troy-Book* Lydgate wrote:

> *Compendiously I purpose to discryve* (II, 5483).

As Caxton refers to this poem in an epilogue to his *History of Troy*, he was evidently acquainted with it.[2] Lydgate's poetry, and the *Troy-Book*

---

[1] Blake, *Neuphilologische Mitteilungen*, lxvii (1966), 129–30 contains a discussion of this word.

[2] Verbal echoes from this poem in Caxton's prologue confirm this, see Blake, *Leeds Studies in English*, New Series i (1967), 26–27.

is no exception, consists of a large number of translations, and is characterized by a continual reverence for Chaucer as the model to be emulated. So at the outset of his printing career Caxton would have learned that translation and appreciation of Chaucer were fashionable. He would also have picked up some of the vocabulary in which to express these ideas, of which *compendiously* is the earliest example. Lydgate used the word to describe his own style, though we today do not consider brevity or pithiness one of its hallmarks. Caxton, however, adopted the word to express one of the desiderata of style and consequently he applied it to his French source. In this way he indicated that it had the same virtues as English poetry written in the Chaucerian manner. That is why he followed his original closely; by doing so he hoped that the fair style of the French text would be reflected in his translation, though he has to imply in deference to the humility formula that his style is rude. It is possible that he also borrowed the words *fair*, *well* and *rude* from Lydgate, in whose works they appear frequently, but as they are words of wide usage, it is not possible to be dogmatic. Yet even though he has started that process of borrowing which we regard as so typical of him, his critical vocabulary is still undeveloped.

It was extended when he started to print Chaucerian works, through which he became aware of the critical commonplaces constantly repeated about those works. The last chapter contained an example of this development from the prologue to the second edition of the *Canterbury Tales*. Even before that Caxton used similar expressions in his epilogue to *Boethius*. Chaucer is described there as 'the first foundeur & enbelissher of ornate eloquence in our Englissh' [37], in which *ornate* and *embellisher* make their first appearance in his original writings. These are borrowed, but unlike many such terms they came to stay. They also show how Caxton's critical vocabulary became enlarged. The final stage in the development of this vocabulary comes about under the influence of the views of the members of court, for it is in the later prologues that he repeats the views of his anonymous clients. The first signs of this appear in *Charles the Great* in which he complains that his style contains 'no gaye termes ne subtyl ne newe eloquence' [96]. This is a far cry from the 'rude language' of the *History of Troy*; he now expresses the humility formula in terms of the absence of rhetoric. From now on his prologues are full of his discussions on rhetoric with his customers. Of these that to *Eneydos* is the best known, but by no means the only example. From those discussions Caxton came to appreciate that there were two styles, that of the court and that of the 'uplandish' men, and that rhetoric and an exotic vocabulary were the characteristic features of the former. He learned not only the difference, but also how to express it.

It might have been expected that as he became more aware of stylistic questions he would modify his methods of translation. There is no evidence that he did. He appears to have learned the critical vocabulary of appreciation without understanding it or letting it influence his own habits. His latest translations show the same stylistic characteristics as the earliest ones, and he uses the critical vocabulary he has learned in a quite uncritical manner. His deferential attitude towards his patrons prevented him from making any but flattering remarks about their work. He praised the translations of Earl Rivers and the Earl of Worcester, even though they have the same stylistic shortcomings as his own, which he claimed were in a rude style. The only difference in his attitude is that as time passed he is able to praise their work in a more rotund manner. This diversity in approach to similar work suggests that he may not have appreciated the style of individual authors with any depth; like many a later publisher, he was influenced more by an author's name than by his writing. His appreciations show no penetration; they follow the fashions of the day.

Fashion may have encouraged him to adhere closely to the language of his French sources so that his English could be enriched with the words from a more elegant language; but even if he followed the dictates of this fashion in a general way, one may wonder whether this was not simply a matter of habit and convenience on his part, rather than one of conviction. When he translated *Reynard the Fox* from Dutch, he adopted the same course, with the consequence that his book is loaded with Dutch loanwords. Yet Dutch was not such a respected and fashionable language as French, and in the prologue to *Eneydos* Caxton implies that Low German resembled older English, which was accepted by all to be 'barbarous' and uncivilized. If he meant what he wrote, he ought to have replaced the Dutch vocabulary of his source by a Latinate one. It was either too difficult a task for him or one that he considered unnecessary. His habit was to translate closely, whether the language of the original was fashionable or not; though mostly he had the good sense to translate from French. Yet he did not always keep as close to the French as he could have done. The chapter 'Caxton as Translator' contains many examples in which he has used an English expression, perhaps a vogue phrase, instead of the French. Someone who was consciously trying to elevate the language ought not to have given consideration to the more common English expressions, which could well be the ones wanting embellishment. These may have been suitable for the rude, 'uplandish' men, but were hardly suitable for the courtly, literate style. In the same chapter we saw that when a word occurs frequently in one of his sources, he sometimes anglicizes that word and sometimes uses an English equivalent. This variation also suggests that he did not pay much attention to the vocabulary he was using. A translator intent upon enriching the language would always have used the French word to make it more familiar to an English audience. In his translations Caxton was not influenced in more than a general way by what he had written about the courtly style; for the most part it was a form of lip service.

Apart from underlining the closeness of his translations, Caxton also in his later prologues refers to rhetorical devices. It is possible to find examples of such devices in his translations, as for example ending successive clauses with the adverbial ending -ly, or pointing clauses by the use of rhyme words.[1] In all such instances Caxton's source exhibits the same rhetorical pattern; the device has simply been carried over into English through close translation. It could be that he did not even appreciate that a rhetorical device was present. Certainly similar ones are not found in his original writings. The only rhetorical decoration he used consciously was parallelism, either of clauses or more often just of words. As we noted, the creation of doublets or triplets was widespread in the fifteenth century because it was a simple way of making one's style appear elevated; as it was fashionable to heighten one's style, the simplest way of doing it was used unceasingly by the less competent authors. Word parallelism is particularly easy for a translator: all he has to do is to transfer the foreign word and then add the equivalent English word. Consequently, it is remarkable not that Caxton used so many doublets, but that he did not use more. But his employment of doublets has been sufficiently dealt with earlier. As we saw, for him it was more of a rhetorical device than a means for increasing the English vocabulary. Furthermore, it is the only rhetorical device he knew how to employ. He can also on occasion attempt a simple form of sentence parallelism, as in the prologue to the *Mirror of the World*; but the more elaborate types of antithesis and sentence balance are beyond his range. He may have written much about rhetorical embellishments, but he used only the simplest form.

So far in our discussion of Caxton's vocabulary attention has been

[1] L. Wendelstein, *Beitrag zur Vorgeschichte des Euphuismus* (Halle, 1902), p. 4.

focused on his translations and original writings. They reveal that he followed the current fashions of the day, translated literally and looked to the English poetic works for help with his own compositions. They do not give any reason to suppose that he was particularly interested in the improvement of English through either loanwords or the creation of new words. They show that his personal vocabulary was limited and that, although he could use the current jargon about style, he was unable to employ any but the simplest methods of stylistic adornment. But he published many English works, and their evidence is of importance, for in them he naturally had to face the problem of obsolete and unfashionable words. To some extent he avoided this problem by choosing texts which did not contain that type of vocabulary. Such works include the writings of the English poets and the translations by such men as Earl Rivers and the Earl of Worcester, which Caxton printed with few deliberate linguistic alterations, as far as we can tell. However, two of the works he printed, Trevisa's translation of Higden's *Polychronicon* and Malory's *Morte Darthur*, did present him with some difficulties, and both were revised before publication.

Although the English of both texts was modified, Caxton refers only to the changes made in the *Polychronicon*. His comments are slight: '[I] somwhat have chaunged the rude and old Englyssh, that is to wete certayn wordes which in these dayes be neither usyd ne understanden' [68]. There is no indication that he has altered the style at all; he has merely replaced some words which had become obsolete by others which were current at his time. The reason for the changes, it is implied, is to make the work more comprehensible rather than to improve its style. As it happens, he also made minor changes in the orthography such as removing ȝ and þ; but these were obviously considered unworthy of comment, though they do give the text a more modern appearance. Since the manuscript he used as his copytext has not been identified, it is uncertain how far this trend towards modernizing the orthography had been carried out in it.[1] This difficulty has to be borne in mind also with reference to his possible word-substitutions, as some of the changes found for the first time in the printed text may have been introduced by the scribe of his copytext. These changes are of the following type. English words are replaced by French ones, as in the following examples where the word in Trevisa

[1] For information on Caxton's copytext see Cawley, *London Medieval Studies*, i (1937–9), 463–82.

which was changed is given in brackets: *a sounder* (atweyne), *departe* (deleþ), *doctryne* (lore), *dwelle* (woneþ), *encrece* (vb., eche), *marie* (wyfe), *reserved* (outakyn), *resseyve* (fong).[1] But there are cases in which one Germanic word is replaced by another: *callith* (clepeþ), *dyches* (meres), *egges* (eyren), *I* (ich), *named* (icleped), *teke away* (byneme); or even occasions in which a French word is altered, *laboure* (travaille), though examples of this are rare. These changes certainly give Caxton's version a modern appearance.

They also reflect the changes taking place in the language at that time: many Anglo-Saxon words became obsolete and were replaced by Romance words in the fourteenth and fifteenth centuries. Similarly, Caxton's replacement of *eyren*, the southern form, by *egges*, the northern one, reflects the swing of the London dialect towards a speech based more on northern forms. Indeed, his translations contain several words from northern dialects;[2] it may be supposed that these words likewise indicate that many such words were finding their way into the London dialect. It is difficult otherwise to understand how he could have become acquainted with them, since there is no evidence that he was ever in the North. On the other hand, in his translations there is only one example of a Kentish dialect word, *flyndermows* in *Reynard the Fox*.[3] But that word can hardly be used to show Kentish influence on his vocabulary as it was suggested to him by his source which reads *vledermuys*, a word which he otherwise translated as 'bat'. The example shows only that he was acquainted with the word *flyndermows*, which was probably not part of his normal vocabulary. Though this may also be true of some of the northern words he used, the very fact that he knew and used them at all is significant, since it suggests that they were known to people in the London area in either the spoken or a written form. Possibly he picked these forms up from ordinary conversation, since many of them are common words like *eggs*.

However, the changes made in the vocabulary of the *Polychronicon* are not carried out in any systematic way. A few are made fairly regularly, but even for these words it is nevertheless possible to find

---

[1] For further examples see C. Babington, *Polychronicon Ranulphi Higden Monachi Cestrensis*, i (London, 1865), pp. lxiii-lxvii.

[2] Hammerschlag 1937.

[3] Hammerschlag 1937 pp. 109-13, and Blake, *Neuphilologische Mitteilungen*, lxvii (1966), 130-1. However, in the recently discovered part of *Ovid's Metamorphoses* Caxton has used 'backes or flyndermyce' once (bk. iv ch. 5).

many examples of the older form which have been passed over. Furthermore, considering the size of the *Polychronicon*, the number of changes is minute. There is no attempt at comprehensive modernization. Consequently Caxton's version may confirm some of the trends in the language, but it is difficult to use his examples independently. He has only touched up his text here and there, he has not submitted it to a complete revision. Its usefulness as a guide to the state of the language in the fifteenth century is consequently small.

Caxton's changes to Malory's *Morte Darthur* are more extensive, particularly in book five.[1] This is the book based on the alliterative poem *Le Morte Arthure;* it therefore contains many words more typical of the older poetic vocabulary since Malory's prose follows the poem closely. However, as book five is the book that Caxton revised most thoroughly for publication, it is not always possible to make a line for line comparison between the two versions. Nevertheless the following passage will give some idea of what alterations have been made to the language, though it should be stressed that as the extant manuscript is not the one he used as a copytext, we cannot be certain how many of the changes are attributable to him.

Malory. And than come there an husbandeman oute of the contrey and talkyth unto the kyng wondourfull wordys and sayde, 'Sir, here is a foule gyaunte of Gene that turmentyth thy peple; mo than fyve hundred and many mo of oure chyldren, that hath bene his sustynaunce all this seven wynters. Yet is the sotte never cesid, but in the contrey of Constantyne he hath kylled all oure knave chyldren, and this nyght he hath cleyghte the duches of Bretayne as she rode by a ryver with her ryche knyghtes, and ledde hir unto yondir mounte to ly by hir whyle hir lyff lastyth. Many folkys folowed hym, mo than fyve hundird barounes and bachelers and knyghtes full noble, but ever she shryked wondirly lowde, that the sorow of the lady cover shall we never.'

Caxton. Thenne came to hym an husbond man of the countrey and told hym how there was in the countre of Constantyn be-syde Bretayne a grete gyaunt whiche hadde slayne, murthered and devoured moche peple of the countreye, and had ben sus-teyned seven yere with the children of the comyns of that land in soo moche that alle the children ben alle slayne and destroyed.

---

[1] It is easy to overemphasize the contribution Caxton made to the language of his edition of Malory's text. Sandved 1968 has not entirely avoided this pitfall, as I have shown in my forthcoming review in *Medium Ævum*.

And now late he hath taken the duchesse of Bretayne as she rode with her meyne and hath ledde her to his lodgynge which is in a montayne for to ravysshe and lye by her to her lyves ende. And many people folowed her moo than v C, but alle they myghte not rescowe her. But they lefte her shrykyng and cryenge lamentably, wherfore I suppose that he hath slayn her in fulfyllynge his fowle lust of lechery.[1]

This passage from the manuscript is not one in which alliterative vocabulary is marked, though Caxton has eliminated many of the alliterative phrases as *wondourfull wordys*, *sotte ... cesid*, *ryver ... ryche*, *lyff lastyth*, and *barounes and bachelers*. Nevertheless, there is much to suggest that it was not alliteration as such that he objected to so much as the older vocabulary. When he found modern substitutes for the older words, many of the alliterating phrases would have been destroyed as well. Yet in the typical moral comment which he added Caxton includes two alliterative phrases, 'fulfyllynge his fowle lust of lechery', though the words used are not typical of the alliterative vocabulary. It is that vocabulary which he wanted to eradicate, and thus he removed words like *cleyghte* and *knave*, even though they are not in alliteration. Since book five was based on an alliterative poem, the prose style is one in which alliteration appears not as a decoration, but almost as a structural principle. Consequently any tampering with the vocabulary is bound to have its effect upon the alliteration. Caxton's revision, on the other hand, is notable for its French words, among which we may note *devoured*, *destroyed*, *meyne*, *lodgynge*, *ravysshe*, *rescowe*, *lamentably* and *lechery*. Many of these were common words in the French chivalric works which he had translated; and several of them help to give the passage an air of pathos which is lacking in Malory. Many are also words of a more general quality which destroy the particularized description in Malory. Caxton's description has become almost indistinguishable from others to be found in chivalric romances: an impression which he intended, but which we today regard as unfortunate.

The differences between the two passages are characteristic of the whole of book five. Caxton will alter or omit such phrases as 'torongeled with lugerande lokys' (196)[2] or 'the gloton gloored and grevid full foule' (202) because many of the words are typical of the old style.

---

[1] Vinaver 1967 i. 198–9. I have not reproduced all of Vinaver's emendations in the manuscript.

[2] Page references in brackets in this paragraph are to Vinaver 1967.

He will change words which were no longer in fashionable use, such as *carp, caste, cragge, freyke, warlow* and *worme*. Some of these were words which had become obsolete in the language, for example in the passage above the substitution of *wynters* by *yere* is the result of the growing obsolescence of the use of *winters* in the sense 'years'; but others were words which had remained in use in alliterative works, though they might have passed out of general currency. Words of this latter type are generally replaced by others of a non-specific character, such as *grete*, or by words from French, such as *piteous* and *innocent*. Sometimes, however, in the course of the revision French words and phrases will be omitted, just as *barounes and bachelers* in the passage is left out by Caxton. This example should warn us against coming to any hasty conclusions about the character of the words omitted in the printed version, since it is possible that some words were omitted through rewriting rather than through being considered objectionable in themselves. Finally it should be stressed that Caxton did not object to alliteration as such. Alliteration was a well-known rhetorical device, used by Chaucer and other courtly writers. Thus Caxton's version of Malory contains alliterative phrases not found in the manuscript: 'He that all weldys' became 'he that alle the world weldeth' (202), and 'waltyrde and tumbylde' became 'weltred and wrong' (203). As long as the alliterative phrase was decorative and courtly, it was considered an adornment rather than a fault.

In Caxton's edition of Malory there are two types of changes: the elimination of common words which had become obsolete and the substitution of words in the alliterative style by those from the fashionable, French-influenced style. The distinction between these two types is important. The changes which Caxton made in Trevisa's English are similar to the changes in the first group mentioned above. Thus the modernization of *seven wynters* to *seven yere* in his Malory can be paralleled from his edition of the *Polychronicon*. It is these changes which give us some idea of the development of what might be called the everyday language. The changes in the second group reflect a development in literary taste; and one cannot be sure that the words of either the old alliterative poetry or the modern fashionable French style were in common use in the fifteenth century. The words were changed because the fashion had changed, and this is why Trevisa's translation, though an older book, was less drastically altered than Malory's *Morte Darthur*, for it was more in harmony with the fashion than Malory's book.

A few words on this change in taste may help to make this development easier to understand. The alliterative metre was the framework for all early Germanic poetry, and it survived in England with considerable modifications as the principal verse form till the fourteenth century. Other metres, based usually on French models, had been introduced into England during the Middle English period, but appear not to have had any permanent success. At the same time prose, though based on foreign models from the beginning, had also been profoundly influenced by the alliterative style, which remained one of its major adornments. In the fourteenth century Chaucer and Gower broke away from the alliterative metre in order to follow French metrical patterns. In addition to abandoning the metre, they also dispensed with the vocabulary which had been handed down with it. By this time that vocabulary, although it had been modified and replenished from various sources, must have been largely a literary one. Chaucer replaced it with a new French vocabulary. To what extent he really introduced into the language many of the French words which occur for the first time in written English in his works is a matter of dispute; but it is clear that many of these words were literary ones which may never have entered the spoken language. Chaucer's great reputation made this new style the fashionable one; and this is why the majority of fifteenth-century poets look back to Chaucer as the founder of the poetic vocabulary in English. He had introduced a French literary language and popularized the use of rhetorical devices. This poetic revolution automatically divided all literary productions into two types: the old-fashioned and the up-to-date. This is why in his prologue to the second edition of the *Canterbury Tales* Caxton refers so scornfully to the old books which contained 'rude speche & incongrue'. It does not follow that all poets immediately gave up the alliterative style, and indeed it survived for a couple of hundred years after Chaucer. It did mean that those who wanted to be in the fashion, particularly perhaps those associated with the court, favoured the new style. This is why so much alliterative poetry seems to have been written in the North and West of the country, since those areas would not have been influenced so quickly by the fashions at the court. Yet even in the court there were people who favoured the older style. In his prologue to *Eneydos* Caxton tells us that some of his clients objected to the new style and preferred the older style, which was more widely known. Possibly they belonged to some of the northern families who patronized the arts. Otherwise his style may have remained more familiar to the non-aristocratic classes, who would have been less influenced by court fashions.[1] Unfortunately, there was no English writer of prose in the new fashion who had the same stature as Chaucer in poetry. Thus those who wanted to extend this linguistic revolution to prose had to do to their prose what they thought Chaucer had done for poetry: they had to use a French vocabulary and rhetorical embellishments. This meant in practice that they followed their French or Latin sources slavishly, as they were able to achieve both these aims in that way. Caxton followed this habit. Once again, this practice was not adopted universally, as the example of Malory makes clear. His prose is much more closely allied to the alliterative prose of the past than to the courtly prose based on French models, even though Malory used many French prose sources.

This brief survey of fifteenth-century literary fashion helps us to understand why Caxton treated the language of his texts in the way he did. He did not alter Chaucer's translation of *Boethius* very much, if at all. Although it was written in the fourteenth century and although it contained many words which were old-fashioned, if not obsolete, by Caxton's time, Chaucer's reputation was such that it was unthinkable to alter what he had written. Trevisa made his translation at almost the same time as Chaucer translated *Boethius*, but as his reputation was not so universally recognized, Caxton felt freer to modify what he had written. Yet since Trevisa did have a certain reputation as a translator and since his translation of Higden's work was based firmly on the Latin original, his style, though it might not have been completely modern, contained little that was unacceptable: at the most his language might be a little outmoded. Such alliteration as he used was employed decoratively, as rhetorical embellishment; it was not based on the old alliterative poetic vocabulary. Hence his work needed a little modernization, but no drastic refashioning. Malory's text, though written in Caxton's lifetime, looked back to the older alliterative style, and had to be modified considerably to make it conform to the new stylistic fashion. Curiously enough Caxton made no reference to these changes. The reason for this silence may be a desire on his part not to offend a member of the court who favoured the older style, for the possession by this anonymous courtier of the Malory manuscript presumably indicates an interest in alliterative prose. Caxton would not

---

[1] In this connexion we may note that J. Burrow, 'The Audience of *Piers Plowman*', *Anglia*, lxxv (1957), 373–84 has shown that *Piers Plowman* was more familiar among the lower clergy.

have wanted to offend him unnecessarily, though he would at the same time have wished to make the book more acceptable to the rest of his courtly audience; so he made his alterations silently. It is clear from his prologue to *Eneydos* that although he favoured the new courtly style himself, he tried to accommodate those who did not share this preference. This led him to claim in that prologue that he had tried to write his translation 'in a meane bytwene bothe' [109] styles.

As I have mentioned, the changes that Caxton made in vocabulary may be divided into two groups: common words which were obsolete and literary words which were no longer fashionable. It is difficult to keep these two groups entirely separate since we cannot always tell whether a particular word was only a literary one. Since the language as a whole was tending to adopt more French words at this time, many of which became words of everyday occurrence, the change in literary fashion was parallel to the general development of the language. Caxton, however, failed to distinguish between these two groups. On the one hand, in the prologue to *Eneydos* he illustrated the changing nature of English by the confusion between the forms *egges* and *eyren*, two dialect forms of the word for 'egg'. Of these two it was the northern form which became the standard one and the example reveals how the speakers of the London dialect, including Caxton, were assimilating northern forms into their speech. On the other hand, he goes on to discuss how ordinary people found it difficult to understand the exotic words introduced by writers to give rhetorical embellishment to their work. These words were those imported from French and Latin by courtly writers. The example underlines the opposite tendency in the London dialect at the time. London speech was gradually taking on a more northern colouring, whereas the literary language of the court was adopting a vocabulary increasingly influenced by French. However, since writers would have been familiar with the common language and since many of the new literary words were also finding their way into the spoken language, it is natural that Caxton should have been a little confused. His confusion confirms that he had no deep understanding of contemporary linguistic changes. This confusion is also seen in a slightly different way in his attitude to the various authors he published. Chaucer's *Boethius* contains many words which he had modernized in Trevisa's *Polychronicon*; these words are not altered in Chaucer's work. But if *clepeþ* is obsolete in Trevisa, it ought also to be considered obsolete in Chaucer, for the two had lived at the same time. Caxton has failed to modernize these words in Chaucer because he was regarded as the father of English style. Thus the purely technical decision of the obsolescence or otherwise of certain words in the English language has been influenced by the literary assessment of an author's style; the same word may be obsolete in one author but not in another. It is this confusion between the literary and the ordinary language which makes the evidence from his printed texts so difficult to evaluate. Consequently it is safest to use such evidence to confirm tendencies which can be discovered from other sources, particularly as Caxton was more interested in the development of English style than in the development of the language as a whole. This is why he is particularly interested in words, but shows little concern for orthography. The stylistic disputes of the time were about the use of foreign words in the literary language. Caxton was aware of this controversy and had gradually learned to express what it was about. But although he tried to emulate the fashionable style by borrowing from others, he made little contribution to the dispute and in the final analysis his own style was little influenced by it. He can steal from others to compose a sentence in the high style; but he never learned enough to be able to write such a sentence through his own unaided efforts.

After orthography and vocabulary, a discussion of Caxton's language and style turns naturally to sentence structure. This subject is not one which need be dealt with in detail here, since the results of the preceding survey on vocabulary can be applied with equal validity to his methods of sentence construction. When Caxton was using a source, his sentences have the virtues and shortcomings of the French because he followed his sources closely. Generally the sentences in his translations are competently constructed, though his policy did mean that constructions of a non-English character do also occur. But as soon as he tried to compose sentences on his own, he lost all control over construction. He can never have viewed a sentence as a complete unit. He seldom looked further than the clause he was engaged on and the one he had just written. Unfortunately, as the elevated style encouraged writers to heap up parallelisms in a sentence, his writing tends to become nothing more than a concatenation of clauses, the relationship among which is very imperfectly indicated. There is in his composition, when it is not based on a French or English model, a sense of looseness amounting almost to disorganization. A clear and harmonious arrangement of the constituent parts of a sentence was usually beyond his capabilities. It was only when he used some organizing principle, as for example the framework of 'he said . . . I said' in the prologue to the second edition of the *Canterbury Tales*, that he managed to construct a series of coherent sentences. Otherwise, he embarked on a sentence and often found it difficult to bring to a logical conclusion. Hence his sentences are long and rambling when they need not have been. The following example from his prologue to the *Polychronicon* exhibits many of these shortcomings.

> Thenne syth historye is so precious & also prouffytable, I have delybered to wryte twoo bookes notable, retenyng in them many noble historyes as the lyves, myracles, passyons and deth of dyverse hooly sayntes, whiche shal be comprysed by th'ayde and suffraunce of almyghty God in one of them whiche is named *Legenda Aurea*, that is the *Golden Legende*; and that other book is named *Polycronycon*, in whiche book ben comprised briefly many wonderful historyees: fyrst the descripcion of the universal world, as wel in lengthe as in brede with the divisions of countrees, royammes & empyres, the noble cytees, hye mountayns, famous ryvers, merveylles & wondres, & also the historial actes & wonderful dedes syth the fyrst makyng of heven & erth unto the begynnylng of the regne of Kyng Edward the fourth & unto the yere of Our Lord MCCCClx; as by th'ayde of almyghty God shal folowe al a longe after the composynge & gaderynge of Dan Ranulph, monke of Chestre fyrste auctour of this book, and afterward Englisshed by one Trevisa, vycarye of Barkley, which atte request of one Sir Thomas Lord Barkley, translated this sayd book, the Byble, & Bartylmew, *De proprietatibus rerum*, out of Latyn in to Englyssh. [66–67].

It would of course be possible to punctuate this sentence in several ways, but I have adopted the punctuation above to try to bring out the loose connexion between the various clauses. As Caxton was writing one clause, it suggested something else to him and he proceeded to go on to elaborate this new idea without considering how he could effectively unite it to what he had already written. The resulting absence of sentence structure underlines how little he had learned from the current fashion for rhetoric. Rhetoric could have taught him how to compose antithetical and balanced sentences, how to point his sentences through rhyme or word repetition, and in general how to organize his sentences. There is, however, no evidence that what he wrote was influenced by his knowledge of the rhetorical fashion. Where rhetoric is found in his works, it comes, as we saw, directly from his sources. When it has no support, his style flounders.[1]

From his own writings we learn that Caxton was unable to compose a sentence with a clear and harmonious structure. But from the works which he revised or translated, we learn that he was not insensitive to the development of word order in English. This cannot be seen very readily in his translations from French, since French and English word order are not sufficiently dissimilar. It may, though, be observed in his translation of *Reynard the Fox* from Dutch. A comparison of his translation of this text with the original is of great interest. English and Dutch are closely related languages, and the older forms of the languages showed similarities in word order. But as English developed, it tended to replace the Anglo-Saxon word order by one which was influenced by French. Traces of the older syntactic patterns were to be found at Caxton's time in English, but they were rare. Yet since English and Dutch still had much in common at that time, he could have transferred the Dutch word order of his source to his translation. This he did on occasion, but in general he substituted a more modern word order, as may be appreciated from the following examples of three different constructions. In Dutch the past participle in a compound tense is placed near the end of the clause: 'Ic hadde doch morghen te houe gecomen'. Caxton usually placed it nearer the auxiliary: 'I had neuertheles comen to court to morowe' [b1][2], though the Dutch word order is found in 'what have I by this pees loste' [c5]. Likewise in subordinate clauses the verb in Dutch is placed at the end of the clause: 'als hi noot hadde'. Caxton gave this construction a more English appearance by putting the verb between the subject and the object: 'whan he had nede' [a8ᵛ]. Finally, Dutch favours the use of inversion to express condition, just as we today can still say 'Were I you, I would do this'. Inversion is replaced by Caxton with the *if*-construction, so that the Dutch 'wil di mi hout ende behulpelic sijn' is translated as 'yf ye wille be to me friendly and helpyng...' [b1ᵛ].

As Caxton altered the vocabulary of Trevisa's *Polychronicon* and of Malory's *Morte Darthur*, it would be natural to assume that he would have done the same with the word order of these texts. In fact there is little difference in the word order between Trevisa's translation and

---

[1] For a discussion of the sentence in Caxton see Aurner, *University of Wisconsin Studies in Language and Literature*, xviii (1923), 23–59.

[2] The references in brackets after the quotations from *Reynard the Fox* are to the foliation of the 1481 edition.

Caxton's edition of the *Polychronicon*. Two explanations for this could be offered. The first is that as Trevisa's text was a close translation of a Latin work, Caxton may not have regarded any modification as necessary. The second is that although it is easy for an editor to replace occasional words in a manuscript, the rearrangement of the word order would mean a comprehensive revision, which could even have entailed recopying the manuscript before it was set up in type. As there are many examples of an older word order in the *Polychronicon* which Caxton could have changed, the second reason should be accepted as the more likely. That this is so is suggested by his edition of Malory. When Caxton revised and rewrote book five, he took the opportunity to modernize the word order as well. This meant that he replaced some of the older forms of word order by the modern arrangement of the subject-verb-extension type.[1] Examples of this change are numerous, though even so not all cases of the older word order are altered. Thus Malory's 'Than broke oute oure buysshemente and the brydge wynnys' became Caxton's 'Thenne brake out the busshement & wan the brydge',[2] in which the word order in only one of the clauses has been modernized. In the other books of *King Arthur* there is very little change in the word order. Since these books were being modified only superficially, Caxton may not have felt it worth all the bother to revise the word order. We may conclude that he was aware of some of the tendencies in the development of English word order, but did not always use this knowledge to modernize his books. It was only when he was translating or completely revising a book, that he bothered to introduce a word order which reflected the state of the language in the fifteenth century, and even then he was often influenced by what appeared in his copytext. He made his changes only when it was convenient for him to do so.

Because Caxton associated language and style, I have thought it best to follow his example and deal with both in the same chapter. Certainly whatever interest there was in linguistic matters in the fifteenth century was directed towards style, and in this Caxton is of his time. He has given us no indication that he knew of the great changes taking place in English. He did nothing to encourage the use of a standardized spelling or to promote the London dialect as the standard for the country. Although he was aware of some of the changes in the language, such as those in vocabulary and word order, he altered his own texts to

---

[1] Šimko 1957 contains further examples.
[2] Vinaver, *op. cit.* p. 243.

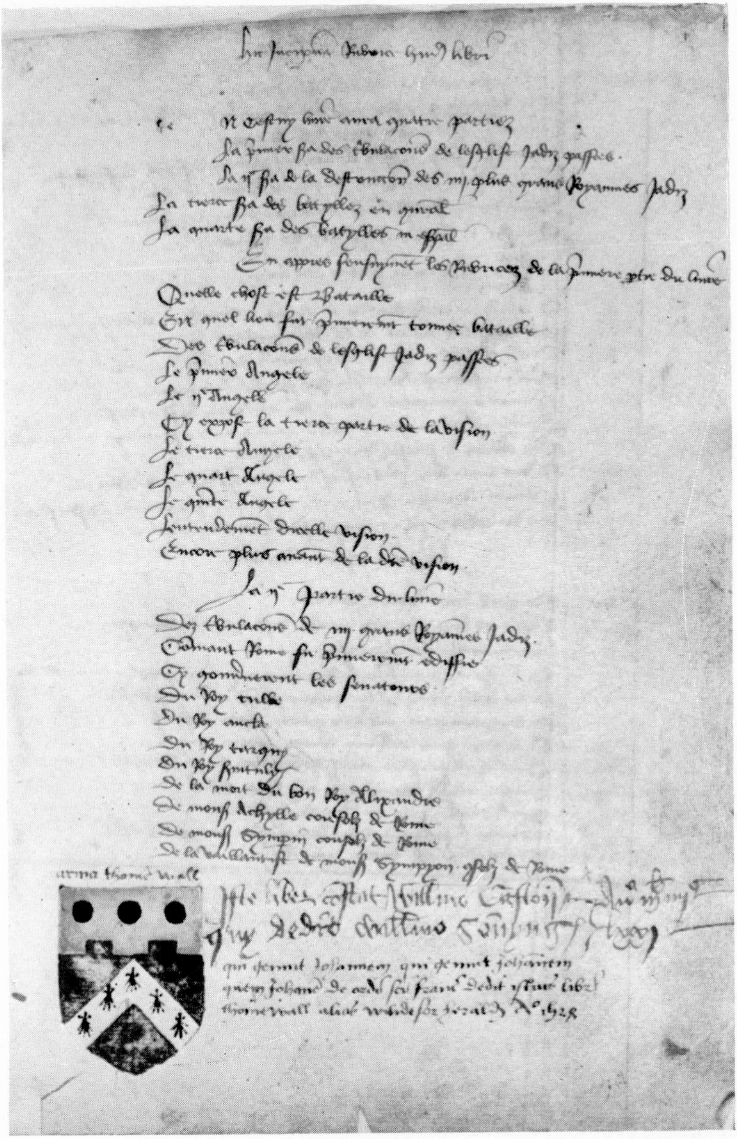

7 *Iste Liber Constat Willelmo Caston*

If it plese ony man spirituel or temporel to bye ony pyes of two and thre comemoraciōs of salisburi vse enprynted after the forme of this preset lettre whiche ben wel and truly correct, late hym come to westmo-nester in to the almonesrye at the reed pale and he shal haue them good chepe ..·

Supplico stet cedula .

conform to the changes in the language only when it suited his own convenience. Such linguistic matters were not very important to Caxton. He does, it is true, comment on the changing nature of the language. It is doubtful whether he had given the matter much serious thought. Comments of this type had been made so frequently that they had become almost traditional.[1] In linguistic matters Caxton must be judged not by his contributions to the common language, in which he had little interest, but by his style and attitude towards the literary language. In this respect I do not think that one can agree with Blades, who wrote: 'As a linguist, Caxton undoubtedly excelled. In his native tongue, notwithstanding his self-depreciation, he seems to have been a master. His writings, and the style of his translations, will bear comparison with Lydgate, with Gower, with Earl Rivers, the Earl of Worcester, and other contemporaneous writers.'[2] Caxton's stylistic accomplishments were limited. He could compose a good sentence only when he had some prop to lean on. Otherwise his sentences become rambling and his vocabulary uncourtly. He had learned the critical vocabulary about style and rhetoric; but he had never learned to apply what that vocabulary implied to his own unaided composition. All that one can say is that he had the good sense not to rely too often upon his own resources. His reliance upon French and English models was forced upon him because he accepted quite uncritically the contemporary fashion in style, which demanded a decoration and elevation Caxton could not produce on his own. The acceptance of that fashion intimates in its turn a lack of independence in stylistic matters on his part, a factor which we must bear in mind in our assessment of the man.

---

[1] As for example in the prologue of *Confessio Amantis* and the concluding lines of *Troilus and Criseyde*.

[2] Blades 1882 p. 88.

G

THE MAN
AND HIS REPUTATION

He who follows one fashion will fall before the next fashion; and such was to be Caxton's fate. He made it his business, as successful publishers must, to provide for the prevailing tastes of his time. Although he did make some ventures into the fields of educational and religious books, the bulk of his publishing career was devoted to providing the upper classes with moral tales of chivalry. If the political conditions had been more settled, he might well have confined his output to chivalric literature, since many of the religious books were printed at times when civil strife and its aftermath made the publication of these books more hazardous. It was necessary to print such books under patronage precisely because they were fashionable. There is a regular, if limited, demand for service books and educational treatises from those who need them; but the books Caxton published, while purporting to be serious moral works, were essentially ephemeral. They appealed to his buyers because they believed them to be what others were reading at the time; but they had to be convinced that this was so by the inclusion of a patron's name. Their implicit recommendations fulfilled the same purpose then as excerpts from reviews in the Sunday papers and the *Times Literary Supplement* do today. People have to be persuaded to buy books of this type, because they are not really necessary to anyone for the conduct of a business or for the functions of everyday life; and in order to make it easier to persuade them, the books have to be both recommended and fashionable.

Naturally a publisher can try to create his own fashion, though this can be a costly enterprise, if unsuccessful. Normally a publisher will take his cue from the general drift of fashion at his time and develop it in a particular direction, within which direction he will hope to establish a monopoly. This is what Caxton did. Close translations from French or Latin texts to enrich the English language were common in the fifteenth century. Similarly the taste for Burgundian chivalry and culture was widespread in northern Europe, but particularly so in England, at this time. Caxton's contribution was to marry these two trends by bringing out translations of books produced in Burgundy. As far as we can tell, this contribution to English letters he made on his own initiative. The realization that such an opening existed and the steps he took to exploit it reveal that Caxton had considerable business acumen. To provide this type of book was his deliberate policy. He started by translating the *History of Troy*, the French version of which was produced five years earlier for Philip the Good, and he continued to produce translations of this type throughout his printing career whenever conditions were favourable. He was thus able to develop a fashion while gratifying it—a combination which was an important factor in his success. However, the taste for translations from Burgundy eventually began to wane, and the books published by Caxton were criticized or simply forgotten. Already in his own lifetime, the dismemberment of the Burgundian duchy following the death of Charles the Bold led to a decline in Burgundy's cultural importance.

An indication of this swing in taste is provided by *The Aeneid* of Gavin Douglas, written in 1512–13. Though Douglas made his verse translation of Virgil's poem only a little more than twenty years after Caxton's death, his whole attitude to the text is different. Not unnaturally, therefore, he criticized Caxton for his translation, of which he says:

> *I red his wark with harmys at my hart* (I. 145)

Douglas's attack is splendid invective, but as it is somewhat long and the language somewhat difficult for a modern reader, it is perhaps best to give a summary of the reasons for his displeasure.[1] His principal complaint is that Caxton's text bore no resemblance to Virgil's poem: they are no more alike than the devil and St Augustine. Caxton had added many tedious passages not found in Virgil, he had omitted much that he should have included (the last six books are missing in his version), and he had also destroyed the ornate language of the original. In his translation, furthermore, the proper names were so muddled that it was hardly possible to follow the development of the action. Finally, because he had followed a French book, his language was difficult to understand. For his own part, Douglas followed the Latin text closely and tried to emulate Virgil's verse, though he treated the characters as if they were sixteenth-century knights and ladies. Caxton, of course, had not tried to produce the sort of translation Douglas thought he

---

[1] See D. F. C. Coldwell, *Virgil's Æneid, Translated into Scottish Verse by Gavin Douglas, Bishop of Dunkeld* (Edinburgh and London, 1957–64), i. book one for Douglas's comments on Caxton.

ought to have made. The features Douglas found so reprehensible had been deliberately introduced. The difference between the two men and their outlook is attributable to the development of humanism.

Humanism had already made some impression on English letters during the fifteenth century. Several Englishmen had gone to Italy where they had picked up some of the new ideas, and many Italians had made their way to England.[1] But these new ideas, though known in England, had failed to make any general impact by the end of the fifteenth century, possibly because men's imaginations were attracted to Burgundy, so much closer than Italy and seemingly more lavish and impressive in its culture. The Dukes of Burgundy have often been accused of delaying the advent of the Renaissance on the continent; their influence on English cultural life, which was profound, had the same effect. Caxton, as we have seen, was closely associated with Burgundy and helped to develop the taste for its literature in England. Nevertheless, he must have been aware at a superficial level at least of the New Learning, since he printed books written or arranged by two scholars inspired by it. These are the *Nova Rhetorica* (1479) by Lorenzo Traversagni and the *Epitome* (1480) of the same work, and *Sex Epistolae* (1483), prepared for the press by an Italian humanist, Pietro Carmeliano. It is possible that his edition of the *Sex Epistolae*, letters sent by Pope Sixtus IV and the Republic of Venice to each other, was reprinted from an Italian edition, though no copy of an earlier edition is extant.[2] Caxton published them, as Weiss has suggested,[3] as models of polite diplomatic literature rather than as news, since few Englishmen would have been interested in the dispute between Venice and the Pope which is the subject of the letters. Even so the Latin in them could hardly be described as humanist. Similarly, Traversagni's work is largely medieval in tone, though there is a strong Ciceronian influence and a new freedom from medieval dogmatism. Both Traversagni and Carmeliano were Italians who had come to England to teach, the former at Cambridge and the latter at Oxford, and they were both involved in teaching Latin rhetoric. That they were teachers is important since it suggests that Caxton may have printed the books as texts for university use; they were not meant for his established clientele. The *Nova*

[1] Weiss 1957, and Schirmer 1963.

[2] Bullen 1892 p. xiii.

[3] Weiss 1957 p. 172, fn. 3. The date of publication (1483) suggests this to be so, though Edward IV had tried to mediate in 1479 between the two parties, and so it is possible the letters may have been of more general interest in England; see Scofield 1923 ii. 265.

Rhetorica was printed from what is now manuscript Vatican, Latin 11441, which was Traversagni's personal copy of the work. This fact indicates that Traversagni was present at the printing and may have been responsible for the edition. Though his *Epitome* was not printed from Vatican, Latin 11441,[1] as it was written in Paris in 1480 and printed at Westminster in the same year, we may assume that Traversagni sent a copy to Caxton, who had already agreed to print it. Although Traversagni cannot have been present at the printing of the *Epitome*, it was no doubt at his suggestion and insistence that it was printed. In the colophon to the third humanistic book, *Sex Epistolae*, published by Caxton it is stated that the letters were 'diligenter emendate' by Carmeliano, poet laureate, at Westminster. As this statement follows immediately after the one which tells us that Caxton printed the letters, it must mean that Carmeliano corrected the proofs of the letters as they went through the press. With all three works, therefore, it would appear that Caxton printed them because he was asked to; and it is quite possible that the two scholars asked for the editions and attended to their distribution, since they would have had the necessary contacts in the universities. That the books were printed on Caxton's press is not evidence that he was influenced by the New Learning, as he may have printed them on a purely commercial basis and by request. He appears not to have taken any interest in the works and made no personal contributions to them.

Apart from these works printed by Caxton, he referred in his prologues and epilogues to other Italian writers. One of these was Poggio Bracciolini. In his edition of *Caton* (1484), Caxton mentions the 'noble clerke' [78] Poggio, who had a large library. He did not value Poggio for his contribution to new developments in scholarship; he used him as an authority in support of his edition, for, according to Caxton, Poggio had said that 'Cathon glosed' [78] was the best book in his library. He used Poggio's name, as he used his patrons' names, as a reference for his book, for Poggio was a modern man of letters with an international reputation. Caxton introduced, or perhaps invented, the information that Poggio had a large library in order to make the importance of the book he was printing more pronounced; it was the best book in the very large library of a modern scholar. There is no indication from his prologue that he understood or had appreciated Poggio's contribution to humanism. It is true that Caxton also printed some of Poggio's *Facetiae* in his edition of *Aesop*. This was simply

[1] Ruysschaert, *Bulletin of the John Rylands Library*, xxxvi (1953-4), 191-7.

because they were included in his French original. And the last tale in his edition, which is attributed to the printer's own pen, has more in common with a medieval fable than with any of Poggio's stories, which can have made little impression upon him. Caxton referred also to Boccaccio's works on the fate of princes and on the genealogy of the gods.[1] Again he used Boccaccio as an authority, this time to correct some facts in the texts he was using. There is nothing to show he was influenced by the tone of Boccaccio's works or that he knew any of his more humanistic works. He is merely another authority. The last Italian scholar referred to in Caxton's prologues and epilogues is Stefano Surigone, who like Traversagni and Carmeliano had taught in England. In the epilogue to his edition of Chaucer's translation of *Boethius*, he wrote that Chaucer was buried in Westminster Abbey, 'by whos sepulture is wreton on a table hongyng on a pylere his epitaphye maad by a poete laureat, wherof the copye foloweth etc.

Epitaphium Galfridi Chaucer per poetam laureatum, Stephanum
Surigonum Mediolanensem, in decretis licenciatum.
[Here there follow thirty lines of verse, after which come:]
Post obitum Caxton voluit te vivere cura
Willelmi Chaucer clare poeta tuj:
Nam tua non solum compressit opuscula formis,
Has quoque sed laudes iussit hic esse tuas.' [37]

Weiss interpreted this passage to mean that Caxton was so impressed by Surigone's eloquence that he asked the poet 'to compose a Latin elegy in praise of Chaucer to be included in the book'. He goes on to suggest that Caxton may have used Surigone's help in editorial activities and that since both men were in Cologne in 1471 they may have met there for the first time.[2] There is evidence that Surigone was in England about the same time as Caxton,[3] but the passage in the *Boethius* epilogue can hardly sustain the hypothesis which has been built upon it. It merely informs us that Surigone's poem was on a pillar by Chaucer's tomb and that Caxton had copied it from there to print it in his book. He added four lines to the original poem, the Latin of which is so

[1] Crotch 1928 pp. 34, 93.

[2] Weiss 1957 p. 139. On Surigone and Caxton see further Blake, *Leeds Studies in English*, New Series i (1967), 28–30.

[3] Dr I. A. Doyle kindly informed me that A. B. Emden, *A Biographical Register of the University of Cambridge to 1500* (Cambridge, 1963), pp. 566–7, suggests that Surigone may have been at Cambridge in 1475–6.

different from the rest of the verses that they cannot have been composed by Surigone. There is thus no need to assume that the two men had ever met, and if Caxton had asked for the epitaph, we may be certain that he would have made more of it in his prologue.

Apart from these Italian scholars, Caxton refers in his work to some Englishmen who had been influenced by the new developments in Italy. For example, he published some translations by the Earl of Worcester. As we saw in an earlier chapter, he did not praise Worcester for his sponsorship of the New Learning. Similarly Caxton knew John Skelton, poet laureate and tutor to the Prince of Wales. He praised Skelton's command of rhetoric, but it was that rhetoric which had been launched in England by Chaucer. He wrote in an aureate diction that was much admired at the time. No doubt it was for his style and because he made translations and was tutor to the Prince of Wales that Caxton praised him. It is interesting to record, on the other hand, that Caxton makes no mention of John Gunthorpe, one of the English humanists. Gunthorpe was secretary to Elizabeth Woodville and apparently on terms of familiarity with the royal family. It seems improbable that Caxton should not have met him, considering the narrowness of the circle in which they both moved. He presumably did not refer to him because he assumed that his name would not help the promotion of his books. This in turn would mean that he was more intent on selling his books than propagating advances in scholarship. His interest in developments of this sort was limited.

Caxton's connexion with the New Learning was, if anything, a commercial one. Being in the booktrade, he could hardly avoid hearing about Italian scholars and their work. But they were outside the scope of his particular publishing interests. He was willing, though, to print books in the new fashion as a printer rather than as a publisher, if he could be persuaded that there was a market for such books. He would print such books to his customer's demands. The same is true of the scribes of the period. For example, a scribe called Werken went from the Low Countries to Italy, and later settled in London. While in Italy he learned how to write a humanistic script. When he came to London he learned the contemporary English script which was both heavy and inelegant.[1] To us it seems a retrograde step that a scribe who knew a beautiful script should have learned to write an ugly one. But he had to live, and his livelihood depended upon the satisfaction of his custo-

[1] R. A. B. Mynors, 'A Fifteenth-Century Scribe: T. Werken', *Transactions of the Cambridge Bibliographical Society*, i (1949-53), 97-104.

mers. Since English people were accustomed to their own script, a scribe would write it for them. Caxton was in roughly the same position and acted in the same manner. He satisfied the demand for a particular type of literature which was fashionable at the time.

It has been necessary to dwell on Caxton's relations to humanism, because his failure to print classical texts or to use the original Latin works as a basis for his translations recurs constantly in criticisms of him from the time of Douglas to the end of the eighteenth century. The criticism is ill-founded. Caxton must have known that classical texts were being produced on the continent and later by his rivals in England. It would also not have escaped him that many of the presses producing such books were not successful financial ventures. A moment's reflection will convince one of the difficulties he avoided by printing translations in English. Although his public was thereby confined to speakers of English, he was able to establish a virtual monopoly. It was only later that others started to print in England or that English books were printed abroad. If he had printed classical texts, he would have had both to compete with texts being produced abroad and to distribute his books all over Europe, for there would have been only a limited market for classical texts in England. He might often as a result have printed texts which were already available on the continent, and would thus have stood to lose his capital investment in that particular edition. He would also have had to employ scholars to produce the texts he intended to print. It is also a reasonable assumption that, if he had printed classical texts, he would presumably not have been the first person to print books in England, for there would be no commercial advantage in returning to England: in Bruges he would be able to acquire classical texts and distribute his printed editions more easily. We cannot tell whether all or any of these considerations had any weight with Caxton, but as he was a businessman he must have considered the economic advantages of different types of books. The choice to print vernacular literature almost exclusively is unusual in the fifteenth century. Most printers, and this is true of the Cologne printers where Caxton learned the art, began by producing classical or ecclesiastical texts in Latin. We might have expected Caxton to start off in the same way; and since he did not, he must have chosen a different method deliberately after he had considered various possibilities. He was first and foremost a merchant: he would be interested in books as merchandise rather than for their contents. From a purely commercial point of view his decision to print English books was apparently a success; which, in turn, suggests that he had considerable business ability.

Because he followed the dominant taste of his own time, Caxton naturally fell foul of the writers who followed him. It is common for one age to scorn the attitudes of the immediately preceding one, and those writers who criticized Caxton were signalling to their readers that they were following the most recent fashion which had by then displaced the one Caxton followed. We expect their comments to be somewhat partisan: they had to convince their audience that what they were doing was something new. We should understand Douglas's strictures in this way. It was not only for his attitude to the classics that Caxton was attacked; his language was also criticized. The following is a good example, but by no means the earliest one, of this type of criticism.

And whereas before time the translator William Caxton, being (as it semeth) no Englishman, had left many words meere French, and sundry sentences so improperly Englished that it was hard to understand, we have caused them to bee made plainer English.[1]

This critic's complaint is that he took over French words bodily into English and that much of his syntax was copied so literally from his French sources that it was often difficult to understand what he meant. As with the question of the subject-matter and approach of his books, this criticism underlines that, because certain developments had taken place within English, Caxton's position had become outmoded. He and his contemporaries had tried to extend to prose the poetic revolution started by Chaucer. To do this they had imported French words and constructions wholesale into English in order to counteract the alliterative style which had been the dominant one in English prose till then. As in poetry, this attitude had been fostered by the common acceptance of the barbarism of the English language—a barbarism which could be alleviated only by relying upon the more elegant French language. Admittedly this borrowing was usually performed in a clumsy and unthinking manner, but it should not be forgotten that it was done consciously and for a worthy purpose. Naturally as time progressed and the language acquired a great many new words, a reaction set in. The flood of neologisms was criticized and adherents

---

[1] *The Ancient Historie of the Destruction of Troy. Translated out of French into English by W. Caxton. Newly Corrected and the English Much Amended by W[illiam] F[iston]* (London, 1607), fol. A4ʳ.

of the native language became more vocal. With the flowering of English poetry in the sixteenth century and the consequent growing conviction that English had reached its maturity, borrowing from foreign languages became less essential. Furthermore, a shift in taste also meant that such borrowing as did take place was of Latin rather than of French words. This change applied equally to syntax, for the sixteenth century saw a fashion for Ciceronianism. Thus although the stage of excessive borrowing both lexical and syntactical from French was a necessary one in the development of the literary language, it was only a temporary stage in that development. The language soon grew out of it and when that happened, it was natural that later writers should look back on the previous stage as somewhat inelegant and rude. When a language is developing in the eyes of its users, each age will think that it has reached a level of refinement not dreamed of by preceding authors. Caxton was as critical of writers in the alliterative style as later writers were of him. So his reputation as a translator was to a large extent the victim of the general improvement of English and the change in literary fashion. Because he was so much a child of his own age, he was inevitably attacked by later writers. This criticism was often stringent because the critics did not bother to consider the history of English prose. For the most part, their attacks were an expression of their superiority over writers of the preceding age. We may perhaps quote Braham as an illustration:

> Yet hath there ben other some so beastly bolde to undertake without eyther wyt or any learning to translate the same historye, namelye the *Eanedes* of Virgyle, into Englyshe, not understandynge scarse any word what Virgile ment in all that worke. As by example, if a man studyouse of that historye should seke to fynde the same in the doynges of Wyllyam Caxton, in his leawde *Recueil of Troye*, what should he then fynde, thyncke you? Assuradlye none other thynge but a longe, tedious and brayneles bablyng, tendyng to no end, nor havyng any certayne beginynge; but proceadynge therin as an ydyot in his follye that can not make an end tyll he be bydden.[1]

That the three passages in criticism of Caxton which have been quoted so far in this chapter were from new editions of his translations

---

[1] *The Auncient Historie and onely trewe and syncere Cronicle of the Warres betwixte the Grecians and the Troyans.* Edited by R. Braham (London, 1555). Also printed in *Prefaces, Dedications, Epistles Selected from Early English Books 1540–1701*, edited by W. C. Hazlitt (Privately printed, 1874), pp. 17–18.

or from reworkings of texts he had issued is significant in several ways. The literary men of the sixteenth and seventeenth centuries who commented on Caxton were led to do so only because they were issuing or dealing with a book that he had printed. Consequently their comments were confined to his treatment of the text with which they were concerned. They did not evaluate his contribution to English literature or the English language as a whole. They were not concerned to discuss his relationship to his own age. In these early criticisms his contribution to English culture is not the major concern: in them a particular example gives rise to random remarks about the printer. Although the commentators approach Caxton with an outlook which is uniform and which was the expression of a new attitude towards humanism and the English language, the random nature of their remarks prevented them from forming a critical tradition to be handed down from one writer to the next. Each criticism was written independently and as a result of a particular publishing event. And there were many opportunities: his works were reprinted or revised many times. Naturally Wynkyn de Worde and Richard Pynson, his former helpers, reissued many of his volumes; but even later in the sixteenth century several of his books went through many editions. The most popular were the *History of Troy*, *Reynard the Fox* and *King Arthur*. Because these comments appeared in reprints or adaptations of his translations, the critics never referred to his choice of texts, which was to become a popular subject with later commentators. It would have been illogical for them to criticize his choice of texts and to republish one of his translations at one and the same time. Or particular importance among the Caxtonian printings which were reissued were the works of Chaucer. The poet's popularity and the fact that the printer had published his works served to keep Caxton's name in circulation in literary circles. Here to some extent a tradition about Caxton was established, the two main features of which were the textual condition of his edition and his foresight and good judgement in printing Chaucer's works. The former represents such a specialized area of comment that it may be discounted here. The latter was incorporated in the general tradition about the printer where it may be most conveniently discussed. It was to become one of his saving graces in the eyes of many critics.

What may be called the major critical tradition was started in the sixteenth century by the antiquarians John Bale and John Leland. Most of the people who contributed to it were not literary figures, in that they did not write or edit literary works. They were antiquarians, bibliographers or historians—or more often all of these. Because they were antiquarians, they naturally consulted what previous writers had said about their subject, and those views often formed the starting point for their own discussion. Furthermore, as recorders of English history and culture, they valued Caxton for reasons which did not carry much weight with men of letters. The antiquarians were always impressed by the very fact that he had introduced printing into England, and they also valued what they understood to be his contribution to the writing of English history. Of the two early antiquarians, Bale was more influential than Leland, possibly because the latter included his remarks on Caxton in his section on Chaucer, where they may have been overlooked by later writers. Bale wrote that he was 'vir non omnino stupidus, aut ignavia torpens, sed propagandæ suæ gentis memoriæ studiosus admodum, multa aliarum gentium monumenta ad id peragendum non parvo quæsivit labore'.[1] The opening phrase of this comment caused considerable anxiety to later commentators, some thinking that Bale undervalued his subject, while others assured themselves that it must be a form of litotes. For Bale's other comments are generally favourable. Caxton was patriotic, industrious and a historian; attributes which many later writers also bestowed upon him. It was particularly his contribution to history which received favourable comment, not only from Bale but from many later authors. His contribution included his continuation to the *Polychronicon* and a work which was mistakenly attributed to him known as *Fructus Temporum*.[2] In this way Caxton was made out to be a scholar rather than a man of letters. Bale misread the prologue to the *History of Troy*: he stated that Caxton had lived in the court of Margaret of Burgundy in Flanders for thirty years. This statement was echoed in all scholarly works till almost the end of the eighteenth century. Bale's work caused Caxton to be remembered and also laid down the lines upon which he was to be judged. He also compiled a list of the works by Caxton known to him, though it was not printed till modern times.[3]

Leland had less to say about Caxton because he was introduced as

---

[1] John Bale, *Scriptorum illustrium maioris Brytannie* (Basle, 1557), p. 618.

[2] This error crept in with Bale's work and was caused by a misreading of Caxton's prologue to the *Liber Ultimus* of his edition of the *Polychronicon*.

[3] R. L. Poole and M. Bateson, *John Bale's Index of British and other Writers* (Oxford, 1902), pp. 119–21.

the first printer of Chaucer. Yet he called him 'hominem nec indili-gentem nec indoctum';[1] and he praised him for introducing the printing press into England and for printing Chaucer's works. Leland also claimed that Caxton had asked Surigone to compose the epitaph on Chaucer (see above p. 198). There is no evidence to support Le-land's view, which seems to derive from a misreading of Caxton's epilogue to *Boethius*. Leland was followed by Pits at the end of the century, who repeated most of what Bale had already said. For him Caxton is pious, learned, patriotic, industrious and modest. Pits also referred to Caxton's historical writings and his publication of Chaucer.[2] This attitude of warm commendation by the antiquarians is continued throughout the seventeenth century, from which period Fuller provides us with a good example. After a comment on Bale's ambiguous phrase, he went on to note that Caxton had been educated abroad and had lived within the court of Margaret of Burgundy for thirty years so that he must have been anti-Lancastrian. Of Caxton's works Fuller mentioned only his continuation to the *Polychronicon*, which was made 'with good judgment and fidelity', and the publication of Chaucer's works, about which he said that 'Caxton carefully collected and printed all Chaucer's works'. He concluded by saying that on many accounts Caxton deserved well of the nation.[3]

Caxton's place in history was thus being carefully marked out by the antiquarians at the same time as the men of letters were rejecting all that he stood for in literary taste. For the antiquarians Caxton was a scholar inspired by the virtues of modesty, piety and industry. They accepted that the introduction of the press, his additions to English historical writings and his publication of Chaucer's works were of sufficient importance to merit him an enduring place in the history of England. At the same time it is clear that few of the antiquarians had read his works and that those works which they had read were not studied very carefully. Most of what was written about Caxton ap-pears to have been taken from previous scholars' works rather than from the primary sources. So it might not be altogether unfair to say that the men of letters attacked Caxton from their intimate knowledge of one of his texts, whereas the antiquarians praised him as a result of their consideration of his general contribution to English cultural life. This state of affairs was modified in the eighteenth century for two

---

[1] *Commentarii de Scriptoribus Britannicis* (Oxford, 1709), ii. 423–6.
[2] John Pits, *De Illustribus Angliæ Scriptoribus* (Paris, 1619), pp. 670–1.
[3] T. Fuller, *The History of the Worthies of England* (London, 1662), p. 157.

reasons. Firstly, scholars began to write full-scale biographies of the printer in which they included many of his prologues and epilogues, both for their quaint character and for their autobiographical information. Secondly, bibliographers began compiling lists of his books and their contents. They also tended to reproduce the prologues and epilogues. The first development was inaugurated by Lewis's biography of 1737, the second by Ames's bibliographical work of 1749. The effects of these developments were considerable. They meant that it was no longer possible to view a Caxton book in isolation, though eighteenth-century readers were anyway less likely to do this than those of preceding ages, since few of his works were reprinted or adapted in that century. The publication of the titles of his works meant that his contribution to English literature could be seen in its entirety, and this naturally led to evaluations of his choice of texts. Since historical works do not form a major part of his output and since advances in bibliography helped to correct some of the errors about his contributions to English historical writing made by sixteenth-century writers, critical discussion tended to concentrate on his moral and chivalric books rather than on his historical ones. Yet although many of the titles of his works were thus brought to light, it is doubtful if the books themselves were often read. The primary reason for this omission was the lack of contemporary editions; only the prologues and epilogues were reprinted. All that most people had read of Caxton then, as now, was his original writings. Since few editions were available and as the taste of the time was not for chivalry anyway, few people read his translations. Hence his services as a translator were not discussed by eighteenth-century critics, though his command of English sometimes was. Finally, the work of the bibliographers highlighted Caxton's importance as England's first printer at the same time as it revealed how scarce some of his books were. Collectors began to value Caxtoniana and his editions started to command higher prices. Avid collecting did not set in till the end of the century and brought with it even higher prices and an increase in the number of forgeries. The collecting encouraged further interest in the man, and it is quite possible that the higher prices contributed to the impression that his work was of some quality, for we all like to think that an expensive object is intrinsically valuable.

Interest in Caxton's biography was aroused by Bagford at the beginning of the eighteenth century, for he collected some material, though he failed to publish a life. Characteristic of his and later work

is the reconsideration of the evidence to be found in Caxton's prologues and epilogues, as the following example from his work shows.

> William Caxton took to the art and crafte of printing right well,
> altho' to his great expense of time and charges of money. Our
> Caxton was of ripe wit, and quick of apprehension in all he under-
> took; I mean in all the books he then translated into English—as
> may be seen by the prefaces he then put forth in print. He was so
> industrious a man, that the like hath not been seen in this our
> kingdom to be the translator and printer of so many books with his
> own hands.[1]

In this quotation we see how some of the printer's attributes praised by
former writers, such as his industriousness, are now linked with some
attributed to him for the first time, and which had been drawn from a
new reading of the prologues and epilogues. This tendency was carried
on by Lewis, the author of the first published bibliography. He complained that Caxton's memory had 'not been treated with the greatest
candour and benevolence . . . considering the public usefulness of the
man, and the little provocation he has given in his writings of such
usage'.[2] He was here thinking particularly of Bale's remarks. Caxton,
however, is praised for his wit and his industry. Lewis also introduced
a new theme in his defence. The printer had published many works,
such as *King Arthur*, not because he wanted to, but because he was
asked to. The age, not the man, was guilty. This defence, which was to
be frequently invoked by later writers, reveals that Caxton was
already beginning to come under attack for his choice of texts.

Certainly by the middle of the eighteenth century it had become
commonplace to attack Caxton's choice of material. An anonymous
writer of 1766 put it this way.

> He was but an illiterate man, and of small judgement, by which
> means he printed nothing but mean and frivolous things, as appears
> from the catalogues of his impressions, given us by Mr. Lewis and
> Mr. Ames. Whereas, had he been a scholar, and made a better choice
> of the works that were to pass his press, it is probable that many
> excellent performances, now lost, would have been secured to us,

---

[1] The material collected by Bagford is now British Museum, MS Harley 5919.
This passage is quoted in J. Ames, W. Herbert and T. F. Dibdin, *Typographical
Antiquities* (London, 1810), i. lxviii.

[2] The Rev. J. Lewis, *The Life of Mayster Wyllyam Caxton* (London, 1737),
preface, p. viii.

especially if he had recourse to some of the more antient pieces; but, as it is, Caxton's works are valuable for little else than as being early performances in the Art of Printing, and as wrought off by him.[1]

I have quoted the passage in full to illustrate that Gibbon's criticisms, which were made only a few years later, followed a tradition. They were in no way exceptional. Gibbon opened his passage in this way.

In the choice of his authors, that liberal and industrious artist was reduced to comply with the vicious taste of his readers; to gratify the nobles with treatises on heraldry, hawking, and the game of chess, and to amuse the popular credulity with romances of fabulous knights, and legends of more fabulous saints.[2]

Gibbon, like Lewis, has shifted the blame on to the period in which Caxton lived. The printer is liberal and industrious, but his taste was corrupted by his contemporaries. Gibbon's disgust was reinforced by his anti-clerical bias, for he was convinced that the monks prevented intellectual inquiry. Somewhat illogically he also suggested that Caxton should have printed some of the classical texts to be found in the monasteries and which were lost at the dissolution. Caxton did not print original texts; he printed later adaptations or translations. Consequently England did not produce the first edition of any classical text. In this respect Gibbon blamed the other English printers as much as Caxton, though all were influenced by their times. However, Gibbon reveals a certain ignorance about Caxton's production. He printed no books on hawking (though one was issued by the printer of St Albans) and it is hardly correct to say that he printed books on heraldry. Gibbon had evidently not read his Caxton. In his estimation he may simply have followed the lead set by previous writers; even though he expressed the sentiment more elegantly. Yet it would not be going too far to say that what he wrote has proved to be the most influential piece of Caxton criticism ever written. This was the result not of what he said, for it had been said by others and was not new, but of the stature of the historian and the quality of his prose. Although Gibbon attacked the age in which Caxton lived rather than the man himself, since his time most writers have adopted a defensive attitude towards Caxton and have assumed that here was a case that they

---

[1] *Anonymiana* (London, 1809), p. 136.

[2] *The Miscellaneous Works of Edward Gibbon, Esq.*, edited by John, Lord Sheffield (London, 1814), iii. 563–4

must answer. In an attempt to find that answer scholarship in the nineteenth and twentieth centuries has tried to decide why Caxton printed the texts he did and to what extent he was influenced by his patrons. These problems have led almost as a matter of course to the question of whether he led or followed public taste.

Even before Gibbon's piece was published, defenders of Caxton were trying to seek solutions to these problems. Thus Thomas Warton in 1778 suggested that at the end of the fifteenth century England was not ready for the classical poets in their original language; knowledge of the classics was insufficiently developed. So Caxton had been obliged to provide translations. Warton concluded that without these translations England would have been deprived of any knowledge of the classics for much longer.[1] The publication of Gibbon's onslaught provided an additional spur to the defenders, among whom Dibdin took up the challenge most thoroughly.[2] His answer was wide-ranging. He admitted that Caxton had been unfortunate in the age he lived in. He suggested that his taste for chivalry was not to be condemned in such an outright way as Gibbon had done, because it had been shared by such famous writers as Milton. Furthermore, he excused Caxton for his production by suggesting that he also had many virtues. Though he had no poetic talent,[3] he had been an excellent judge of poetry as his critical writings about Chaucer revealed. He not only wrote English 'with fluency, simplicity, and occasional melody and force', but he also knew Dutch, German and French. One is thereby led to assume that Caxton's personal accomplishments were considerable and that whatever faults there might have been in his production were to be attributed to the age in which he lived.

Others followed where Dibdin had led; and nineteenth-century scholarship culminated in the monumental work of William Blades. His two-volume life of Caxton may be said to be the first modern one of the printer, in which full account was taken of the prologues and epilogues as well as of such other documents as Blades could find.[4] Yet when it came to evaluating the character and achievement of the

---

[1] T. Warton, *The History of English Poetry* (London, 1778) ii. 123–4.

[2] J. Ames, W. Herbert and T. F. Dibdin, *Typographical Antiquities* (London, 1810), i. cxiv–cxxi.

[3] This was stated by J. Ritson, *Bibliographia Poetica* (London, 1802), pp. 51–52: 'Our venerable typographer does not seem (in his own language) to have "dronken" very deep "of Elycons well", as he translated Virgil and Ovid, out of French, into English prose'. It has been generally accepted since.

[4] Blades 1861 i. 74–82.

man, he repeated many of the views which had already appeared. For him Caxton was a pious man of remarkable industry. He was a fluent writer of English as well as an excellent linguist. He was, however, circumscribed by the age in which he lived; though considering its 'barbarity', he printed much that was estimable. The times prevented Caxton from printing the Bible or the classics, but he showed a fine discrimination in English poetry and he printed all that was of any poetic value. The only new element that Blades introduced was Caxton's conservatism: it was evident that he had been slow to adopt improvements in printing that were made on the continent. He was 'eminently conservative'.

Blades was the last scholar to study Caxton with a good knowledge of many disciplines, though he knew more about typography and bibliography than about manuscripts and the literature of the fifteenth century. His book, which has become a classic, is somewhat uneven, because the bibliographical material overshadows the story of Caxton's life. Since his time these two sides of the subject have usually been studied separately, for the growth of information within these disciplines has been such that it would take an exceptional man to have an intimate knowledge of both. As for the study of the man and his character, with which we are concerned here, the effect has been two-fold. Either biographers have paid too little attention to bibliography and have relied too much upon historical documents to assemble the facts of Caxton's life;[1] or else the biographies, freed from the restraint of bibliography, have become speculative and even romantic.[2] As for literary studies two major trends can be traced. Firstly, particularly under the auspices of the Early English Text Society, many individual Caxtonian translations have been made available in modern editions. The availability of these texts and their editing have stimulated interest in Caxton as a translator and in his contribution to the English language. Differing estimates of his powers as a translator have been offered, though modern editors, like their sixteenth-century counterparts, have not generally praised his translations. Secondly, increased knowledge of fifteenth-century literature, the greater study of patronage and a deeper understanding of the book-trade have kept alive the controversy whether Caxton led or followed public taste. Unanimity has not yet been reached. As an example of how modern scholars try to reconcile the differing opinions, we may consider the synthesis by

[1] As in Crotch 1928.
[2] Particularly in Cunningham 1917, and to some extent in Plomer 1925.

Dr Bühler.[1] He accepts that Caxton showed little flair for poetry and that his prose style was often harsh and muddled. Nevertheless, because his works were printed, they must have been more influential than those of better writers. Many of the faults in his translations are attributable to his French sources; but as a result of his translating activities he enriched the English language by introducing many new words. As for the taste for chivalric translations, Bühler suggests that Caxton did not initiate it, but he certainly emphasized and promoted it. Even so he instinctively chose to publish what was best in that type of literature. Like all other scholars, Bühler praises Caxton's industry, though he also stresses his versatility. Finally, he raises the question whether Caxton was not something of a snob, who was more interested in the aristocratic classes than in the common people.

This survey of opinions about Caxton indicates that some of the disputes have been unnecessary. The judgements that have been passed have varied in accordance with the disposition and interests of the critics. Thus the students of literature, who have come to know Caxton through one particular text, have generally found fault with his work. Here a modern scholar's 'hasty translation' is no different from the sixteenth-century editor's 'brainless babbling'. It is not difficult to understand why an editor who has to tackle the tautologies, rambling sentences and muddled constructions of his prose should reach an unfavourable verdict about his talents. To such a scholar the fact that his translator also introduced printing into England may well seem irrelevant. To the historian, however, this is Caxton's great achievement, and he might also feel that the infelicities of a particular text are of little importance when weighed against the impressive body of literature printed. The value of his achievement is not uniform.

The historians have praised Caxton because he introduced printing into England and because he printed so many books. To be the first to do a particular thing is always an achievement, even though Caxton's feat was not of great significance for the country. He did not invent printing, he merely brought the process to England. And if he had not done so, the country would not have had to wait long for a press. Theodoric Rood was printing books in Oxford from c. 1478 to 1485; an anonymous printer was active at St Albans from c. 1479 to 1486; and John Lettou started printing in London in 1480. Lettou came to England at the invitation of a mercer named William Wil-

[1] Bühler 1960 pp. 7–15.

cock; merchants other than Caxton were impressed by the financial possibilities of the press and sought to exploit them. Although Caxton was the first printer in England by only a couple of years, these three rival presses did not survive long and offered little competition. The presses at Oxford and St Albans each lasted for seven years; and Lettou was forced to enter into partnership with another printer, Machlinia, in 1482. The collapse of these ventures is attributable in part to their policy of printing Latin texts, whether classical or ecclesiastical. Rood naturally sought to provide the students of Oxford with scholarly texts in Latin. There was less reason for the other two printers to issue Latin works, though the St Albans printer did try to diversify his output by printing two courtly treatises on hunting. At first Lettou published modern scholastic works; and after the merger with Machlinia, the press tended to specialize in legal works. Consequently these three presses were subject to the competition of foreign printed books. As foreign printers often had greater experience, their books were usually technically of a higher standard than the English ones and generally they contained better texts. And as the book-trade was in a healthy condition in the fifteenth century, it may be surmised that foreign books were not much more expensive in England than native ones. The output of these three English presses resembles that of their European counterparts very closely: the printers had not benefited from Caxton's example; and the competition was evidently too much for them. Without Caxton, the history of English printing in the fifteenth century would be very like that of other European countries: small presses operating for a few years producing a few Latin texts before going out of business or being forced to amalgamate. Whereas if Wynkyn de Worde's press is regarded as the proper continuation of Caxton's, England is unique in that its first printing house continued in business for almost sixty years. This is Caxton's real achievement; though it would be unfair to deny Wynkyn an equal share in it. Because he knew what policy to follow in his choice of texts, Caxton was able to maintain a virtual monopoly—and hence to survive. It was because he enjoyed this monopoly, for foreign printers did not start printing books in English till after his death, that he could afford to fail to keep abreast of the technical improvements developed on the continent; his books often appear primitive when compared with many produced in Europe at the same time. Whatever the technical backwardness of his books, his clients could not go anywhere else for books in English on fashionable topics unless they were prepared to pay more for a manuscript. As a merchant Caxton could appreciate the position of the market, and he based his publishing policy upon that assessment.

In the literary and linguistic spheres Caxton's achievement is less; it is also more difficult to assess. His printing of Chaucerian works has been most loudly acclaimed, though I have shown that in publishing those works Caxton was following a practice which was common in the fifteenth century. It is, however, possible that Caxton's editions put the seal on Chaucer's popularity. Even if Caxton had been a very different man and had, for example, settled in York to print alliterative texts, it is to be doubted whether English literature would have been much different. The pull of London and the influence of the court were already too pronounced. Caxton himself recognized this by behaving in the way he did. However, by his printing of Chaucerian texts, he may have made a small contribution to the development of those poets known as the Scottish Chaucerians. It has been suggested, for example, that Robert Henryson had access to Caxton's *Aesop* and *Reynard the Fox* when he composed his *Morall Fabillis* in the late fifteenth century.[1] And Henryson's *Testament of Cresseid* is modelled on Chaucer's *Troilus and Criseyde* and *Anelida and Arcite*, both of which were available in editions by Caxton. While it would be rash to assume that the *quair* (*Testament of Cresseid* 40) which Henryson picked up was Caxton's edition of *Troilus and Criseyde*, it is possible that the relative cheapness and the availability of his editions contributed to the knowledge of Chaucer's poems in Scotland and elsewhere and hence to the many Chaucerian imitations. Viewed in this way Caxton's contribution to English literature may be greater than is usually accepted; but even so, he confirmed Chaucer's position as the premier poet of England. It was not the result of a new critical assessment of English poetry; Chaucer's pre-eminence was already accepted widely.

Caxton also confirmed the trend towards translation in English letters, a feature of English literary output in the fifteenth and sixteenth centuries.[2] Once again, he did not start the fashion and it is doubtful whether he could have stopped it; he no doubt gave it greater emphasis and authority. Many vernaculars at this time used translation to expand

---

[1] Most recently in John MacQueen, *Robert Henryson, A Study of the Major Narrative Poems* (Oxford, 1967), Appendix III. While many of the parallels MacQueen adduces are not convincing, it seems probable that Henryson did have access to some Caxton editions.

[2] See particularly Bennett 1952 pp. 152–77.

their vocabulary and to set a standard. In England this reliance on translation may well have made it difficult for much important literature to be written at the time, but it could be argued that it paved the way for future literary excellence. It certainly meant that the Chaucerian revolution of looking abroad for one's vocabulary and literary models became a permanent feature of English letters. Unfortunately it also entailed the neglect of native English writers, particularly prose authors. Caxton did not print any earlier English poetic romances or prose treatises, as Wynkyn was to do. This might mean that some treatises are lost which would otherwise have been saved, for a romance like the *Squyer of Lowe Degre* or the prose version of the *Chevalere Assigne* are known today only from Wynkyn's prints. Whereas Gibbon criticized Caxton for not printing classical texts, modern scholars regret that he failed to print earlier English works. Caxton was content with translation and with a style which was a blend of English poetry with French prose. In this he set an example for future printers, who even copied his habit of composing prologues out of the stock phrases that Caxton had popularized. The language they use and the reprinting of Caxtonian texts, some of which in revised forms were to catch the imagination of later writers, shows that Caxton's influence lived after him.

Caxton's achievements are thus the establishment of a viable printing house and the confirmation of many trends in English letters which were already established. For although it is possible to point to certain areas in which his editions may have had some influence, it would be difficult to prove that the course of English literature would have been much different in the sixteenth century if he had never printed a book. Yet it is only when Caxton's aims, methods and achievements are put in perspective that one can pass judgment upon him and discuss whether he might have acted differently. In this respect all previous commentators have underestimated his mercantile experience, even though the basic facts about his early life have always been available. It is as though critics assume that he could cast off the habits of some forty years as easily as he might change his clothes. Instead of considering how his life as a merchant might have influenced his attitude to books, commentators have labelled him a scholar or a 'vir doctus'. As a result they have invited attacks upon Caxton from his opponents, for a scholar ought to be interested in improving the language and in printing scholarly texts. A merchant may be allowed to act in another way; and this is true of Caxton. He was industrious and produced many books for, although printing may not have been his sole source of income, his livelihood depended upon his output. He produced his books hastily because he was more concerned with keeping his presses working than with the quality of his texts. He was a businessman, not a scholar. Similarly he needed to sell his books in order to live and therefore he had to produce books which would appeal to his public. The public he chose to supply with books was the one that he had learned to know through his activities as a merchant adventurer and Governor of the English Nation at Bruges. In Bruges he had been on the fringe of the courtly society, and he no doubt wanted to continue living within that circle. To produce learned works for scholars of the universities would obviously have held less appeal for such a man. This may mean, as Bühler suggests, that he was something of a snob, as the middle classes often are. They liked then, as they do now, to associate themselves with the aristocracy and to gain a foothold in polite circles. It was necessary for Caxton to follow the fashions of the time, for the court usually set the lead in such things as literary taste. So he printed what he thought was courtly literature and neglected what he thought of as provincial work. His work as publisher served a small clique which had its own taste in literary matters, but it was this clique which set the tone for the development of English letters. It may be appreciated, then, that many of his actions as a bookseller and printer are attributable to his training and life as a merchant, and it seems nonsensical to complain that he did not do certain things which he would have done only if he had been a different man. It may be unfortunate that our first printer was a merchant and not a scholar or a gentleman or even an artisan—but that is another matter. Possibly the history of the English language and of English literature would have been different if our first printer had belonged to a different class of society; but that is mere speculation. Caxton should not be blamed for being the person he was. He might perhaps have done the things he set out to do better. When he intended to make an accurate translation, he should have taken enough care to see that he carried it through properly. Similarly one might suggest that just as he let others do the actual work of printing, so he could have let others make the translations. He might have remained the financial overlord, while letting others do the more menial tasks. The translations might then have been better than they are. Even if he had done this, the choice of books would have remained unaltered, for he was supplying a limited public with what it wanted. If more of them had wanted classical texts, we may be certain that he would have provided them. He was evidently not prepared to take the financial risk of being a pacemaker.

Unfortunately we have no authenticated portrait of the printer or any handwriting that can safely be attributed to him. Our assessment of him must be derived both from what is known of his life and from his writings. As the facts of his biography are subject to various interpretations and as his writings follow traditional formulas, it is often difficult to get behind them to the man. In this book I have tried to show how the evidence may be interpreted so that we may reach a fuller understanding of the man and his work. I hope I have underlined the dangers inherent in the common procedure of dividing his life into two disconnected parts. He was essentially a businessman all his life, and he possessed the virtues and limitations of that class. As for his impact on English literature, I think it would be fairest to conclude that his individual contribution to English letters is not so important as the evidence he gives of the taste and culture of the fifteenth century. Perhaps Caxton himself would not have wished for a different verdict.

NOTES ON THE PLATES

CHARLES THE BOLD PRESIDES OVER A CHAPTER OF THE GOLDEN FLEECE
Cambridge, Fitzwilliam Museum, MS J 187, f. 129

The plate represents the chapter of the Order of the Golden Fleece held at St Paul de Valenciennes in 1473. At the top of the hall Charles the Bold, Duke of Burgundy, sits in a canopied throne which is surmounted by his shield enclosed in the chain and pendant of the order. Charles and the knights of the order are dressed in the robes of the order, but Charles also holds a book. At the bottom of the hall there is a table with four richly bound volumes; a fifth is held by a bishop. The bishop is flanked by two courtiers and a member of the order dressed in a short cloak. The manuscript, completed in 1563, contains the statutes of the order and the arms of the knights in it till 1559. It also contains a representation of Duke Philip, the founder. A somewhat earlier version of the statutes is in British Museum, MS Harley 6199, which also contains full-length portraits of Charles of Burgundy and Philip of Austria. A picture similar to the plate reproduced here is found in Brussels, Bibliothèque Royale MS 9028 (see Cartellieri 1929 plate 8).

The Order of the Golden Fleece was founded in 1430 in Bruges by Philip the Good, the first chapter being held in Lille in 1431. The order, dedicated to the Blessed Virgin and St Andrew, consisted of a Grand Master (the Duke) and twenty-four knights—later increased to thirty. The model for the order was at first Jason, frescoes of whose exploits were to be found in the ducal palace at Hesdin which Caxton had seen. Later under the influence of the Church Jason was replaced by Gideon. There was a close connexion between the chivalric orders and the Church, and this was especially true of that of the Golden Fleece. The chancellor of the order was always a cleric, and heresy remained one of the crimes for which a knight could be expelled from the order. The plate underlines the important role played by the bishop in the chapter; and from the plate we are reminded of the close association in the fifteenth century between chivalry and religion—an association also revealed in Caxton's publications.

1. THE MERCHANT

Caxton's Second Edition (1484) of Chaucer's *Canterbury Tales* [John Rylands copy], fol. a8^v.

The earliest Caxton edition provided with woodcuts was the *Mirror of the World* (1481), which contains diagrams based on the manuscript and some illustrations. The former are necessary to explain the text and may have prompted the inclusion of woodcuts in this volume. Some, however, are incorrectly placed, and all the rubrics were written in by the same hand which suggests that the woodcuts, which also show signs of the influence of the Low Countries, were made in Caxton's office. Woodcuts were also provided with the 2nd ed. of the *Game of Chess* (1483). In 1484, *Aesop* and the 2nd ed. of the *Canterbury Tales* have woodcuts. Those in the former are modelled ultimately on Johann Zainer's Ulm edition of *Esopus*; those in the latter are original. They consist of simple views of individual pilgrims and a picture of the assembled pilgrims at supper (see Blades 1863 ii. plate 42). Many of the woodcuts are used several times. The one reproduced here is also used in the General Prologue for the Franklin (b2^r) and the Summoner (c1^v), and at the head of the Merchant's Tale (l8^r) and of the Summoner's Tale (t6^v). The woodcut at the head of the Franklin's Tale (p2^v) is the one used for the Manciple (b8^r) in the General Prologue. It is not clear what model the artist used, for the pictures are very different from the illustrations in the Ellesmere MS (see E. F. Piper, 'The Miniatures of the Ellesmere Chaucer', *Philological Quarterly*, iii (1924), 241–56); his merchant is more sedate. It is to be doubted whether he read the description of the merchant in the poem, for his picture is very different from it; though it is more suited to the Merchant than to either the Franklin or the Summoner. The picture may have been based on the artist's idea of what a merchant was like; though it is reproduced here more to exhibit the style of woodcuts in Caxton's books than to give an accurate representation of a fifteenth-century merchant. The beads strung across the Merchant's chest belong to a rosary, which every pilgrim is provided with in this series of illustrations. For further information on the history of woodcuts see Arthur M. Hind, *An Introduction to a History of Woodcut* (New York: Houghton Mifflin, 1935); and *Collected Papers of Henry Bradshaw* (Cambridge: University Press, 1889), pp. 84–100.

2. THE LIVERY PAYMENT

Wardens' Account Book [Mercers' Hall] fol. 176^v.

This plate illustrates a section of the accounts for 1453. The four names at the top are those of the Wardens of the Company for that year. At the side of the first column of names is the entry in French explaining that the amounts listed were received as livery payments for the first year. The mercers' names are arranged in groups, though this grouping seems to be without significance. Sixteen mercers paid 6s. 8d. each for the first of their three annual instalments; but in the right-hand column Henry Lytelton paid 20s. 'pur toutz iij Ans' (a composition fee for the three years). Caxton's name is entered at the bottom of the left-hand column. However, his name and that of Richard Burgh have been crossed out, and a note in the margin has been added, which reads 'quia inter debitores in fine compoti' (i.e. because they are among the debtors at the end of the account). Their names are duly listed at the end of the year's accounts. Underneath the livery payments the total revenue from this source is given. Below that the fines of those who failed to accompany the Mayor, the mercer Geoffrey Fielding, to Westminster are recorded. The plate includes only thirteen of the thirty-six names in the list. Each mercer was fined 3s. 4d. Caxton's name is to be found at the bottom right-hand side of the page. He evidently paid this fine, though he omitted to make his livery payment.

3. MARGARET OF BURGUNDY
Oxford, Bodleian Library, MS Douce 365 fol. 115.

The plate shows Margaret of Burgundy, the sister of Edward IV of England and the wife of Charles the Bold of Burgundy, at prayer. It comes from the *Traités de morale et religion* written by David Aubert at Ghent in 1475; Aubert carried out several commissions for her. There are four miniatures in the manuscript which are attributed to the Master of Mary of Burgundy; see Otto Pächt, *The Master of Mary of Burgundy* (London: Faber, 1948). Margaret was a patron of the arts and had many religious and moral works copied (though as her arms are added in the margin of MS Douce 365, it is possible that the manuscript was not made originally for her). In manuscript illuminations she is frequently depicted at prayer (cf. British Museum, Additional MS 7970 fol. 60; Brussels, Royal Library MS 9296 fol. 1 & 17, and MSS 9272–6 fol. 187), or otherwise as the recipient of a book from a scribe (cf. plate 6). One famous engraving (in the Huntington copy of Caxton's *History of Troy*) shows her receiving a book from an author or scribe, who is often thought to be Caxton (see Pächt plate 5; Aurner

1926 plate 3). Though the woman is certainly Margaret and though the designer of the picture can be identified stylistically with the Master of Mary of Burgundy, its connexion with Caxton remains doubtful. The picture is not found in any other copy of the *History of Troy* and may not have been intended for that work at all. Hence it is best to be cautious over accepting the identification of the donor as Caxton.

A woman of outstanding beauty, Margaret was also pious and of a determined character. Although she was the patron of the first book in English, it is interesting that many of the manuscripts written for her were executed after the printing of the *History of Troy*. Although she had patronized the printer, it is possible that she preferred the luxurious manuscripts from the Flemish and Brabant workshops to the printed texts which Caxton and Mansion produced.

See further *Marguerite d'York et son temps* (Brussels: Exposition organisée par la Banque de Bruxelles, 1967).

4. A MEDIEVAL BOOKSHOP

British Museum, Cotton Tiberius A VII fol. 91^v.

This illustration is said to represent a medieval bookshop (Thompson 1939 pp. 643-4), and as such is the only known representation of a bookshop before the introduction of printing. The work of Manly and Rickert on the *Canterbury Tales*, of Laura H. Loomis on the Auchinleck manuscript, and of Hammond and Doyle on John Shirley has proved the existence of secular bookshops. They appear to have arisen in the fourteenth century or earlier, but they developed considerably in the next century. There were during this period many private libraries, big and small, which may well have been supplied through these bookshops as well as through individual scribes. For the shops were active in both the production and the sale of manuscripts.

The illustration shows the books arranged for display on two stands; and the keeper of the shop is talking to a prospective purchaser. Perhaps the conversation was not unlike those which Caxton said he had with his clients. The picture is one of many in a fragment of Lydgate's English poetic version of Deguileville's *Pilgrimage of the Life of Man*. The pilgrim with his wallet and staff appears frequently, as here. The lady is the Hagiography of the poem; though the scene may well be modelled on a bookshop.

5. DEATH AND THE PRINTERS

La grante danse macabre (1499) [British Museum copy].

This is the earliest known representation of a printing office. The compositor is on the left. In his left hand he holds a composing stick which he is filling with type, arranged in little compartments on the trestle table in front of him. The page he is setting up is attached to a stick fixed to the table. There are some formes on the bench beside him. When he had completed the formes, they would be inked by the man standing behind the press, who is holding an inking ball in his hand. The formes would then be put in the press, and the turning of the handle would force them on to the paper. The man in front of the press (possibly an apprentice) was presumably responsible for operating it. At the right of the picture is a little cubicle where the finished products were assembled and displayed. All the volumes appear to be bound, but this would in practice have been unlikely. The man behind the counter is probably the master printer in charge of the office.

6. EARL RIVERS PRESENTS HIS BOOK TO EDWARD IV
Lambeth Palace Library, MS 265 fol. 1ᵛ.

Lambeth 265 contains a transcript of Earl Rivers's translation of the *Dicts or Sayings* written by a scribe Haywarde, who finished his task on 24 December 1477. It was once thought that he had copied the text of the first edition of Caxton's *Dicts or Sayings* as he included Caxton's colophon dated 18 November 1477 (cf. Caxton's Publications No 29); see Montague R. James and Claude Jenkins, *A Descriptive Catalogue of the Manuscripts in the Library of Lambeth Palace* (Cambridge: University Press, 1930), pp. 412–14. But C. F. Bühler, 'Some Observations on *The Dictes and Sayings of the Philosophers*', *The Library*, 5th Series viii (1953), 77–88, has shown that Lambeth 265 shows similarities with both Caxton's first and second editions as well as some differences from both versions. He suggested that Lambeth 265 might be a transcript of a different manuscript from the one Caxton used, though closely related to it. For at the end of his text Haywarde inserted the note: 'And one William Caxton atte desire of my lorde Ryuers emprinted many bokes after the tonour and forme of this boke whiche William saide as foloweth etc.'. It is only at this point that Haywarde inserted Caxton's additional material and epilogue. Haywarde may, Bühler suggested, have got hold of a copy of Caxton's edition as he came to the end of his own copying, and noticing the additional material, he may have decided to insert it in his own manuscript.

The illumination shows Earl Rivers kneeling; he is dressed in a surcoat, embroidered with his arms, over his plate mail. Next to him is a man in black with a tonsure, possibly the scribe Haywarde. The book,

bound in green, is being presented to Edward IV, who is in full
regalia. Behind him is the Queen, Elizabeth Woodville, and in front of
her is their son, the future Edward V. Rivers was the governor of the
Prince. The presentation is portrayed as taking place at court. Such
presentation scenes were common in fifteenth-century manuscripts
(cf. note to plate 3).

7. *ISTE LIBER CONSTAT WILLELMO CASTON*
   Boston Public Library, Mass., MS 1519 fol.1ʳ.

This manuscript of 196 leaves was written by V. C. Moris of Calais and
another scribe in the latter half of the fifteenth century; it has a contemporary Flemish binding. It contains works in Latin, French and
English. The two principal English works are the poems the *Libel of
English Policy* and Lydgate's *Churl and Bird*. The latter was printed by
Caxton in 1477; but as the manuscript version does not contain the
usual prologue, it cannot have been used as a basis for the printed
edition. The manuscript also contains an account in English of the
retinue of Edward III. The major French work is *L'arbre des batailles*
by Honoré Bonet (*c.* 1382–7)—a schematized account of the international law on war. The Latin pieces are prophecies and interpretations
of dreams. This diversity is not uncharacteristic of manuscripts of this
period, which often have the nature of commonplace books. However,
unless it is known that a manuscript was made at the request of a
particular person, it is dangerous to assume that the contents necessarily reflect the interests of the first owner.

The manuscript has aroused interest because it belonged to a
William Caston. Towards the bottom of the plate are the entries
recording ownership. One reads 'Iste liber constat Willelmo Caston
quy dedit Willelmo Sonnyng Anno mliiij°lxxj' (i.e. This book belongs
to William Caston, who gave it to William Sonnyng in the year 1471).
Another records the gift of the manuscript to Thomas Wall, whose
arms have also been added to the page. It has been suggested that
William Caston is to be identified with the printer and that the first
entry is in the printer's own hand. Even if the first assumption were
correct, the latter need not be deemed so, for the entry is perhaps
more likely to have been included by Sonnyng, of whom we know
nothing. However, the first assumption is far from proved, since as
part of the manuscript was apparently written at Calais by Moris it is
probable that Caston was a stapler rather than a merchant adventurer.
Although the contents would be quite appropriate for any manuscript